AF423051

BACK 2
OMNIPARK

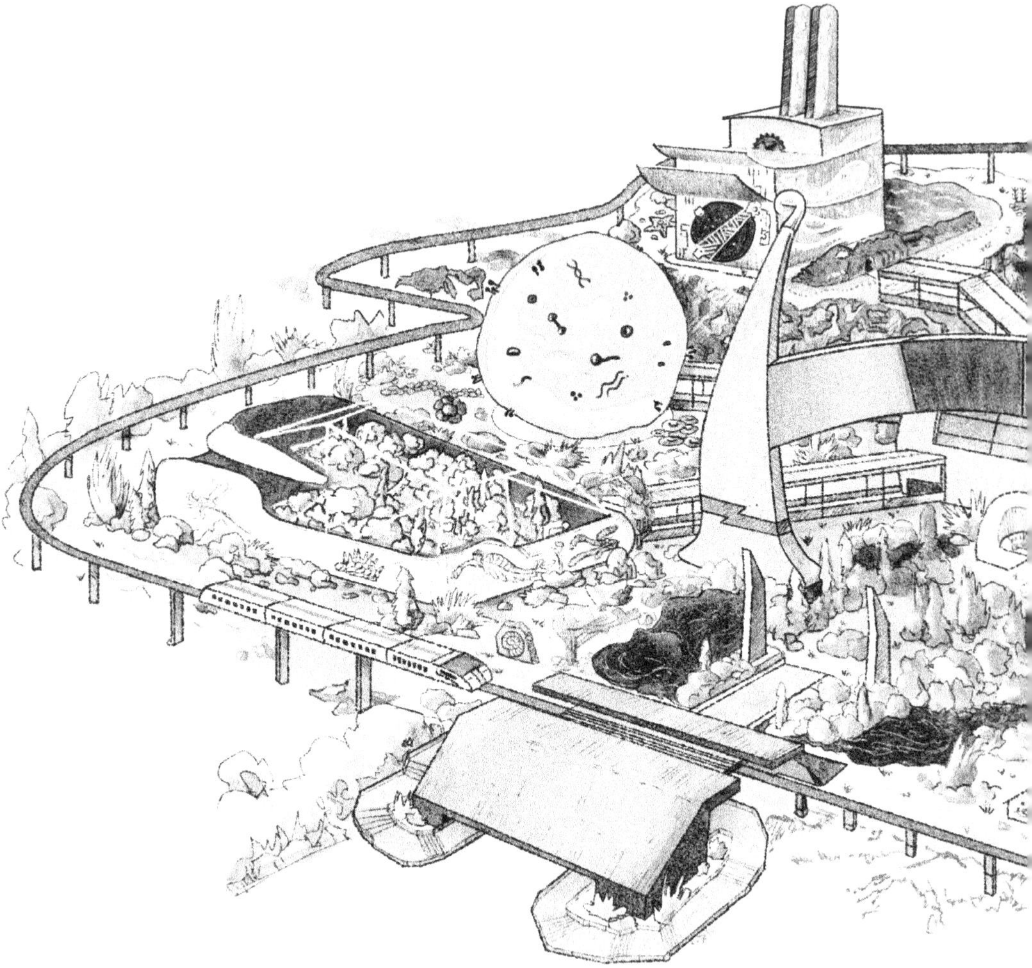

IN ARKADIA

BACK 2 OMNIPARK

EDITED BY BEN THOMAS AND ALICIA HILTON

ILLUSTRATIONS BY ANTHONY R. RHODES

Table of

CONTENTS

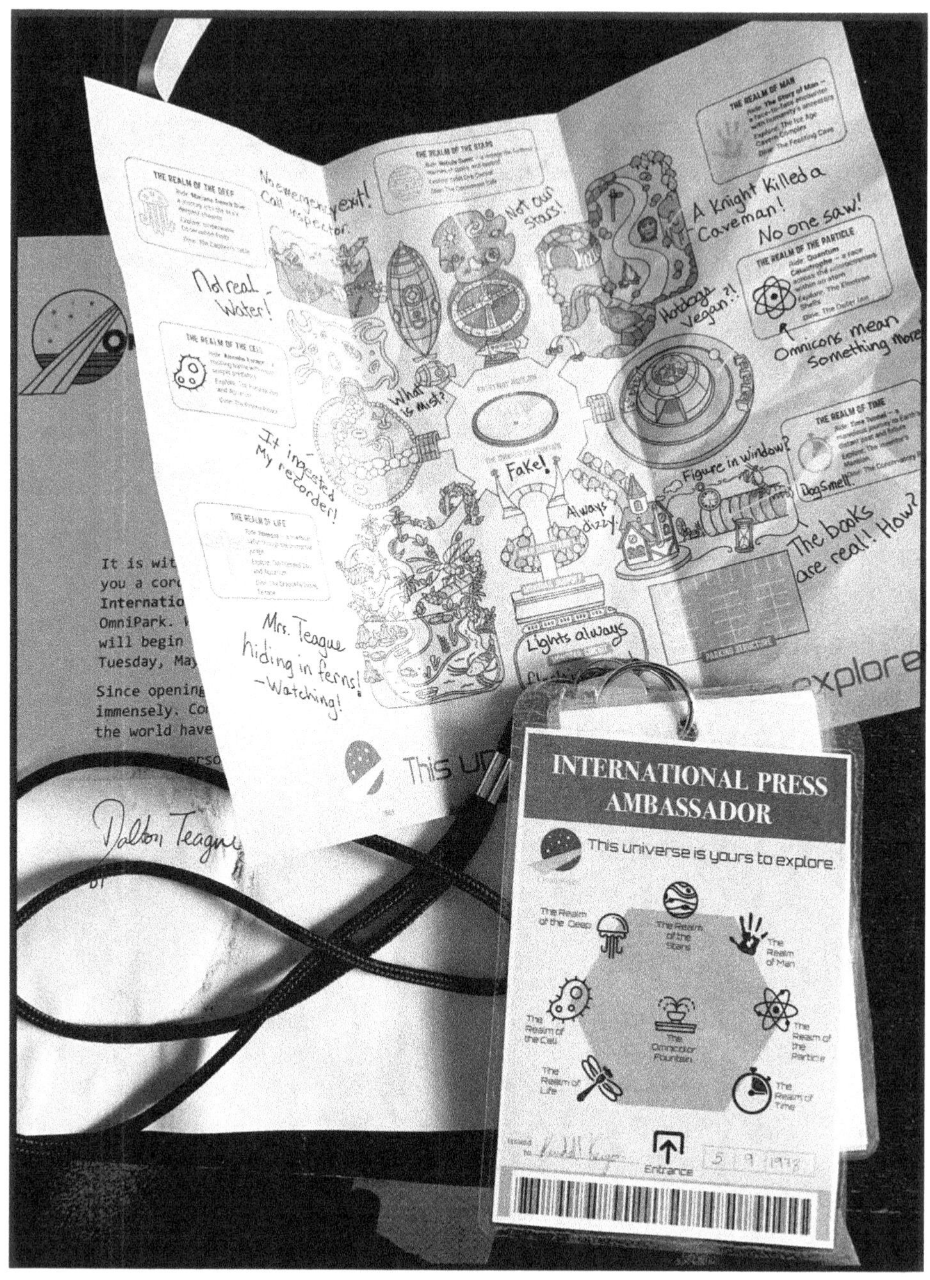

Materials collected from the home office of reporter Kendall Kenyon. Kenyon was one of OmniPark's most prolific and aggressive public detractors, writing a total of 13 articles about the park throughout the 1970s, primarily in the Odessa Sun Chronicle and The San Antonio Light Review. Kenyon participated in several press tours of the park before becoming permanently banned from the grounds in 1988. He died three years later, after selling his research and notes on the park to an undisclosed benefactor known only by the initials "SOT."

Foreward

Alicia Hilton, co-editor

Truth is a matter of perspective.

When my great uncle Elstner first told me about OmniPark, I thought he was joking. A liminal space that was a portal to other worlds? How could that be possible? Parallel planes, interstellar travel, and time travel weren't real. Monsters and extraterrestrials only existed in horror stories and science fiction.

Sometimes you can't believe that the impossible is possible until you venture down a tunnel, smell a strange, musky scent, hear tentacles thrashing, feel an invisible talon grazing your cheek.

Evil is a matter of perspective.

Are the most horrid monsters found on Earth or in other dimensions? When I was a child, I used to fantasize about rescuing people from monsters — serial killers. I was a realist and believed that the most dangerous apex predators were diabolical humans. I thought that cryptids, kaiju, extraterrestrials, and spirits didn't exist — until I met a ghost. I finally realized that Uncle Elstner's stories were real. When you open up your mind to the supernatural, you enter a new world. Welcome to OmniPark.

Surviving a ghostly encounter was a traumatic experience that was forever etched in my brain. It changed me. I felt compelled to seek out others who'd experienced the impossible and lived. I heard about Ben Thomas and his quest for stories about OmniPark. My story "Stellar Nucleosynthesis and the Infinite Power of Love" was published in *Tales from OmniPark*, the first OmniPark anthology.

When Ben sought a co-editor for *Back 2 OmniPark*, I jumped onboard. I was ready to delve into OmniPark's darker mysteries. To finally unburden my soul and recruit authors who would reveal their own terrible secrets.

Together, the authors returned to OmniPark's ruins, traveled back in time to the park's early days, and opened the portals.

We faced our monsters.

(Top, left) Dalton Meadowcroft
Teague's yearbook photo, Texas
Tech University, 1941.
(Top, right) Dalton Teague in a
CBS News Interview. 1979.

(Bottom, left) Evelyn Sheridan Teague
(born Evelyn Kincade) yearbook photo,
Midland Senior High School, 1941.
(Bottom, right) Last known photo of
Evelyn Teague, circa 2005.

Introduction

Ben Thomas, co-editor

Like a lot of people, I first heard about OmniPark conspiracy lore in the early 2000s. I'd visited the park with my family a couple times as a kid — back in the pre-internet era, when you had to actively go looking for weird stuff. At the time, I had no idea how weird this stuff could get.

Around 2004, I fell down the rabbit hole of forum posts and chat room debates about the park's clandestine side: Founder and CEO Dalton Teague had deep connections to the Kennedy and Bush families. OmniPark served as a black site for mind-control experiments by Project MK-ULTRA; for communication with extraterrestrial intelligences; for genetic engineering; for research on wormholes and time travel. All allegedly, of course.

At some point, I stopped asking myself how much of this I actually believed. I just loved reading about it. I screencapped wall-of-text OmniPark posts; collected them; showed my prize specimens to friends, who marveled at the strangeness of it all. We kept saying it'd make a perfect setting for a novel, or maybe a *Myst*-like video game. But despite all my attempts, I never managed to find the right core narrative to weave such a project together.

Flash forward to 2020. Stuck in quarantine with too much time to think, I began to wonder if an OmniPark project might work better *without* a single narrative thread. Maybe it needed to be a collection of stories told in a legion of dissenting voices, like the chat room arguments that had drawn me to the park's underground lore in the first place. Maybe that was the whole appeal.

I was surprised by how many authors agreed, and by how excited they were to tackle OmniPark in fictional form. The resulting anthology, 2021's *Tales From OmniPark*, made the preliminary ballot for a Bram Stoker award. We seemed to be on to something.

So in this book, we're going back for seconds. Back to the origins of OmniPark, to explore the questions raised in all those forum threads back in the day: What research took place in the honeycomb of tunnels beneath the park? What went on in the VIP area known as the Realm Between the Realms? What were the Teague family's connections to the CIA and the White House? Was OmniPark itself just a cover for some top-secret ultimate purpose?

We've let our imaginations run wild here, and come up with some truly nightmarish answers. But in case it's unclear, all the stories in these pages are fictional. Unless... maybe some of them aren't, entirely. Maybe we'll never know for sure.

It's up to you how much of this you believe.

A jar of "photons" sold at the Everything in Particular General Store, in the Realm of the Particle. The "photons" emitted a mysterious glow without any discernible power source, making these jars popular souvenirs throughout the 1980s. Reportedly, the jar would continue glowing for months. However, breaking the seal would lead to immediate decay in intensity.

One Is the Only Number

Hailey Piper

Alonzo thinks of numbers while he digs. A construction site of any purpose or scale runs by invisible numbers stretching between steel shafts, buckling beneath churning cement, hiding in the depths to be opened by handheld shovel or yellow crane digger. Alonzo works with a pickaxe to clear stones from a three-by-four-foot hole where steel will stand. And he thinks of numbers.

It's the mid-1970s, and the temperature is in the mid-seventies, and his father turned seventy-five years old yesterday. The synchronicity feels relevant — but then, he always sees significance in these patterns. Maybe he has an architect's mind, or maybe he should be running OmniPark's construction instead of scraping at its earth, and he's distracted by the numbers and maybes until he hears a firm metallic *clang* at his next pickaxe strike.

That's no rock below. He draws the pickaxe back in blistered hands and peers into the shallow three-by-four-foot hole.

Where another man's face smiles up at him from a tiny opening in the bottom, as if there's a tunnel under the worksite. Like Alonzo, he wears a yellow hardhat, sweaty wifebeater, denim shirt and jeans, and he wields a similar pickaxe.

"Excuse me, I was digging here," the man says. "We're building a theme park too. On our side. Would you like to see it?"

Despite the outfit, the man doesn't resemble Alonzo. He might be younger, might be older. Hard to tell. The tan on his dust-coated cheeks suggests he works in the sunshine despite his subterranean-looking position. There's a perfectness to the man's smile that Alonzo can't quantify, and his mind again drifts to numbers, whether the mid-seventies in some degree might explain the man's too-straight teeth or the radiance in his blue eyes.

"Well?" the man asks, raising one arm to offer Alonzo a hand.

The man's arm does not reach above the lip of the hole, and Alonzo wonders how deep he's dug. He was distracted while clearing rocks, could have cleared the wrong ones, to the wrong place. But where?

The man's fingers flex together, each digit signaling, *Come hither*.

Alonzo looks for solace in his numbers, but there's nothing calculable to help him right now. He only knows he shouldn't take a strange man's hand. Shouldn't let himself be led into the ground.

He taps his pickaxe against a flat rock, wedging it into the hole, blocking out the man below. There should be ample room to press a steel column here and fill the foundation with cement. No one visiting the theme park later needs to know there's a man in the hole and an entire other side to him, with that word *our* suggesting more men elsewhere.

Alonzo hefts the pickaxe onto his shoulder. "Hole's ready," he tells his foreman; then he moves on to another.

And this time, he makes sure not to let the numbers distract and coalesce.

On Alonzo's way home, a cop pulls him over for a busted taillight. Alonzo tells the cop that it's Tuesday, and it takes three tries before he can elaborate.

"Pay's on Friday," he says. It's almost a whisper.

The cop tickets him, officially for the broken taillight, but his grumbling suggests it's unofficially for *being a smartass*. He's already strolled back to his police cruiser, off to ruin someone else's evening, before Alonzo can explain the ticket will cost him the taillight money. Before he can ask how he's supposed to make these pieces fit together.

And he wonders if the man in the hole, the one building a theme park on *his* side, has to deal with cops and tickets and taillights.

When exactly does that man get paid?

Alonzo parks on the curb outside the dust-coated brick apartment building where he lives with his father. He forces himself to stand straight as he steps inside, no stooping. Father is pacing the small kitchen, trying to scratch together a meal of rice and leftover chicken cutlets, but he burns more than he cooks. He and Alonzo sit on a tattered couch at the kitchen's edge for a crunchy meal of black-scaled rice.

"Landlord stopped by again," Father says when they've finished. "Told him today was my birthday, since he don't know the difference from yesterday. Asked him to have a heart. Guess he did, maybe buried somewhere in that bank account of his."

Alonzo says nothing as he washes dishes in the sink basin. The sponge is crumbling in his hand, but it's a tough hand, same as its fellow, and he's grateful for both. Needs them to make what he can while numbers run through his head again. No seventies or sevens this time, but the hundred and twenty-two dollars socked away under his mattress. That plus pay will make rent, electric, gas, and groceries — but now there's the taillight and the ticket, too.

Father's slippers scuff the linoleum floor. "Need to get out there with you, like the old days. Social's not balancing the scales, kid."

A scratchy, full-throated coughing fit stops him at the kitchen's center. While Alonzo only puts buildings up, Father has dabbled in taking them down, and the years of shattering ancient walls with sledgehammers have tinged his lungs with asbestos, cigarette smoke, and every other vicious particle swirling on the winds of progress.

Alonzo presses Father into his living room chair and fetches him a glass of water.

Father only sips it. To gulp too hard will bring on another coughing fit. He sets the glass down on a wooden crate beside him and picks up the television control, its black cable snaking over the living room's orange carpet to the blurry little TV set. There's a ball game on, but none of Father's favorites are playing. He only wants the noise.

Alonzo sits on the floor beside him. "Father, I was thinking again."

"They'll dock your pay for that." Father leans over the arm of his chair and offers a grim smile. "And?"

"I was digging while thinking," Alonzo says, settling into himself. No one's presence eases him like Father's. His fingers relax over his knees, like they've forgotten they have to work for a living, and he can simply enjoy having them as parts of his body. "I think my thinking did something. Like when you find a small rock, big rock, small rock, and you wonder if the pattern will keep up?"

"Patterns are patterns," Father says. "Used to think they were neat, only ever messed me up. Seeing where the pencil scratches match on a junior high exam only dumped me out of school. Numbers matter if they're green, nothing else."

"I saw an impossible thing." Alonzo thinks of the man in the hole, and he wonders the same thoughts as when that cop strolled back to his car. About how much the man in the hole gets paid, and when. "I think something right might come from it, but if it's impossible, I don't know how to make sense of it. Sort of feels wrong to hope it could help."

"What's it matter?" Father presses himself harder into the groove his body has formed in the chair. The TV's flickering gray light deepens the shadows creasing his face and fills the bags beneath his eyes with black hollows. "You decide all that."

Alonzo stares up at Father, his face twisting, perplexed.

"When you're a kid, the hard world teaches you to be grown too soon," Father says. "And at wrong angles. We don't know it until too late, and then we take eons digging up decayed dreams. Most of those who go digging tire quickly, set down their shovels and pickaxes, and they laugh at everyone who goes on digging, their hands mapped with blisters, their hearts too, clinging to hope. *Maybe it's not dead*, the hopers pray. *Might I'll at least find bones or something. Anything.* And none can say who's the bigger fool — those laughing, or those still hoping."

Another coughing fit takes Father's voice. Alonzo waits as Father sips his water again.

"Well, kid?" Father asks, swallowing hard. "Will you be a laugher in the end? Or a hoper?"

He turns then to the TV, lets the ball game take him. His favorite teams aren't playing, but he's said and thought and done enough today.

Alonzo has more thinking to do, of green numbers and grander chances. If he can make today's impossibility happen again, he can then take the man's hand. See that other side. How different it is, and how similar, and how it might help Alonzo and Father on this side of the hole.

The numbers drift in again, practice for tomorrow. Alonzo is thirty-four years old. He was thinking about his father's age, the temperature and the decade, and he was picking rocks from a three-by-four-foot hole. How far down? A number relating to seven, or evenly divided from seventy, he's certain. And shouldn't all these sevens and pieces of seven mean Alonzo is lucky? Maybe the man in the hole, and his *other side* will bring good fortune.

Except while numbers are absolute, luck is a human construct, same as a theme park. Always the chance something will go wrong. But Alonzo won't laugh at any man who goes looking for better. He can hope instead.

If nothing else, he can always be the something wrong that happens to someone else.

Alonzo manages to avoid any cops on his return to work, taillight still busted, but maybe not for long. He's going to come into a minor amount of funds soon.

It feels petty to murder a fellow worker, especially for what's likely a small sum, but the man in the hole is from one side, and Alonzo is from another. Whatever else that means, he can get away with this, and he has good cause. Money is money; numbers only matter when they're green. The landlord who comes by to harass Father is not going to count Alonzo's wrongdoings, but he'll be absolutely certain every dime's accounted for when collecting the rent.

Besides, the man from the other side is in a hole in the ground. All men, even Alonzo, will someday be in holes in the ground. A convenient fate, dying the way he lives, and the burial will be as easy as overturning a stone.

Alonzo rejoins the worksite, already busying in the early morning light. A bulldozer flattens a stretch of earth in preparation for asphalt. A pair of workers carry a narrow metal beam. Someone is shouting, and someone shouts back, and neither can hear the other clearly over a ceaseless jackhammer.

No one will notice what Alonzo's doing.

He returns to yesterday's hole to find it filled with concrete and a steel column. That's right — he told his foreman it was ready.

Time to move down the site, find another hole to clear of rocks. Pickaxe ready, he begins another clearing, three feet by four, but he finds no man in this hole. Not in the next, either.

He briefly wonders if he imagined the man yesterday. Or summoned him in thought. Aligned the numbers in his head *just so* and broke through some cognitive barrier into the unfathomable, but only once and never again.

At another hole needing to be cleared of debris, Alonzo lets go of green numbers and thinks again in the abstract. It's the mid-1970s, and the temperature is in the mid-sixties now but will reach the mid-seventies later, and Father turned seventy-five years old two days ago, despite what the landlord might believe. Here lies another hole, three feet by four, and no one expects much but a pickaxe swing, broken rocks, and a hole ready for its steel column.

Another metal *clang* rings out from the earth. Pickaxe head meeting pickaxe head. Alonzo peers down.

The man in the hole is back, dressed the same as yesterday. He stares up from where Alonzo has moved a rock, as if there's a whole tunnel beneath the construction site. A whole other side.

"You're back," the man says. "We've made fantastic progress on our side. Way ahead of you, I'll bet. Would you like to see? But mind your manners."

His hand rises from the bottom of the hole. There isn't room to hurt him here, and Alonzo wouldn't mind seeing this other side. It might make his task easier, quicker, and he can get a lay of the land this man comes from.

Alonzo doesn't ask if he's allowed to bring his pickaxe. He simply takes it along.

Gravity twists Alonzo's stomach as he slides through the bottom of one hole and out the top of another. He's bony enough to fit after too many lean dinners. On his hands and knees in the dust, looking up as the man helps him stand, he can briefly imagine he hasn't gone anywhere. The sun beats his gaunt face the same, no subterranean tunnel here. He can almost be certain that gravity tugs down and does not flip on its head when you slide through a hole in the earth.

But then he sees the looming structures, and he accepts this is not his side of the hole. The impossible has taken him elsewhere.

The construction site on the man's side of the hole has indeed progressed further than Alonzo's. Where there are few steel columns standing on Alonzo's side, this man walks him between several dozen, the skeletons of multiple structures. Great glass slabs stand uphill from the site, containment of some kind. There's a railway forming, and the beginnings of what looks to be a Victorian mansion in the distance, though whether it's beginning out of newness or because it's only being restored is a mystery to Alonzo. There's something funny about the place, but he isn't sure why.

"Can't pretend we're nearly finished," the man from the hole says, elbowing Alonzo. "But unless I find a side that's already figured it out, we have this project in the bag."

"A theme park?" Alonzo asks.

"Yes. Specifically, OmniPark." The man waves to fellow crewmen, each wearing similar hardhats. "Can't you tell?"

Alonzo can't. He's never seen OmniPark's blueprints, the end goal, only focusing on his assigned tasks. That's why he can't take the progress here personally. Progress has never been his responsibility, one reason he likes his job, where only so much is expected of him. He has enough responsibility caring for Father.

A twinge of guilt halts Alonzo in his tracks. Yes, he can physically drive the spike of his pickaxe head through the back of this man's skull and tug it free, leaving a gory red socket into unknown brain matter, but what if this man, too, is caring for an elderly father? Or a mother? Maybe siblings, a spouse, children, grandparents, more? Countless relatives.

Alonzo shakes away the concern. All things can be counted, but only green numbers matter.

He hurries to catch up. "When's pay?"

"Funny question," the man from the hole says.

Or is Alonzo now the man from the hole? He's never asked the man's name, and the man hasn't asked either, as if they each know they won't meet again.

"Friday," the man goes on. "Likely same as you. One side's much akin to any other, for now. But in case you're thinking they'll offer you a job here, I'd better warn you, the pay's the same. Though I don't blame you for wanting to hitch a ride on the winning side. If you sabotage your side, I'll put in a good word. You can be my little rat. Would you like that?"

Alonzo says nothing, only studies the man's perfect grin. He must be paid enough to visit the dentist. "What day is it here?"

"Wednesday, same as for you. Why, planning to steal my paycheck?" The man cackles, slapping his belly with both hands.

Alonzo almost blushes. His fingers curl tight around the pickaxe shaft.

"Peanuts for you, peanuts for me," the man from the hole says. "When you know what I know about the different sides, then you'll see there are bigger prizes than money. Or is it money that lets someone set us different sides against each other? That sounds like Dr. Teague. Now *his* is a plump purse."

Alonzo eases his grip. "Teague?" he asks. The name sounds familiar, but he can't figure why.

"You know, the big boss. Fella who runs the show." The man gestures across the grandiose worksite. "Never met him, but you hear rumors. They call him a visionary. I didn't really believe it though, not until I made the same mistake as you."

Alonzo wants to get his mind back on green numbers, but he can't help his curiosity.

"Which mistake?" he asks.

The man lowers his arm and turns his grin again to Alonzo. "You broke open the world's heart."

Alonzo glances over his shoulder. The hole he climbed out of lingers open about three hundred yards back. He can't fit that into his numerical patterns, but he's sure he has a way back home to Father before he turns again to the man from the hole.

"The crew broke something?" Alonzo asks.

"No, not the crew," the man says. "Specifically you. Exactly the right place, the right moment, the right depth and pressure, thinking the right thoughts."

Alonzo blinks at him. "The numbers."

"They synchronize. Boy, do they ever." The man pats a jeans pocket. "Sometimes they're a winning lotto ticket. Sometimes they're a traffic ticket. And sometimes, they're the equation to calamity. Or fortune. You broke open the world's heart, like I said, small and fragile as your own, but far more precious. And we on the other side? Our voices are the weakening heartbeat, and our deeds are the flowing lifeblood. You break through to another side, it gives something of an advantage, can figure out what you're dealing with, but it sure fucks with your sense of self. I lost many nights of sleep worrying over what I learned. That was before I finally took a chance and put my side on the winning path."

Alonzo shakes his head. "I don't understand. How many sides are there?"

The man shrugs. "Who can say? Yours is only the second I've broken into. You learn a lot when you break open another side. And… I don't know, this seemed like my one chance to gloat. Clearly our side has a better shot at winning than yours." Another grin breaks across the man's face. "Who cares about Friday's pay? It's no good if there's no *you* to spend it, no *where* to spend it, and what plumper purse is there than your assured reality?"

Alonzo hefts his pickaxe. He should end this now. What the man is saying about losing nights of sleep, about fucking with the sense of self — these aren't troubles Alonzo needs. He's got plenty of his own.

He starts back toward the hole he crawled from, hoping the man will follow. They can finish this at the path to Alonzo's home, where he will empty pockets and gather up green numbers to bring to his side.

The man does follow. And he keeps speaking.

"I learned about OmniPark's plans the first time I broke into another side. One part of Teague's vision is the Realm of Time. But you can't build anything like that without causing ripples, and these ripples are to Teague's favor. For a project of this magnitude, you need the right somewhere. But sometimes *where* isn't a geographic location, it's a cross-temporal one. It's a matter of chance."

Alonzo parrots last night's thoughts without meaning to. "Always the chance for something to go wrong." He and the man are now about a hundred yards from the hole.

"Exactly," the man says. "And Teague can't really afford to take chances. Imagine if OmniPark never came to be? Too big a gamble, and I take it you know what gambling is? You make a bet, and if you wager right, you win. Maybe numbers go up. Wager wrong, you lose. To hedge your bets is to wager on multiple sides. Better your chances by taking control."

"Of the numbers," Alonzo says.

They're now seventy-five yards from the hole, he estimates, and this synchronicity gives him momentary comfort. Let the man blabber. All will be well in the hole in the end.

The man forms a claw with one hand. "Yes. Take control of the numbers, like grabbing them in your fingers. You can't win every bet, but maybe you don't care how much you lose so long as one of the sides you're betting on wins. You need to win. Period."

Alonzo licks his drying lips. Squeezes the pickaxe. Fifty yards from the hole.

"In this case, Teague rolled a pair of dice. Metaphorically speaking." The man pantomimes the gesture. "Or it could have been three dice, four—"

"Seven," Alonzo offers.

"Sure, seven," the man says. "And for every combination, there's a side working on OmniPark's construction. Different factors, different possibilities. Your side might be a three and a four of the dice. Mine might be a five and a five. Point is, when Teague set construction in motion, it forked across time. Cross-temporal possibilities. Right now, every side co-exists, but that won't always be the case."

Alonzo picks up his pace. Sweat now beads across his forehead, and the sense of a terrible truth breathes warm air down his neck. They're maybe twenty-five yards from the hole, and he needs this conversation to end.

The man beside him flails an open hand. "Do you get it? In the end, there's only going to be one OmniPark." He turns to look over one shoulder and scans the worksite again. "We're making progress. But you're only the second parallel park I've encountered, so who knows where the other sides have gotten?"

Alonzo bites at his cheeks, his tongue, his bottom lip, trying to stop the questions, but they come anyway: "What was the first you found? What were their numbers?"

"The dice roll is an analogy," the man says, scoffing. "Let's say they were snake eyes though. Much closer to the finish line than either of us. I had to hobble them, get it?"

Alonzo slows ten yards from the hole. Looks the man in the face.

The grin is marvelous and terrifying. "They would've won. I gave my side a chance, your side a chance — all sides, really. But knowing there are other sides, that means picking up the pace. Sure, maybe cutting corners, but none of that matters if we lose. We can only try to be the side Teague wins on. Or the horse he likes, if that's more your gamble. We're going to win, and our horse will be that one OmniPark, even as the other horses' legs fall out from under them. Even if we have to break those legs, get those horses ground into glue. You know how it goes at the track."

Alonzo has stopped walking now without meaning to. He feels the pickaxe dangling from his fingers, ready to fall on the ground.

"That analogy too much for you?" the man asks. "Maybe you're more a rat race kind of fellow." His upper lip peels back from his front teeth, and he suctions his tongue against the backs of his incisors in a verminous *tut-tut-tut-tut*.

Alonzo retreats two steps, nearly falling over his own heels. "Why?" he asks. "Why tell me?"

"Thought I said." The man's full grin returns, and there's a laugh in his voice. "I'm from one side, and you're from another. A losing side. Might be my only chance to gloat."

Alonzo tenses his muscles and swings the pickaxe at the man's head. He's been building to this moment since last night, and now that it's here, he doesn't care about green numbers, only the ones he shouldn't have thought about. The ones he shouldn't have let synchronize.

The pickaxe swings through open air and flies out of Alonzo's grasp. Its iron head strikes the earth four feet away, bounces, and then lands three feet past that.

Alonzo doesn't make to fetch it. He turns from this other side and its construction site, and he barrels for the hole he crawled from, the hole back to his side. His pitiful, slow-moving, no-chance side. There won't be a park there, or a fated hole in the earth for its men, not even Father. Only too-slow failure, and then oblivion. Ground into glue.

"You'll never finish before we do!" the man from the hole calls. "And there's only going to be one OmniPark. Good luck, my little rat! *Tut-tut-tut-tut!*"

Gravity twists Alonzo's guts as he emerges from the hole on his side, and this time he vomits. Some of his sick might have traveled to the other side. He doesn't know; he covers the opening with a rock and climbs out. Tells the foreman the hole is ready. That he should hurry about it.

Alonzo eyes the open construction site, everything paced with steady efficiency. Nothing paced with a winning attitude.

They're going to lose.

He spends the day not resting, not taking breaks, only moving from place to place to offer any help he can. To cut corners on the project might buy more time. But then, cutting corners might result in accidents, and then delays, and then—

Alonzo works into the dusk. He only pauses long enough to hide from his crew as they shuffle to their dusty pickup trucks, pretending he's gone home, but he can't waste time on the commute, let alone risk being stalled by another cop for his taillight. Not when this side might blink out like a dead bulb.

The foreman and other workers find Alonzo in the morning kneeling at the center of the worksite. His eyes have sunk into his head, and soil covers his clothing. He's rambling to himself about numbers, trying to make patterns and then interrupt them, but he isn't certain whether he hopes to hide from other sides, or to find and disrupt them.

Deep down, he's really hoping to finish OmniPark here, on this side of the hole. Fast as he can. Even if he has to wear down every tool to a metal nub.

He's already done the same to his fingers. Some have been scraped to red muscle between stones. Others have worn down to bone.

And he keeps on digging. Teague isn't going to count Alonzo's intact fingers. He only needs to count to one, when he sees a finished OmniPark, never knowing the many combinations of sides that have fallen from existence.

Alonzo has to be sure OmniPark stands here, first and only. It seems impossible against the titanic stature on the far side of the hole, but he has to try. Not a rich man; can't hedge these bets.

But at least if he keeps digging, keeps working, there's hope for a chance.

Chimera

Alicia Hilton

July 7, 1973

Nine coyotes tipped up their heads and howled at the massive, silver disc that silently hovered over the arid plains on the outskirts of Midland, Texas.

The disc began to *hum*. A hatch on the underside slid open.

The alpha male's howl turned to a bark, warning the pack of danger. The coyotes bolted for their burrow, a tunnel they'd taken from a badger. The smallest pup was the first to fall. Three seconds later, all their bodies were twitching in spasms.

Dust, but not dust — the powdery substance sprayed from the hatch was nearly invisible.

May 18, 1977

Gwen carried a balisong butterfly knife. Denise had become an expert at hurling shuriken, the ninja stars she'd inherited from her granddad. Up until their senior year of high school, they'd followed all the rules they'd learned from horror movies: always go armed, avoid cabins in the woods, don't have sex, and you'll survive.

In slasher movies, teens who had sex got whacked with axes, stabbed with knives, carved up with chainsaws, shot, hung, strangled, or burned alive. All damned good reasons to keep your pants zipped, but following the abstinence rule wasn't easy.

Gwen yanked down her zipper, wriggled the denim fabric past her hips, and tossed her jeans on the floor next to the calculus textbook.

"Hurry up," Denise said. She was already reclining on Gwen's bed, naked.

Gwen stripped off the rest of her clothes and climbed on the bed. It was twin size, so there wasn't much room to maneuver. She lay on her side and caressed Denise's shoulder. Her skin was hot. "You want me to open the window?"

"Someone might hear us." Denise giggled.

They kissed — first tentatively, then with passion. Gwen stroked Denise's breast. Someone knocked on the bedroom door.

"Just a sec," Gwen said. She got off the bed and grabbed her underwear.

The door swung open. Gwen's father strode into the room. He kept walking until he was close enough to touch Gwen if he'd reached out his hand. The smug grin on his face conveyed that he was enjoying their embarrassment.

Denise screamed and pulled up the sheet, covering herself.

"Dad, get out!" Gwen said. She curled her hands into fists. She wanted to smack Dad but lacked the courage.

Instead of leaving, he laughed before he turned away. "Denise, would you like to stay for dinner?"

"No, thanks, Mr. Slouka." Denise blinked rapidly, like she was trying not to cry.

"I'll drive you home," Dad said.

Gwen picked up Denise's shirt and handed it to her. "I'm sorry," she whispered.

Dad walked into the hallway, leaving the bedroom door open.

After Gwen's father's Chevy C10 truck pulled out of the driveway, Gwen wrote a note and put it on the kitchen counter. *I've got a stomachache. Took some Pepto. Going to sleep now.*

Her mother wasn't home yet. Mom worked late on Wednesday nights — therapy appointments. She was a psychologist at Midland Memorial Hospital.

Gwen really did have a stomachache, but she also wanted to postpone the inevitable "sex talk."

She took a slice of leftover pizza and a can of soda to her room. Pizza was her favorite food, especially pepperoni with green peppers, but she set down the slice after only eating one bite. She opened the can of root beer and took a swig. Her nausea was getting worse. She kept replaying the moment when her father barged into the bedroom.

It was embarrassing that he saw her naked, but she felt even sicker about him staring at Denise.

Denise lived less than three miles from their house but being stuck in a truck with him must've been awful. Did Dad grill her about sex? Make comments about her body? Gwen had seen nudie magazines in the toolchest in the back of her father's truck.

Fifteen minutes later, the Chevy still hadn't pulled into the driveway. Dad should've been home by now.

Another forty minutes passed. She got out of bed and tiptoed to the hallway. She was heading towards the phone in the kitchen when the sound of an engine made her bolt back to her bedroom.

She peeked through the blinds. It was Mom's AMC Pacer.

Dad's truck arrived home at 11:29 PM. Gwen stopped pacing and peered out the window. Where the hell had he been for nearly four hours?

She stomped to her bedroom door and grabbed the knob. It was tempting to fling the door open and yell at him, but Dad hated emotional displays. He'd bawl her out if she acted hysterical.

She let go of the doorknob, sat down on her bed and sighed. She'd talk to Dad in the morning and ask him to apologize for invading her privacy.

She was still awake but calmer when her alarm clock buzzed at 6:45 AM. She hurriedly dressed and stopped in the hall bathroom. Her eyes were swollen from crying.

Mom and Dad were in the kitchen, dressed in running clothes, which wasn't a surprise since they jogged together in the morning a couple times a week. In late spring, it got hot early in the Permian Basin.

Mom was standing by the stove, cooking pancakes. Dad was sitting at the table, nose buried in today's edition of *The Odessa American*. The headline at the top of the fold said, *OmniPark Grand Opening: Explore the World's Greatest Theme Park!*

The grin curving Dad's lips made Gwen want to scream. She took a deep breath to calm herself. He was probably smiling because he was glad he'd quit his engineering job at Halliburton to take a position at OmniPark. He'd been smiling about that big raise all week.

"Morning," Gwen said.

"You want two pancakes or three?" Mom said.

"Two, please." Gwen sat beside her father. She had no appetite for pancakes, but shoving food in her mouth was easier than opening herself up to criticism for skipping breakfast.

Mom put two pancakes on Gwen's plate, served herself three pancakes, and joined them at the table. She poured syrup on her own pancakes and handed the bottle to Gwen.

"Thanks," Gwen said. She poured a dollop of syrup and capped the bottle.

Dad was only drinking coffee, which was strange since he always ate breakfast. "That's a lot of syrup," he said. "You're getting chubby."

Heat rushed to Gwen's face. His comment reminded her of how he'd laughed when he saw her naked. She shoved her chair back and stood.

"Honey, stay." Mom turned to Dad. "You're being insensitive."

Gwen sat down but didn't eat.

"Just stating a fact," Dad said.

"Our daughter has a lovely body and a healthy attitude about food."

Dad set down his coffee cup. "Christ, quit jumping on me. I'm sorry."

Gwen looked down at her plate. She used her fork to slide the pancakes away from the syrup.

Before Dad had barged into her room, she was already self-conscious about having big breasts. She hated it when guys looked at her chest instead of her face.

"Do you want to talk about what happened last night?" Mom said.

"Not really." Gwen cut off a bite of pancake but didn't put it in her mouth.

Mom smiled. "Exploring your sexuality is natural."

"I don't want to talk about it," Gwen said, "Dad, why did you get home so late? I was worried."

He jabbed a finger at the newspaper. "The Scalar Portal needed to be recalibrated. Dr. Teague wanted everything to be perfect for OmniPark's Grand Opening."

Gwen didn't think she could feel any worse, until the phone rang.

Dad stood, grabbed the telephone receiver from where it was mounted on the wall by the fridge, and answered.

It was Denise's mother, wanting to know if she was there.

"I dropped her off three blocks from your house." Dad passed the phone to Gwen. Denise's mom said, "Do you know where she is?"

"No. I haven't talked to her since she left our house."

"Do you know where she might have gone?"

Gwen suddenly felt cold. She started trembling so hard, she almost dropped the phone. "Maybe she went for a run and fell?"

"I'm going to call the police," Denise's mother said. She hung up the phone.

Gwen couldn't hold back her tears. She glared at Dad. "Why didn't you pull into their driveway?"

"She wanted to walk."

"What did you say to her?" Mom said.

"We talked about the calculus test."

"Bullshit!" Gwen shouted.

Dad slammed his fist against the table. "Don't raise your voice at me, young lady."

Ten minutes later, Gwen grabbed her father's keys while he was in the shower.

Mom followed her to the foyer. "Where are you going?"

"To look for Denise."

"The school bus will be here in twelve minutes." Mom tapped her watch.

"There's an assembly first period," Gwen lied. "I'll be back in less than an hour."

"Forty minutes. Dad needs to leave for OmniPark."

Gwen ran out the door. The Chevy was parked in the driveway. Water beaded on the truck's light saddle paint. She felt a sudden wave of nausea. Why would Dad have washed his truck? He'd just washed it two days ago.

Denise's backpack wasn't in the cab. The bed was empty, except for Dad's tool chest. Gwen's hand shook when she stuck the key in the lock. She held her breath as she lifted the lid. Nothing inside the chest except tools. If her father had hurt Denise, he would've dumped her backpack. He loved to read crime fiction. When he talked about the plots, he made fun of characters who got caught with incriminating evidence.

Footsteps approached, startling Gwen.

"Looking for something?" Dad asked.

Nine hours later, Denise's body was found forty miles away in Big Spring State Park, in a ravine below the vista. She had been strangled.

Gwen wept nonstop for two days. She couldn't sleep or eat.

Denise had been her closest friend for ten years, since they were in elementary school. Their homeroom teacher had assigned desks alphabetically by last name. Gwen's last name was Slouka and Denise's last name was Sagara, so they sat next to each other. They were two nerds who'd bonded over their shared interest in scary movies.

A year ago, friendship had turned to love. Gwen felt like part of her had died. If a loss cut so deep that you felt hollow inside, had you survived?

While her parents slept, Gwen hunted for clues.

She foraged in Mom's purse for her car keys. Backed the Pacer out of the pitch-black driveway with the headlights off.

When she arrived at Big Spring State Park, she didn't see any police tape cordoning off the vista. She climbed down the ravine.

TV shows and movies made analyzing evidence look easy. She shone her flashlight around, but saw only dirt, boulders, scruffy-looking trees, bushes, and cacti.

❧

Two more days passed, and the police hadn't made any arrests.

Dad was still working at OmniPark and acted super nice when he was home, but his kindness made Gwen more suspicious. When the police asked him to come down to the station for an interview, her wariness spiked. Was Dad capable of murder?

Gwen and her mother were waiting in the living room when Dad returned from the station.

"Did you find out if they have any leads?" Mom patted the sofa cushion, motioning for Dad to sit beside them, but he remained standing.

"Bupkis. They had me in an interrogation room for four hours. Acted all friendly at first, offering coffee and soda. The younger officer wasn't much older than you." Dad glanced at Gwen. "He said they wanted my advice on what kind of man might have done it."

"What did you say?" Gwen clutched her hands in her lap to stop them from trembling.

"I told them to look at truckers and construction workers. Someone strong enough to snatch her off the street and force her into his vehicle."

Mom nodded. "That makes sense. Denise was a smart girl. She wouldn't have hitchhiked."

"Why did they keep you for four hours?" Gwen said.

"Standard procedure. I was the last person seen with Denise. They're tracing her movements." Dad ran his hand through his hair. His face was getting sweaty.

"You're a suspect?" Gwen said.

"Of course not!" Mom said.. "Dad was at OmniPark when Denise was killed."

"Someone was working with you?" Gwen said.

"The security guard at the main gate clocked me in and out."

"What about the other gates and the underground tunnels? Are they monitored at night?" Gwen said.

Mom grasped Gwen's arm. "Don't be rude."

She yanked her arm away and stood. "I'm not being rude. Dad doesn't have a real alibi."

"That's enough!" Mom said. "Go to your room, young lady."

Before school, Gwen knocked on doors and rang doorbells, hoping to uncover clues that she could pass to the police.

She cornered a middle-aged man mowing his lawn. He shut off the mower and looked at the picture she showed him of Denise. "Yep, I've seen her."

"Where?" Gwen leaned closer.

"On the news. She was your friend?"

Gwen's eyes stung with tears. "Yes."

"I'm sorry for your loss."

After she quit crying, Gwen peddled her bike to the playground closest to her high school. Though it wasn't summer yet, it was sweltering hot. Sunlight reflected off the metal slide. Gwen raised her hand to shade her eyes.

A woman wearing a yellow sundress and a floppy hat was pushing a toddler on the swing set. She showed the photos of Denise and Dad to her.

"Sorry, I don't recognize them," she said.

"Take another look." Gwen shoved the photos in her face.

The woman's smile vanished. "Sugar, I said I didn't know them." She picked up her child and put her in a stroller.

Gwen followed them. "How would you feel if someone murdered your daughter?"

The woman's face twisted in fury. "Are you threatening me? I'll call the police."

Gwen sprinted towards her bike. Her gut hurt like she'd been punched.

During one of her insomniac bike rides, Gwen saw a flier for *Josiah Crone's Psychic Readings* taped to the dumpster outside the Horseshoe Restaurant. When you're obsessed with avenging your soulmate's death, you'll reach out to almost anyone for help. She'd called Josiah's number and told him what she wanted. He hadn't laughed. He told her to meet him in a sketchy neighborhood in the southern part of Midland.

Josiah Crone's bald scalp was speckled with liver spots, and his face was so wrinkled that he looked a hundred years old, but he moved like a much younger man — quick and menacing. He shut the motor home's door and turned the bolt, locking Gwen inside with him. No one would have heard her if she screamed. Josiah's Winnebago was parked at the end of a dirt road. No other RVs or houses were in view.

"Where's the cash?" Josiah asked.

Gwen held out her wallet. "I've got forty-five dollars."

He took the money. "That's not enough. We'll do a trade."

"A trade?" She glanced towards the kitchenette. A skillet sat sizzling on the hotplate. The slab of meat looked like beef but smelled sweet. She hoped it wasn't human flesh. Goosebumps rose on her skin. She rubbed her arms to comfort herself. Was it strange that she was afraid to die? Maybe death would be a mercy. She would be reunited with Denise.

"I'll take your hair." Josiah's chapped lips parted in a smile, revealing crooked teeth stained the same shade of yellowish gray as his linen tunic and trousers. He looked like he'd traveled in a time machine from Medieval England. Josiah Crone, an appropriate name for an elderly sorcerer — or a con artist who pretended to have psychic powers. He beckoned for her to follow him.

The Winnebago's bathroom was small, and it smelled medicinal, like strong mouthwash. A white lab coat with the OmniPark logo hung from a hook on the door. *Did every weirdo who lived near Odessa work at OmniPark?*

He opened a cupboard under the sink and pulled out rusty hedge clippers. He pointed a gnarled finger at the wavy hair that flowed down Gwen's back, almost to her waist. "Cut it all off."

The shears were so dull that Gwen had to saw at her hair. She cut off the bangs first, then started on the left side of her head. The tugging sensation, combined with her fear, made her temples throb. *What if the spell didn't work?* As her dread built, a tear rolled down her cheek. "Do you have anything sharper?" she said.

He chuckled. "Not for you."

She reached into her jean's right pocket and pulled out the butterfly knife.

"Put the knife away," Josiah said.

"I'm going to use it to cut my hair."

He tilted his head to the side and peered intently like a bird of prey preparing to pounce. His eyes took on a strange glint. "In a hurry, are we? Magic takes work. Keep cutting with the clippers."

Desperation made her comply. She'd thought that her hair was her best feature, but it was a small sacrifice for a hex that might reveal the truth. *Snip, snip, snip.* She trimmed until she'd cleared a bald patch on the top of her head.

Josiah picked up a clump of hair and sniffed it. A weird expression flickered across his face. Was it her imagination, or had his left pupil dilated and the right pupil shrunk?

Gwen's mouth went dry. She worked the clippers faster. The pile of hair on the floor grew thicker. Her wrist ached. Except for stubble, her scalp was almost bald. She was chopping the hair at the nape of her neck when Josiah opened the medicine cabinet and pulled out a straight razor. "Give me some blood," he said.

Gwen set the hedge clippers on the sink. Her hand shook when she took the razor.

"You squeamish? No refunds if you back down."

"What if he's innocent?" she said.

"Blood for blood. If your daddy didn't kill your friend, he'll be spared. Only the murderer will be turned to stone."

Gwen pressed the razor against her scalp until the blade bit into flesh. The wound stung, but it didn't hurt nearly as much as Denise must've suffered.

Josiah snapped his fingers. "Bend down. No, closer to me." He took a handful of shorn hair and rubbed it against the wound.

She gritted her teeth, stifling a scream, but couldn't hold back a whimper.

"Hush," he said. He sopped up the blood.

Gwen started feeling dizzy. She grabbed the sink.

Josiah chanted, "Forked tongue, lovely rattle. Forked tongue, lovely rattle." After the sixth repetition, his voice changed, softening and rising in pitch. "Forked tongue, lovely rattle."

He sounded exactly like Denise.

"Do you have any bandages?" Gwen said.

Josiah picked up a stained handkerchief from the counter. It smelled like beer.

Gwen handed it back to him and stumbled from the Winnebago.

She felt Josiah's eyes drilling into her back as she climbed on her bicycle. She yanked a bandana from her pocket and wrapped it around her head, then biked further down the dirt road instead of heading home.

No trucks or cars passed her. The road veered to the right as she approached a chinkapin oak tree with a gnarled trunk. A dilapidated shack near it had collapsed.

The sun beamed hotter and hotter, scorching her face. It felt like she'd entered an alternative reality, a dystopian world where she was the last human survivor.

When she arrived at the desolate spot that Josiah had described, she didn't see any wildlife, except for a Red-tailed hawk that circled overhead, screeching. She left her bike on the side of the road, broke off a branch from a dead sugar hackberry tree, and began to forage.

The ground was dry and cracked from lack of rain. She had to be careful where she stepped to avoid falling on loose rocks or getting jabbed by thorns. She stepped around a horse-crippler cactus with spikes longer than her thumbs. A group of prickly pear cacti were strangely deformed. All the pads were twisted, and none of the plants were blooming. In late spring, the prickly pear should've been coated with bright yellow flowers.

Blazing sunlight gilded the sweat glistening on her skin. She panted with exhaustion, but she kept shoving boulders with the branch. She found no critters underneath the rocks, except bugs. "Forked tongue, lovely rattle. Forked tongue, lovely rattle," she called.

As her voice was carried by the warm wind, her chest constricted, squeezed by a corset of grief. Pushing past the pain, she repeated the phrase until it became a song, melodious yet thick with sorrow and frustration.

Finally, after she'd chanted for an hour, a juvenile diamondback rattlesnake slithered from underneath a dry mesquite shrub. The snake was nearly two feet long — mature enough to have potent venom.

Gwen pulled off the bandana, shoved it in her pocket, and drew a dead mouse from her other pocket. Its fur was sticky with the blood Josiah had rubbed on it. He'd insisted it would "draw the serpents."

The snake swallowed her gift. As the lump slowly traveled down its brown-scaled body, Gwen tentatively reached out her hand. She held her breath and stroked the diamondback.

Instead of embedding its fangs in her hand, the rattler lapped her wrist with its forked tongue.

Gwen grasped the snake behind its head and said, "Forked tongue, lovely rattle."

The rattler thrashed.

She yelped and almost lost her grip. Squeezing tighter, she repeated the chant until the rattler stopped struggling. Gwen palpated the brown and tan scales, searching for the seam between the heart and lungs, the secret spot Josiah had described to her. She felt a pang of conscience as she used her butterfly knife to slice open the reptile's flesh. Her fingers probed muscles and tendons. She plucked a rib. The bone was sharp but tasted like hope. She ground the rib between her molars, swallowed, and placed the wounded snake on her head.

Rattler blood blended with her sweat. The diamondback writhed and *hissed*, but finally wrapped itself around her bald scalp.

Gwen climbed over more rocks and found another young rattler. She gave the second snake a mouse. After she consumed the second rib, Gwen began to change. The tip of her tongue split and became forked. Her canines lengthened. What a strange sensation, scales bursting forth from her skin.

When her transformation was complete, the two snakes on her head rattled their tails, writhing like a Gorgon's crown. Gwen *hissed* along with the coronet of diamondbacks. If Josiah hadn't lied, the snakes would have the power to slay Denise's killer.

As she pedaled toward home, one of the rattlers nipped her left shoulder. She patted the snake's head and crooned, "Forked tongue, lovely rattle."

The venom sent a rush of adrenaline streaking up her spine. Within seconds, the puncture marks had healed.

Gwen arrived at the street that led to her family's house. She parked her bike on the shoulder and waited. Mom would be in the kitchen preparing dinner. Dad usually got home by 7:00 PM.

A dented pickup whizzed past her, followed by a Ford Pinto station wagon with fake wood paneling.

The wind whipped up. Dust blew in Gwen's face. When she rubbed her eyes, one of the snakes licked her hand.

The sunset painted the sky an angry red when her father's truck appeared. She walked into the road. Blazing headlights, a blaring horn. The Chevy screeched to a stop. Gwen ran toward the truck. For a moment, she thought that she saw Denise sitting in the driver's seat, wearing her softball uniform and a wide smile. Gwen yanked on the door, but it was locked. "Denise!" she shouted.

Her soulmate's image disappeared, and Gwen saw her father. For a split second, his face looked like it was carved from granite. Then the hallucination vanished, and Gwen realized her father was screaming.

"Dad," she cried. Her heart pounded so hard it felt like it was going to burst through her ribs. Relief, shame, and frustration made her burst into tears. Her father hadn't turned to stone. He hadn't killed Denise.

The Chevy's motor was still running. Dad unrolled the driver's side window.

The rattlers *hissed.* The snake curled atop her head lunged at him, but did not bite.

"What've you done?" Dad stared at her in horror. "Get rid of the snakes!"

"I can't! They're stuck to my skin!"

By the time she'd finished telling him about Josiah Crone, Dad was crying as hard as she was. "What'll I say to Mom?" she said.

Dad wiped his eyes. "Get in the back of the truck. I'll make him change you back."

The truck lurched when he put it in gear. He drove to Josiah's motorhome and pulled up behind the Winnebago.

"Wait here," she said.

Dad shut off the engine. "I'm coming with you." They stormed up the driveway. Dad pounded on the RV's door. No one answered, but Gwen heard a TV blaring. It sounded like an old Western movie:: horses running, and gunshots.

Dad twisted the doorknob, and the RV's door swung open.

The elderly sorcerer sat in a recliner, within striking distance of the rattlers, but he didn't look nervous. He set down his beer bottle. "No refunds."

"Change her back," Dad said.

Josiah ignored him, but raised his eyebrows at Gwen. "What's the matter, missy? Don't like being a Chimera?"

Gwen stepped in front of her father. "He didn't kill Denise!"

"Coulda told you that if I'd seen him. Daddy's got a clean aura."

The snakes rattled their tails and *hissed*.

"Forked tongue, lovely rattle," Josiah said.

The rattlers quieted.

Dad said, "Change her back, or we're calling the police!"

Josiah picked up his beer. "Won't do no good. You swallowed the ribs. Your cells have meshed. No take-backs."

The Chevy's tires spun, kicking up dust as they sped away from the Winnebago. Though Gwen sat in the truck bed, she could hear her father shouting from the cab, "There has to be a scientific explanation!"

"Dad, are we going to the hospital?" Gwen shouted back.

"No, I'm taking you to the Biologist."

"Who?"

"Dr. Fiona Clark. She's a biologist who works as a special contractor at OmniPark. All of the Park Ambassadors who teach visitors about science are based on Dr. Clark."

The truck surged forward. Her father must've been driving twice the speed limit. Gwen grabbed onto the side of the bed when the truck fishtailed, enveloping her in a cloud of dust. The sensation of the snakes slithering on her head should've been driving her mad, but it was strangely soothing.

Dad finally stopped in Odessa, parking in the circular driveway of a plantation-style home with white Corinthian columns flanking its front door. "Wait here," he said.

Her mouth went dry as she watched him standing on the doorstep.

A woman with wild red hair opened the door. Dr. Fiona Clark looked more like a hippie than a scientist. She wore a long batik dress and stood barefoot on the stone steps. Gwen couldn't hear their conversation, but it didn't last long. Dad led the way to the truck.

"I hear you've had quite an adventure," Dr. Clark said. Her voice was soft, as if she was talking to a small child.

"Ye — yes," Gwen stammered, so nervous she could scarcely get the words out. Her heart hammered in her chest.

"Josiah Crone told you to swallow the ribs?"

"Yes. I was trying to figure out who killed my girlfriend." Gwen burst into tears.

"What did he promise the snakes would do for you?"

Gwen rubbed her eyes. She felt like an utter fool. "He said they'd turn the killer to stone."

"Like Medusa." Dr. Clark smiled. "Is that what you want?"

"I want justice! The police haven't arrested anyone!"

"Change her back!" Dad said.

"Can you do that?" Gwen said.

"There's a chance." Dr. Clark glanced at her watch. "I'll fetch my shoes and purse."

How could a theme park ride counteract magic?

When they arrived at OmniPark, it was nearly 10:00 PM. Dr. Clark unlocked the main gate and led them through the cavernous Entryway Pavilion. Except for the sound of their footsteps, it was eerily quiet.

"We'll enter the Realm of the Cell through the Scalar Portal," Dr. Clark said.

Gwen turned to her father. "Is the Scalar Portal the project you worked on?"

He nodded, his lips set in a grim line.

Dr. Clark paused in front of an archway decorated with giant paintings depicting bacteria and amoebas. "You'll need to ride the Amoeba Escape on your own. Are you afraid?"

Gwen's stomach clenched. "Is it dangerous?"

As if they understood her words, the snakes *hissed*.

"Be honest and open about your feelings, and the snakes won't harm you," Dr. Clark said.

Dad raised his eyebrows. "What about the ride?"

"The Amoeba Escape is a facilitator — it has the power to strengthen or loosen links between cells. The ride should be perfectly safe, but it's never been used on a Chimera." She beckoned for them to follow her through the archway.

"That's what Josiah Crone called me!" Gwen strode faster, matching her brisk pace.

"A Chimera is a person who has more than one set of DNA within their cells. Human and foreign DNA. Scientists have tried to produce Chimeras in laboratories, by introducing pluripotent stem cells, but none of the experiments have succeeded. I believe you are the first true Chimera," Dr. Clark said.

"Human and Western diamondback rattlesnake?" Dad said.

Dr. Clark shook her head. "No. Those are not ordinary rattlers."

Being shrunk to the size of a cell would've been a truly disorienting experience if the Scalar Portal's science had been real. But Gwen knew that it must be an illusion — her dad was an ordinary engineer — not a mad scientist.

The wall next to the entrance of the Amoeba Escape looked like it was made of solid metal, but when Dr. Clark pressed it, a hidden panel popped open, exposing glass beakers that held colorful liquids. She picked up a small beaker filled with sapphire fluid and handed it to Gwen. "Drink this. It will improve the effectiveness of the ride."

The glass was cool. No scent wafted from the liquid. It seemed like she was holding a beaker full of tap water.

"What is it?" Dad said.

"A special blend of enzymes that reduce inflammation, and soften the links between human cells and foreign cells."

"You sure you want to do this?" Dad asked.

Gwen lifted the beaker to her lips. When the liquid touched her tongue, it warmed instantly to her body temperature. She drank deeply, gulping until the beaker was empty.

"You may feel dizzy," Dr. Clark said. "Have a seat in the ride vehicle. Close your eyes if you feel disoriented. We'll be watching. If you feel like you're in danger, squeeze the stabilizer bar three times — hard. We'll stop the ride."

The stabilizer bar latched against Gwen's chest with a clang, pinning her in place. Her seat began to vibrate. "I love you, Dad!"

"I love you, sweetie!" His eyes were moist as if he was about to start crying again. She'd never seen her father cry so much.

The cart glided down the "cell membrane" path. The floor, ceiling, and walls were painted to represent close-up views of cells. Projected images moved as a voiceover told the story of The Amoeba Escape. The animatronic sculptures were so lifelike, Gwen felt like she was traveling through the bowels of some giant creature that was infested with parasites.

As the vehicle rounded a curve, a giant amoeba pulsed and reached for her. She jerked back and cringed. Sweat rolled down her spine.

The twisting tunnel seemed as if it was never going to end. Gwen's heartbeat accelerated. She had experienced claustrophobia before, but never so strongly. She took a deep breath, trying to calm her agitation, but the fear clenched her gut. The snakes wound around her scalp raised their heads and swayed back and forth, as if they were dancing.

The cart lurched when it took a sharp turn. The vehicle hovered above a pit filled with shimmering cells. A scream tore from her throat. The sound of her voice echoed and grew louder, turning the tunnel into a terrifying auditory hall of mirrors. She closed her eyes, pressing the lids together. *Denise, I miss you. I miss you so much. Tell me what to do!*

"Forked tongue, lovely rattle."

Gwen's eyelids snapped open. Had the snakes spoken?

A diamondback swayed in front of her face. The snake's mouth opened wider. Fangs dripped venom. "Justice," the snake hissed.

Chimera. Maybe that was her purpose in life, a teen whose DNA bonded with extraterrestrials and snakes. A human who would seek justice when cowards and fools said it was impossible to catch Denise's killer.

After Gwen graduated from high school, she applied for police officer jobs. She sent resumes to more than two hundred law enforcement agencies. None granted her an interview. They'd heard about "The Gorgon Queen," the moniker reporters had given her. How ironic — police were afraid of Gwen, a five-foot-four lesbian who wanted to solve a murder.

Dad encouraged her to enroll in courses at Texas Tech. "Become a psychologist like you planned. Have a normal life," he said.

"How can I be normal?" Gwen said. "You want me to pretend Denise never existed?"

Dad sighed. "I wasn't talking about Denise. I know you love her."

"She needs closure," Mom said.

Gwen sent one more letter, a thank you note to Dr. Clark. She wasn't expecting a response. A week later, Dad knocked on her bedroom door. He waited in the hallway until she opened the door. "There's some visitors here to see you," Dad said.

Dr. Clark and a white haired man were sitting in the living room with Mom. Dr. Dalton Teague, the billionaire who founded OmniPark. Gwen recognized Dr. Teague from the photographs of him she'd seen in the newspaper.

"I understand you'd like to solve a murder." Dr. Teague smiled.

Gwen opened her mouth but was too shocked to speak. She nodded.

"Thirty-five thousand people walk through OmniPark's gates every day. Where else can you interrogate so many suspects?" Dr. Teague said. "I'd like to offer you a proposition."

Gwen swallowed "What do you want me to do?"

"A special internship. You'll spend an hour each morning with Dr. Clark. Let her study you. Fluid samples, physical training, mental acuity. The rest of the day, you can work in one of the OmniPark Realms in a position of your choice. Waitstaff or Park Ambassador."

"My daughter's not going to be a lab rat," Mom said.

"Of course not." Dr. Teague smiled. "The salary is competitive and comes with excellent benefits."

Gwen found her haven in OmniPark. "My World is yours to explore," Dalton Teague had promised. He hadn't lied. As a special intern, she was given free admission to the attractions in all of the seven Realms.

The medical tests weren't nearly as painful as she expected. Having her mouth swabbed and spitting in tubes wasn't a big deal. Dr. Clark only stuck her with syringes once a month.

Gwen started working as a Park Ambassador in the Realm of the Particle. Dressing up as a scientist was cool, but narrating the same ride every day got boring. Her request to be transferred to a waitstaff position in the Realm of the Cell's Protein Palace was approved. She liked the restaurant's bustling atmosphere, and the frozen yogurt bar was awesome—there were new toppings every day.

On the busiest days, thousands of customers looked at Gwen with curiosity, amazement, and horror. Some guests asked her on dates. She turned them down.

Four years, one month, and sixteen days after Denise's death, a sunburned jerk patted Gwen's butt as she walked past him. "Can I get a refill?" He leered, looking from the snakes to her breasts.

His coffee cup was nearly full, but she said, "Sure. Be right back." As she strode towards the counter, a little boy pointed at her head.

The rattlers *hissed.*

"Look Mommy, look!" the boy said.

Gwen pressed her lips together. She wanted to yell at the brat, but he was just a kid.

Someone near the restaurant's main entrance screamed. Gwen was used to hearing kids goofing off, but this voice was low. It sounded like a terrified man.

Gwen turned around.

A man wearing a cowboy hat was kneeling on the floor, as if in prayer. His mouth yawned wide, as if his expression had frozen mid-scream. His face was pale. His teeth were shinier than teeth should ever be, clear as quartz crystals.

Color drained from the man's skin until his epidermis became completely transparent, like glass wrapped around pulsing muscles.

"Forked tongue, lovely rattle," Gwen said.

The rattlers *hissed* louder. It sounded like there were hundreds of snakes coiled on her head.

People panicked, shoving each other as they fled the Protein Palace.

"Forked tongue, lovely rattle!" Gwen shouted.

The rattlers thrashed.

Energy coursed through Gwen's body, an electric shimmer that zoomed from the snakes to her toes. Time seemed to slow down as the snakes *hissed, hissed.*

The kneeling man's flesh morphed, blackening and becoming glossy — exactly like the volcanic rock obsidian in the desert outside Odessa.

The snakes' tails vibrated like maracas, faster and faster, until the obsidian man imploded, collapsing inward with a blinding flash of light.

As the smoke cleared, Gwen's knees buckled. She knelt on the linoleum, stunned.

The only trace of Denise's killer was a scorched mark on the floor.

Eat the Rich

Angela Yuriko Smith

Giselle tapped her clipboard with impatience.

"Is it ready yet? This needs to move faster. I'm expecting."

The aquarium tech looked up from the oversized filtration unit at Giselle's thin, almost brittle frame. Wafer thin, she certainly didn't *look* pregnant. Always best not to question Giselle Worthington, though. He learned that the hard way.

"Yes ma'am, no ma'am. I can't rush the temperature now. The water is gonna do what the water is gonna do."

She narrowed her eyes at him. "Make the water go faster, or you will be done..." She made a point of reading his name tag. "...Richard."

The tech felt like her frigid attitude was probably not helping the water heat up any, but again, he thought it best to keep these thoughts to himself. He ducked his head and fiddled with his test tubes, checking the salinity for the hundredth time under her gaze. The specifications she had given him were wrong. No fish could live in water with this much salt in it let alone the additional chemical cocktail that included sodium thiopental and pancuronium bromide but he wasn't going to question that either. Trying to reason with her earned him her clipboard thrown into his face. He had a cut over his eye to show for it.

She started tapping the clipboard again and he flinched, waiting for another blow.

"I'm going to call the delivery crew and see what is taking so long."

She turned on her wooden platforms and stomped off.

He relaxed only when the sound of her footsteps went into the foreman's makeshift office and she slammed the door behind her. He could see her through the glass window, stabbing the phone buttons with her talons.

"That's high class people for you. Eat the rich before they eat you."

He had muttered this low, to himself. There was no way she could hear him, but she whipped her head around to glare at him as if she had. He ducked down and fiddled with the vials again, as if that could somehow hurry the water temperature along.

She was screaming into the phone now, pointing at the clock on the wall as if the victimized listener on the other end could see her pointing. Whoever it was, they weren't able to please her either. She pounded the heavy receiver against the tempered glass window a few times before she slammed the phone back into the cradle where it promptly bounced out to dangle from the wall by its cord. In a full rage, she swiped all the papers, books and schematics off the work desk and onto the office floor. When the foreman returned he would just pick them all up without a word and spend an hour sorting them. He'd had a stapler thrown at him. The door to the office burst open.

"I have to check on these incompetents in person. Don't you dare leave."

Richard nodded, keeping his eyes glued to the water sample.

"I mean it. I want you here when I come back. If you aren't, not only will you not be paid but I will ruin your career, and subsequently your life."

Richard nodded again, still focused on his test kit. He knew she could and would make good on her threat. Without another word, Giselle stomped through the manmade cavern that would soon be a busy theme park attraction and slammed the outer door behind her.

Only when he heard the golf cart she had waiting for her drive off did he relax. He didn't regret taking the job — the pay was phenomenal — but he did wonder if he was going to survive this. If he did, he promised himself he would cash the check, change his number and consider a new line of work. There was no way any fish were going to survive in the toxic stew she was demanding he concoct. There was no way he was taking the blame for this later.

Aside from Giselle, he would have loved this job.

The Realm of the Deep was classy, no doubt. All gleaming brass and cherry wood paneling, the submersible looked like it was ready for Captain Nemo to board at any moment. Instead, there was a fisherman animatronic overlooking the artificial wharf. The craft would be filled with sticky, overly excited children and their parents. A sign proclaiming this the Mariana Trench Dive leaned against the faux rock wall, waiting to be posted. A voice echoed out in the empty room, making Richard jump in his skin. He dropped the test tube he was holding and it shattered.

"For a thousand... eons, as the ocean brine laps across the ancient bedrock, a protean creature will grow fat, thriving on human waste..."

It was the fisherman animatronic going off for the first time Richard had been here. Metal gears squeaked under its latex skin as it mimicked humanity. *"...it is finally stirring awake."* The Fisherman ended the prerecorded spiel and settled back into place.

Okay, maybe this job would be stressful even without Giselle.

Richard could hear the phone beeping in the office, still off the hook. He grabbed a small hand broom,swept up the broken glass and headed to the office to take care of both annoyances. He dumped the glass in the small office trash, trying not to walk over the schematics scattered across the floor. A drawing of a tentacled creature's life cycle caught his eye. He didn't recognize this mollusc looking animal. Its shape was irregular. Maybe it was a bad rendering, but it was drawn with pieces of refuse protruding from it. He could see pieces of a broken ship, airplane propellers and what looked like a bicycle. He squatted down, studying this thing that would grow from a footlong egg to a creature large enough to wrestle a skyscraper. It was labeled as a Gulaplast, as presented by one Flavius Gauntius in a spidery thin signature in the corner. *What the hell is this?*

The Fisherman squeaked to life again, and again, Richard felt his soul try to jump out of his skin. *"For a thousand unparalleled eons..."* the mechanical voice boomed. The automaton went through his speech about human waste and wound back down to a stop.

"Thanks for turning the robot on, ma'am. Much appreciated."

He picked the Gulaplast chart up and left it on the desk. Dalton Teague had really gone all out for this park, down to the last detail, including realistic life cycles for fake monsters. Richard picked his way back through the scattered charts and to his post to check the water temperature. Still not warm enough.

Her highness probably wouldn't be back any time soon and there really wasn't anything too pressing for Richard to monitor. The water was toxic and she wanted the enormous lagoon far too warm. Richard figured this was a good time for a smoke break to calm his nerves. He lit up.

A long slow exhale, and he followed the smoke's path up to the carefully painted styrofoam ceiling. It looked just like he was in some sort of sophisticated underground lagoon — like a European Casa Bonita. There was a partially built library to one side, all mirrors and Tiffany lamps. Brass fixtures and leather seats gave the place a real *Thousand Leagues* vibe. Still smoking, Richard walked to the water's edge to get a closer look at the submarine floating in the manmade brine.

It didn't seem large enough to hold many people, but there probably wasn't a lot of room in the observation pods either. A map outside sold the pods as the Trench ride's destination, reported to be "full of wonders." Sure, enthrall the kiddies with glowing jellyfish. He imagined the real Mariana Trench was where all the ocean garbage settled like a great septic tank of the deep. He squatted down on the artificially aged wharf and looked sideways through the water, trying to see the pods.

The water was black after just a few feet, and looked much deeper than what Richard expected from the dimensions Giselle had given him. It could be that the sides were just painted, but there seemed to be a depth to the inky dark. No guidelights, no cable to hang on to the tiny craft as it traveled. The water gave Richard a sense of the infinite, the same uncomfortable feeling he got when staring up at the night sky. *Endless depth, liquid cosmos...*

"For a thousand unparalleled eons, as the ocean brine..." blared out from behind him. Richard jumped for a third time and dropped his half smoked cigarette in the water.

"That's it you hunk of junk. I'm pulling your plug."

He took two steps toward the automaton that was winding down his small speech with a mechanical whine, when Richard heard a different noise behind him. A whoosh, and a sudden heat warmed his backside. He turned around to see a small fire spreading across the water.

"Those damn chemicals!" Richard yelled to no one. "I said it was a lethal combination!"

He stood for thirty seconds, watching, not knowing what to do. It wasn't like he could just throw water on the flames to douse them. The gas rising off the boiling water made him choke and he backed up. He was aware the fisherman robot was performing again, but Richard wasn't listening. He had advised against the added chemicals. This wasn't his fault---except he'd been told smoking wasn't allowed near the water.

The flames were spreading like a drink he'd once seen served at a fancy bar. They rose up from the lagoon in a twisted blue dance, spreading over the water far too fast. Frenetic, the flames were engulfing everything. He could feel his eyebrows singing. The submarine was shrouded in fire, the flames licked the wharf, reaching toward him. They shot toward the ceiling, tendrils of black smoke antiquing the airbrushed rocks. The air was acidic, the odor burning his nostrils from the inside. Richard realized the whole fake lagoon could fireball and he would be trapped inside. He backed up, tripped on something and fell backward. Overhead, the fisherman was waving his arms manically and finishing another canned performance.

"...human waste, it is finally stirring awake."

Then, just as suddenly as it started, the flames seemed to go out.

Richard sat up. The flames had burned off the chemical, he guessed, just like in the fancy drink. The exhibit seemed dark in the sudden absence of light. Nothing looked damaged. The submarine and the rocks all looked a little stained from the smoke and heat, but it made them look more realistic.

The door burst open, and with it came a blinding flash of outside light, and Giselle.

She stopped just inside the door and looked at Richard sitting down in front of the automaton. She sniffed the air and smiled.

"Smells like you've been busy working in here. Good. How's the temperature? My baby is on the way."

Stunned, Richard jumped up and started fiddling with his water test tubes again. He checked the thermometer.

"96.8 degrees Fahrenheit! Damn, way too hot!"

Richar knew it was the fire, the fire had heated the water too fast. The fire was his fault. He would be dismissed, fired and have to face Giselle's wrath. He braced himself. Instead...

"Perfect! Well done! I honestly didn't think you would be able to get the water warm enough in time. Richard, you are a miracle worker."

He looked up at her, dumbfounded.

"In fact, there will be a nice bonus for you at the end of today."

He didn't trust Giselle. He had only worked for her a few days, but she had a vicious, cruel temperament. "Really?"

She clomped her way across the cavern floor and put her arm around him reassuringly.

"Really. And I don't blame you for your air of distrust. I know I can be... driven. I have even been told I'm a bitch."

"No..." Richard tried to look shocked.

"Yes, to my face."

"No...!" He wondered if he looked like a cartoon character as he tried to ramp up the shock on his face.

"Yes, but it doesn't matter. What *does* matter is that we did it. Nothing great is ever accomplished without a sacrifice, wouldn't you agree?" Giselle released him, and relieved, Richard inched away and nodded.

"I'm glad we are of the same mind, then. I appreciate everything you've done, sincerely. In fact, why don't you take a smoke break while we wait? There's nothing left to do now. As soon as my baby gets here you can help me get him installed and be on your way. With that bonus I promised, of course."

"Sure thing. I'll just step outside to have a smoke. And watch for the delivery."

Giselle walked to the office and looked in. "What a mess I've made in here for the foreman. It's a wonder anyone will work with me at all. I certainly don't know why Dalton does." She turned back to Richard.

"Don't worry about this. I can clean this up and then I'll get you that bonus. Go smoke. Relax, Richard. You did fantastic work."

Richard shrugged and exited. He certainly wasn't one to argue with a lady.

Outside, he let out a long exhale of relief. He would have to grab a lottery ticket on the way home, because he had some strange luck going on today. His head was still reeling — from fireball to fired to on fire in 60 seconds flat. And, her majesty was actually *happy* with something? He felt like a miracle worker, all right.

He groped in his pocket for his pack, tapped a smoke out and lit up. Still under construction, OmniPark was already an amazing feat of engineering. The sun glinted off silver and white towers rising to the blue sky, connected by skyway rails. *This is what oil money can build*, Richard thought to himself. *Money builds the future. The future belongs to the rich.* But Giselle was nice enough to give him a bonus. She wasn't all bad. He finished his smoke and tossed it across the parking lot to die out on the asphalt. At a distance, he heard a motor vehicle driving through the park instead of the usual electric whine of golf carts.

"Ma'am, your delivery might be here!" He called in and got no answer. Richard walked back into the Realm of the Deep.

His eyes were struggling to adjust from the brightness outside, but he could see the office was now empty. He walked in, looking around. On cue, that cursed fisherman spouted off again. Richard did his best to ignore it. He could hear gears grinding somewhere off over the water, around a faux boulder corner, and then sunlight blasted through the dim chamber.

"Be careful, mind the tentacles."

Giselle's voice, but Richard hadn't noticed another entrance on the tank schematic he'd been shown. He had assumed the corner was the end of the chamber. There was a splash, followed by a yelp.

"I told you, mind the... oh sweet baby..."

Curious, Richard reviewed the park map he'd been given to see what was around the bend. Just as he'd thought, it showed a relatively small area for the Mariana Trench ride. He went over to his charts. They matched the map. By all accounts, the ride stopped at what was painted to look like a bend. There should be nothing past there but a maintenance room full of pumps and equipment. *This would explain why everything was taking longer than it should.* A man yelled out followed by a bigger splash followed by silence. The grinding around the corner began again, and the blast of sunlight was pinched out.

"Ma'am?" Richard called out. He walked back to the water's edge but he couldn't see anything from his vantage point. He did notice some soot floating in patches across the water, now slightly iridescent in the lamp reflections across the oily surface. Whatever just splashed in there wasn't going to live long. He had advised against it. Not his fault. Best to get his check cut and run.

"Ma'am?" he called out again.

"Yes, sorry. Let me write your check."

This time Richard almost fell into the water. Giselle was a few feet behind him, smiling.

"I... er... didn't hear you come in." He glanced at her feet, still entombed in her clunky platforms.

"I can be sneaky when I want to be. Would you mind checking the water composition one last time before you go? I'll get that check written."

She was staring at him too brightly, a wide smile plastered across her face. Somehow, this intense focus was worse than Giselle in a tantrum. Richard felt a trickle of sweat slide its way down his spine. He shuddered involuntarily.

"You're tired. Check the water composition. I'll be right back. And I'll unplug Flavius."

"Who?"

Giselle grinned and pointed a thumb over her shoulder at the automaton that had given him so many jump scares recently. "Flavius the Fisherman." She clunked her way back toward the office. "Wait here. I'll be right back with your bonus."

Richard retrieved his water testing kit from his makeshift work table. He knelt down next to the submarine. He didn't need to test the water again. It was too hot and toxic for anything to live in. He would make a show of it, humor Giselle and go. Just get the bonus and go. If she called him to complain that her... baby had died, he'd hang up. Why call up an expert just to ignore him? He was only following directions.

Something swished under the surface of the water and bumped the submarine. Out of the corner of his eye he thought he saw an oily tentacle slither across the water's surface. A grimy island of froth sat on the surface of the water a few feet out. It reminded him of glassy, dead eyes staring. He looked away and scooped a water sample up into his vial.

"What kind of creature is your baby anyways? I figured you guys were just going to do some basic tilapia or something. That's the usual amusement park fish." He raised his voice so Giselle could hear him.

"Oh... it's called Gulaplast. Very hard to find. They don't reproduce in the way we think of reproduction."

Richard saw an expanse of skin slide through the shadows to vanish beneath the wharf. Black, iridescent like the water, it slid across his field of vision with barely a splash. It was a pretty big fish.

"Gulaplast? Like the chart in the office? I thought that was just for the park guests — like make-believe. I never heard of one. How big do they get?"

"Oh, pretty big."

Richard yelped with surprise. Somehow she'd managed to tiptoe behind him in those noisy shoes of hers again.

"How the heck...?"

"To be honest, we don't really know. Maybe there is only one Gulaplast and it leaps back and forth across space-time. Maybe it reproduces and grows to match the environment. Certain scholars speculate the Biblical Leviathan is actually Gulaplast. To even see Them is a rare blessing. To actually interact with Them is quite the bonus."

Richard backed away from her, trying to angle his way sideways. He wasn't comfortable with the water behind him.

"Gulaplast is grand, cosmic... They are the eons and the depths. They are beyond our understanding. They dwarf our comprehension." Her eyes were so feverish Richard worried they might physically sear him. He felt real fear of this woman, cold shivers in his gut as if he'd swallowed a bucket of iron nails.

"Don't worry, Richard, we agreed. Nothing great is ever accomplished without a sacrifice, remember? Do you remember when I said that? You agreed."

"Okay, I have to go. You can mail me the check."

Behind him, Richard heard a splash. Something wet and solid landed on the wharf. Giselle glanced at it behind him and cooed.

"Oh, They like you," she beamed. "You both have the same goal, in a way."

Richard was afraid to turn around. Giselle was speaking gibberish.

"What? What goal? I need to clock out."

Something snaked around his ankle and tugged. Richard yelled and tried to jump forward but whatever had a hold on him pulled him down. He slammed onto the dock. He kicked at what he could see of a tentacle, rainbows playing over the slick skin in the lamp light. It was dragging him toward the water. Richard screamed as more tentacles rose up followed by a three foot gaping maw filled with shards of rusted metal and glass. The eyes were just boils on the skin, pockets of pus and poison set in a horror semblance of a face.

"Look at that baby go," said Giselle. "He wants the same things as you, as any of us really. He just wants to eat the Rich."

Richard screamed again as he was drug toward the toxic brine, nails digging into the artfully aged wood. He looked to Giselle for help, tears of terror streaming down his face. He raised his hand, almost as if waving farewell to the world, in a last, desperate attempt to elicit her aid before he vanished over the edge with a kerplop. A grimy island of froth bubbled up to the surface of the water a few feet out, glassy and stained pink.

From behind her, a mechanical voice rang out.

"... *a protean creature will grow fat, thriving...*"

Giselle smiled.

"I think it's just about opening time."

(Top, right) Main entryway of the enormous faux submarine, the Pequod, located in the Realm of the Deep. (Top, left) The Captain's Table Restaurant in the Realm of the Deep, circa 1979.

(Bottom, right) A hallway with windows looking out on a "starship manufacturing plant" in the Realm of the Stars. (Bottom, left) Orbit One Central located in the Realm of the Stars, as it looked circa 1985.

OmniPark's Founding Team of Technosophers

(Top, left) Beth Bachmeier, Realm designer. (Top, right) Chuck Walcott, lead writer.

(Bottom, left) Denise Olivetti, storyboard artist. (Bottom, right) Harry Peale, systems engineer.

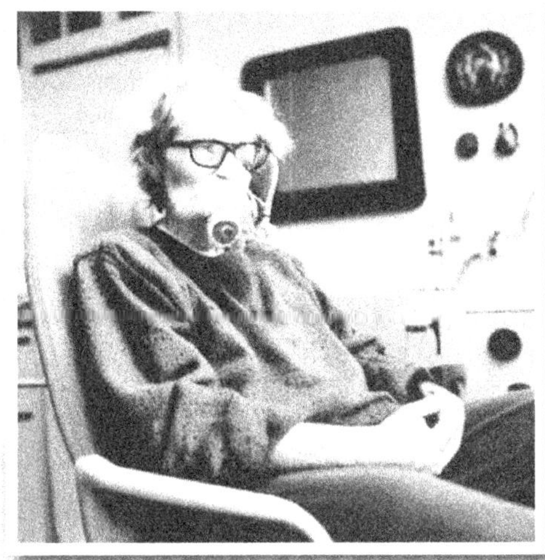

*(Top)
Elijah Shattuck,
ride designer.*

*(Bottom, left)
Roger Clarendon,
ride engineer.*

*(Bottom, right)
Yamasato Masaru,
ride and Realm
interior artist.*

The Nebula Quest

Laird Barron

The Ice Age iteration of Ace Pilot Shaw would've worn a mammoth hide cloak and carried a flint-tooth spear. His mantra: *Cave. Dog. Fire.*

The Nuclear Age incarnation of Ace Pilot Shaw disappeared after many years of exemplary service. Nobody could explain it. There were rumors he'd been arrested and informally imprisoned while on a top-secret intelligence mission overseas. Some claimed he'd gotten killed putting a cutting-edge jet through its paces, although he was well past his flying prime. His daughter latched onto that last theory. In her recurring dream, Ace Pilot Shaw's experimental fighter jet slammed into the earth at some ungodly speed. Countless nightmares from countless angles.

Ace Pilot Shaw often quipped, *I'm no Chuck Yeager, but I know how to land a plane.* Grinning behind his weathered hand: *Truth is,* anybody *can land a plane.*

Ace Pilot Shaw often said, *Enjoy me while I'm around. One day God will snap His Fingers and I'll blink into the infinite.*

Our present shapes the past. Ace Pilot Shaw's aviator glasses melted.

History is how we remember it. Ace Pilot Shaw's face curled and crisped.

Imagination is a Power, not a plaything.

Flames leaped higher. Smoke roiled. Tasted like bones.

People's problems are the same everywhere.

A haunted planetoid orbited a dwarf star near the rim of Galaxy Gamma-Zed.

The Imperial Star Catalog designated it Planet X-9 followed by a dash and sixty-eight-thousand-character alphanumeric code. Inhospitable to nonindigenous carbon organisms. Hollow, volcanic, tenanted by creatures of legendary vileness. As if local conditions weren't sufficiently challenging, a large black hole called Light Eater lurked near enough to precipitate a number of temporal anomalies.

A survey expedition was dispatched to evaluate X-9's resources: mineral, biological, and strategic. Matters went to hell from the outset. Imperial servants were conditioned to eschew melodrama, but the expeditionary forces were soon convinced the rock was cursed.

Firstly, they discovered an ancient planetwide graveyard of ships. Primitive vessels of myriad shapes and models embedded in X-9's crust. The surveyors studied the wreckage and the bones of the crash victims to determine these vessels generally originated from mythical Terra, a world forgotten by most Imperial cartographers and historians. Bizarrely, these wrecks didn't possess engines or any other apparent means of propulsion; they were clever *replicas* of spacefaring vehicles.

Secondly, whether by accident or doomed interactions with hostile entities, equipment malfunctioned and the army of surveyors and laborers rapidly dwindled. Case in point: try as they might, Servitors Frang and Colv couldn't repair the Titan Crawler following its collision with a stalagmite of unusual density, so the vat brothers donned battle exoskeletons and descended into Cavern L9 on a twelve-strand obsidiron cable to undertake manual mapping. Forty seconds later, the cable danced wildly. Warning beacons lighted the winch's control panel. The anchor dragged up the line and received Servitor Colv's slagged suit. Green acid gushed from the exoskeleton's burst seams and bubbled on the rocky ground. Servitor Frang was just gone.

The dearth of peons concerned those in supervisory positions.

"The perils of going lo-fi," Ordinator Vennen said. This was his one-thousand-and-forty-second expedition conducted over the past three cycles. *To spread the influence of humanity, we must never forget our humanity,* went the Plenum slogan. By that justification, the Plenum imposed draconian restrictions on expeditionary protocols — a hindrance to complement a host of similar self-imposed handicaps, such as physical and mental throttles. Eons past, the peoples of the Empire abandoned supreme godliness in favor of mere demi-godliness. They'd seen firsthand evidence that ennui was the greatest threat to any sapient species. The struggle was the all.

Rak the Techmaster dialed a lethal dose into his replica Mark V plasma rifle. "Always send a synthetic. Always. Or a drone." Emboldened by youth, he spoke out of turn. On the other hand, he carried a plasma rifle. Leveler of mountain ranges, rearranger of continents.

"Androids are expensive," Ordinator Vennen said. "They also have distinctive personalities. Deactivate your shackles and hook onto the gangline. The mission must proceed, and it must proceed according to sanctioned parameters."

"Whoa, no need to risk our own precious hides. Radio the mothership to spawn more expendables."

"*Everyone* is expendable. Mind the rules. Defiance will be rewarded with agonies beyond measure. Worse, it'll blacken your permanent record."

"Buddy, I'm not jumping in that pit no matter how much you sweet talk me."

"Oh, I beg to differ, my mutinous friend," Ordinator Vennen said directly into the left barrel of his subordinate's rifle. "Don't make me assume a less collegial form." His dominant hand sprouted titanium alloy claws.

Rak the Techmaster decided to unload the entire coil into his boss. Such a wanton expenditure of power could be expected to blast a quarter of the planetary crust into space. Guaranteed self-annihilation. He mildly wondered if that would be enough to get the job done.

Proximity alarms on their belts chirped. Purple skull pips of danger flashed in sync.

"An object materialized in a cavern half a klick southeast," Ordinator Vennen said around multiple sets of diamond fangs he'd spontaneously grown to complement his whirligig eyes. "Multiple carbon-based lifeforms. Anthropoid. Interlopers from beyond the stars?"

Rak the Techmaster grudgingly relaxed his trigger finger.

"They stand between us and the extraction zone. Let us roll out the welcome wagon and crush them under its iron wheels."

Back on Earth:

As a child, H Shaw's dreams of becoming an astronaut were endorsed by her hotshot pilot dad. *I'm secretly an astronaut!* he said. The old man didn't express disappointment when she eventually ditched hard science and majored in drama. A few months before Ace Pilot Shaw vanished, the powers that be had clipped his wings, assigned him a comfy desk job — he most definitely hadn't died in a wreck despite his daughter's technicolor nightmares to the contrary (the odor of barbecue smoke provoked her gorge). He smiled supportively at every rehearsal, sat front row at every rinky-dink production, looking razor-sharp even out of uniform. Paid the rent of her shabby apartment and stocked the fridge. Footed the bills for dancing and voice lessons. Politely ignored the fact her siblings pulled their own weight or at least married well. *You're doing precisely what the universe built you to do,* he'd say with an enigmatic smile. She pretended the setbacks didn't faze her as Broadway dreams faded.

Then Dad dropped off the face of the earth and the military brass remained suspiciously mum. Time, a hell of a lot of time, rolled by and the world kept spinning. H Shaw's courage faltered as the years passed. Auditions dried up. After a six-month stretch with no callbacks, and bill collectors hounding her day and night, she answered a classified ad for a job opening at a newly-constructed theme park near Odessa, Texas. Dreamchild of Dalton Teague, eccentric billionaire, it had been in development for gods knew how long. The ad said, *Position: Navigator. Charisma and extemporaneous wit a plus. Theater experience preferred.*

Navigators directed the course of vessels for safe passage. Why would a Navigator require theater experience? Nonetheless, she dressed in her smartest, most conservative pantsuit and hopped a bus for Odessa. The bus deposited her at a transfer station where she boarded a shuttle with "OmniPark" embossed on its side. She was the sole passenger for the half-hour trip across a prairie to the threshold of a futuristic cityscape. As the shuttle approached its destination, Shaw removed her shades to gawk at what she initially assumed to be an intricate mural or façade. The gates swung wide, dispelling her skepticism. Sunlight bounced off impossibly vibrant spans of plasticized steel spires and sugar-delicate glass domes. EPCOT Center by way of a baroque new-wave science fiction novel. Unspoiled at the moment by throngs of guests who'd soon descend in a cacophony of excitement, sullying the immaculate paths with discarded trash and a million shoe-scuffs.

H Shaw was greeted by a blandly smiling man in a starched shirt with rolled-up sleeves. He introduced himself as the Operations Coordinator. He escorted her past a service entrance, through a warren of corridors, to a dim auditorium similar to any number of other theaters she'd performed in. He asked her to stand near the edge of the stage on an X of black tape and await further instructions. She stared out over several rows of empty seats at a light beaming from its recessed aperture. She thought of the Operations Coordinator's sinewy arms, their whiteness, the metallic glamor of the light as it pierced her eye into her brain.

An intercom crackled and a cordial voice said, "Ms. Shaw, on behalf of our benefactor, Dr. Dalton Teague, welcome to OmniPark. Astride a carousel of infinite timelines, you could've been anything. Perhaps in this go-round, you'll fulfill the role of Navigator. Management hopes so." The voice paused, then continued, rolling with the supreme confidence of a seasoned narrator, a master mesmerist.

"Are you familiar with remote viewing? Astral projection? Telepathy? Quantum entanglement? Mass hypnosis? Psychotropic techniques will serve as an integral component of the OmniPark experience."

She inhaled to question, to protest; ashes filled her mouth, burned her throat. Her skull perked like Vesuvius.

"Fix your gaze upon the lamp," the voice commanded. "Don't blink. Don't even think of blinking. Blink and we will terminate the interview."

The blue spotlight rippled, widening into the molten yawn of a galactic core. The taped X supported her blackened boots above a rift of fulminating stars. She wore the charred remnants of a space suit. Her left arm ended at the wrist, the rest of it peeled to the bone. Painless, cold. Her father waved from the bubble-domed cockpit of a futuristic spacecraft zipping toward Pluto on a red-hot rail.

Goodbye, kiddo. Goodbye! I aim to thread this needle through a gap in the Great Filter — His taillights flared and winked out.

"The tarot reveals your destiny," Radio Voice said. "Worry not. If you survive the mission, the Prop Department will fit you with a prosthetic. Please, don't scream. It's perfectly normal to mourn one's absent father. Even if he's alive. In another universe, your mother is the one who vanished. In another, you were never born and I'm speaking to a genetically enhanced canine. No matter which way we turn, each of us has one foot in the Lagerstätte."

The stage resolidified. She was whole again, albeit wobble-brained; dressed in her smart pantsuit, unscorched. Dread suffused her every fiber, and a pins and needles sensation of waking to a new, vicious reality. Fleeting fear gave way to euphoria, and beneath that, a steely belligerence. She didn't understand the game, only that they were playing one.

Radio Voice said, "I trust you've read the script. Take it from the top."

Except, no one had provided her a script. She cleared her throat and began to recite the *Iliad*. Radio Voice let her go on for nearly forty-five minutes before interrupting to say, "We've heard enough. The role is yours. Always has been."

H Shaw was ensconced in spartan-yet-serviceable dormitory quarters. The room came with mandatory literature: a four-hundred-page manual detailing the park's architecture and purpose (enlightenment via entertainment!), as well as an employee code of conduct and biographies of Dalton Teague and his inner circle of fellow dreamers, the Technosophers. The naked bones of the park were awesome feats of engineering technology, akin to sumptuous movie sets featuring colossal structures and intricate costumes. Details were minute, down to nebulae arabesques on the floor tiles. Her contract included ominous language regarding nondisclosure. Not that she could disclose much of anything — employees were discouraged from departing the premises during the first six-month rotation which coincided with OmniPark's grand opening. Outbound letters and phone calls were forbidden except in cases of emergency.

The core OmniPark attractions were divided into Realms: The Realm of the Cell; The Realm of Life; The Realm of Mind; The Realm of the Deep; The Realm of Man; the Realm of the Particle; and the Realm of Stars. She undertook the lead role in the Realm of Stars; specifically, the Navigator of the Nebula Quest event. The Realm of Stars was modeled as a space station called Orbit One. Created in the shape of a vast ring and cleverly (perhaps eerily) designed to immerse patrons with the sense they were touring the real McCoy — computer terminals, utility robots, an orbital view of Earth and shuttle jets cruising to and fro, while more exotic vehicles launched on missions beyond the solar system. Employees wore jumpsuits and remained unfailingly in character via painstaking method acting. From the outset, H Shaw was exclusively referred to as the Navigator. Soon, she thought of herself as the Navigator as well. Within weeks, her former life as a struggling actor and mourning daughter were figments of a hazy dream.

Preparing for the Nebula Quest consumed her waking hours. In addition to the expected line readings, she attended lectures on basic psychology and introductory physics, and adhered to a strict exercise regimen. Every moment under the scrutiny of company tutors, trainers, and bureaucrats. Designed as the most ambitious ride ever conceived, a substantial portion of the park's future depended upon Nebula Quest's success. Through artifice, Tesla-worthy special effects, and a proprietary gyroscope to simulate faster-than-light velocity, guests would embark on a guided tour of the "cosmos" in search of a wandering nebula. The engineers of OmniPark were responsible for generating the broader illusion of perilous star travel, posing as techs, scientists, and cosmonauts (the space travelers of park lore); H Shaw's task was to deliver the human element, the compelling narrative, and the requisite stagecraft. Per company policy, maintaining the illusion of reality was paramount.

Come the day they embarked upon their Nebula Quest dress rehearsal, she'd slavishly memorized the script and prepared herself for every contingency from mechanical breakdowns or medical emergencies, to irate hecklers. The Operations Coordinator introduced her to the critical personnel: Engineers Peters, Kowalski, and Sondergaard. These individuals would monitor and adjust the systems, and also serve as an audience for H Shaw's performance. Strange she'd not met them prior — management preferred to isolate certain personnel from one another.

The team skipped breakfast, but was administered a mildly brackish tonic, which the head physician promised would mitigate motion sickness precipitated by the immense gyroscopic forces. They gulped it down and headed for the "ship." The sphere seated eight passengers. Engineer Kowalski officially suggested a more compact design to avoid potential long-term hazards with structural integrity. The Operations Coordinator, dry as ever, assured Engineer Kowalski that his concerns would be relayed to the appropriate Technosopher, who was likely drafting other prototypes.

In keeping with the theme of complete immersion, the Props Department went full bore on costumes, rigging the team with lightweight faux spacesuits, reflective as the type worn by volcanologists. The engineers assembled before the airlock and dutifully nodded along as H Shaw recited her speech concerning a nebula spotted by the station telescope array and how the celestial body had vanished soon after. The best way to track the nebula would be to engage the hyperspace drive and go for a jaunt across the galaxy, so, everybody pile in!

Radio Voice said over their headsets, "Good luck, secret cosmonauts." And to H Shaw on a private channel: *Feel free to improvise. When you recite your lines, imagine color; vivid, rich, coruscating. Stunning cold and crushing heat. Soundlessness. The prickle of creeping radiation. Imagine the wandering nebula is the great fisherman of the universe. He has a hook set in your mouth. He's reeling your poor souls across the cold white black.*

The channel clicked dead.

According to the Nebula Quest script, each hyperjump not only projected the ship and passengers into deeper space, it would also reveal, at a crucial moment, they'd been flung millions of years into the future with no sure way home. The first couple of "jumps" went well, uncomfortable g-forces notwithstanding. Jump three provoked an exclamation from Engineer Sondergaard as she gaped at the vista of an alien starscape dripping across the view screen. Surreal as a Dali painting, yet solid enough to touch.

"Either I'm overdosed on Dramamine or we've got wizards in the F/X department," she said.

"A hundred-million-dollar lightshow for sure," Engineer Peters said. Less than an hour in, his contempt for management shone through the veneer.

Engineer Kowalski breathed heavily as he gripped his armrests.

"Smaller, gotta go smaller, gotta get compact. This bucket is coming apart at the seams. Too much surface area."

Engineer Peters, warming to this opportunity to share his antipathy, said, "A contractor told me the park is an elaborate cover for some clandestine agenda of Teague and his investors."

"Clandestine agenda?" Engineer Sondergaard's faceplate reflected the pretty lights. "Besides making piles of money?"

"Mr. Billionaire doesn't need money and I doubt he's particularly sincere in regard to educating the public. There's an ulterior motive. Remember that story about how Teague secretly funded a fleet of manned rockets with experimental engines to explore the edge of the solar system? Had the blessing of the Pentagon."

"Nope."

"Exactly. None of those 'cosmonauts' ever returned to tell the tale. Allegedly, a garbled radio transmission warned the ships were destroyed by an alien intelligence that wants mankind to stay in his own yard."

"This contractor pal of yours must be well-placed," Engineer Sondergaard said.

"The contractor does business with the government. He says OmniPark operates like a big ol' black ops project the CIA loves to run. Farfetched, but you gotta wonder... Tourists will flock in here by the tens of thousands. Hell of a lot of guinea pigs, eh? Mind control experiments. Think of the reservoir of psychic energy a mad scientist could harness." Engineer Peters inclined toward the fake control panel. "If anybody happens to be eavesdropping, for the record it's a joke."

H Shaw gamely continued inhabiting her Navigator persona.

"Kindly direct your attention to the port side of the craft, you'll see we've arrived on the rim of Galaxy Nemesis Minor. Still no nebula, alas..." This last comment was accompanied by a nervous chuckle. A detached portion of her mind agreed with Engineer Sondergaard — the imagery felt and appeared astonishingly authentic. "Hold tight, folks. We're making a big leap this time!" Her tongue moved sluggishly.

Radio Voice crackled over her headset: *You've done well. Now, visualize the eye of a hurricane, the Eye of Jupiter's angry grandfather glaring from one-hundred-million years in the future-past. Visualize your rocket ship threading the eye of God's Needle...* And thus compelled, she did.

On cue, the gyro-arm shuddered into action and swung their cage along its hidden rail. Incredible force crushed them into their padded seats. The viewscreen went black. Rivets popped and bulkheads wailed. The men also wailed. H Shaw scream-laughed as her harness raveled and her limbs whipped about and her head slammed sideways against a support beam. Amidst these distractions, she did her level best to imagine a soft landing.

The viewscreen flickered and strobed, blinding bright. Colors of the cosmos bled together redyellowgreen—

The ship stopped, a yoyo snapped at the end of its string. Folding, unfolding, a tightly wound origami sculpture sprung, disjointed. Eventually, the team emerged from their cage to find themselves in what appeared to be a cavern. Total darkness gave way to weird, sulfurous illumination. This infrared glamor suffused the chamber. Humid and stifling. The air was thick and foul. Water thundered somewhere below.

H Shaw's skull rang.

"Where are we?" Engineer Peters said. "This isn't on the park schematic." He tried his two-way radio. Static. It was the same for each of them.

"Hey, Emergency Services, get a move on!" Engineer Sondergaard's shout was swallowed by the gloom. Her helmet was cracked nearly to pieces. "We've got injured people down here!" She moved forward between stalagmites studded with obsidian crystals. The rest followed. "Gotta be an exit. Disguised as a boulder or what-have-you."

Kowalski cursed. His left arm hung limp.

"Something went far wrong. We're cooked. We're in the fire. I knew Teague was jerking our chains."

Time passed.

"Good lord," Engineer Sondergaard said. "What's that?"

Sulfurous mists parted. Two humanoids loomed, partially concealed by ruddy shadows. Both were enormous — three meters tall; lanky, and clad in dull metallic scales that could've been armor or naked flesh. Chromatic specks of gold and red flickered across the nearer giant's torso. The farther giant's eyes glowed. It carried a sinister rifle-like device in both hands.

"Identify yourself," the chromatic one said in a mellow and resonant tone. Its features remained softly blurred.

When none of the men answered, H Shaw said, "I am the Navigator." The fact she couldn't see the giant's mouth bothered her on an instinctual level. Its language reached her ears as flawless English, but she couldn't shake the sense it started as something else. Her inner hominid recognized death.

"Oh, the Navigator," the chromatic one said. "That strikes a chord of memory."

Engineer Sondergaard tilted her head back to cry, "Teague! Are you watching? This isn't funny."

"Easy, Sondergaard," Engineer Peters said. "Easy."

H Shaw grappled with the impossibility of the situation. The entire premise of The Nebula Quest revolved around ill-fate. Perhaps this seeming mishap represented a stress test to determine her coolness under fire and had simply spun out of control, as evinced by her minor injuries. The "cavern" was an elaborate soundstage and the "aliens" were animatronic characters or actors on stilts. Other explanations were entirely too bizarre for a sane mind to entertain.

Improvising, she said to the giants, "How shall we address you?"

"However you will," the chromatic one said. "Amuse us, I beg."

She spat a mouthful of blood.

"Very well. I'll call you Polyphemus. Your friend is Saturn."

Engineer Sondergaard laughed crazily. She tossed aside her shattered helmet.

"And I'm Jack. Fe, fi, fo, fum!"

Polyphemus pointed a sickeningly long, sharp nail.

"I smell the blood of an Englishman."

"I smell the blood of *four* Englishmen," Saturn, the rifle-bearer, said. Neither mellow nor soothing, its voice ebbed and crashed like scratchy speakers amped to the maximum. "I propose we eviscerate them and lick the stains..."

"These are *Terrans*."

"Authentic Terrans?"

Polyphemus wiggled its fingers.

"Evolution is a hell of a drug. Allow me to introduce our ancient ancestors."

"I don't see the resemblance. So puny, so feeble. Shameful."

"Scans are conclusive. DNA corresponds to pre-Imperial catalog. One hundred percent Terran. And speaking of drugs, they are saturated with synthetic hallucinogens."

"Hallucinogens?" Engineer Kowalski clutched his injured shoulder.

Engineer Peters said to him lowly, "What was in that anti-motion sickness tonic the doctor gave us?"

"Protocols are clear," Saturn said to Polyphemus. "Primitives are forbidden to leave their solar systems upon pain of death. Emphasis on pain."

"I am curious how they materialized and by what miracle," Polyphemus said. "Behold their rude technology. Behold their rude minds. It bears investigation."

"These arrived the same way as all the other ships full of dead primates," Saturn said.

"Indeed, but since there are survivors on this occasion, we should embrace the opportunity to solve a mystery."

"Are you seriously considering preserving them as specimens?"

"Fetch a jar, drill holes in the lid, we're in business."

"My father always said, when the first roach appears, start spraying."

"Apparently, you inherited his lack of imagination. She, on the other hand…" Polyphemus regarded H Shaw. "Navigator, our scans detect no engine on your craft. What means of locomotion propelled you?"

"Hyperspace!" Engineer Sondergaard sneered. Her demeanor indicated a woman on the precipice of doing something reckless.

"Faster-than-light travel is a fairytale," Polyphemus said. "Quantum folding and wormholes are the known methods of interstellar transcorrespondence… Oh, you naughty gremlins. You were dosed with psychotropic agents, yes? Then beamed here via a crude mode of psychic projection? Are you the answer to the greatest riddle plaguing our species — the chicken or the egg?"

"We rode a gyroscope," H Shaw said, bewildered. "A gyroscope powered by a wish."

The aliens exchanged glances.

Engineer Sondergaard, said, "Whoops, don't spill the beans, lady! The gyroscope is proprietary tech! If Management is watching, you're canned for sure!" She cackled, lifted a sizable rock, and chucked it toward Saturn. The rock plinked against the giant's hip. "Open the goddamned service entrance already, you lousy sonsabitches!"

"Prop rocks are made of Styrofoam," Engineer Peters said to Engineer Kowalski. "Medics should be on the scene by now. There's one explanation… This isn't a stage and these aren't props."

"Oh shit," Engineer Kowalski said. "Sondergaard, no!" He and Peters tried to restrain their lunging colleague. Engineer Sondergaard twisted free, advancing with her arms raised in what H Shaw thought to be an absurd pantomime of menace.

Saturn swiveled the bore of its mortar-sized rifle to cover the engineer.

"Wait," Polyphemus said. And to Engineer Sondergaard, "Relax, my friend. Behold yon vent in the wall? There lies the service tunnel. Go forth, be rid of our company."

Indeed, at the alien's gesture, loose stones rattled and collapsed, exposing a ragged hole extending into the cavern's face. Engineer Sondergaard didn't hesitate; she bolted for the hole, scrambled upward over the pile of rocks, and disappeared within. Saturn's petty laughter echoed in H Shaw's ears. And she knew Engineer Sondergaard was a dead woman walking even before her short, agonized shriek erupted. Came a dry-twig snapping, a gurgle slosh of viscid fluid violently released. Presently, vitriolic green slime egurgitated from the opening and sluiced downward, bearing chunks of the woman's space suit.

"Oops," Saturn said. "There's an example of first contact gone wrong. We confine you primitives to your home systems for good reason. Gods know what might follow you home…"

Polyphemus said, "My associate speaks a brutal truth. The cosmos teems with organisms thirsty for our blood. Creatures that dwell in the cubbyholes of this rock are but fingerlings of a greater abominable consciousness. As abominable consciousnesses ourselves, we glean the hazard."

H Shaw listened with half an ear, distracted by the bubbling mess of her erstwhile comrade. Engineers Kowalski and Peters shouted incoherently and stumbled backward like a pair of terrified drunks. Polyphemus' chest shimmered brighter. It stooped, uttering a series of oddly soothing glottal clucks while beckoning them. The men quieted. Now they approached the giant; no longer drunks, but sleepwalkers, or moths, jittering toward an electric light.

Engineer Kowalski said, "Please, for the love of God—"

Polyphemus' enormous claws made a cat's cradle gesture. It flung a net of glistening barbs over the engineers and snatched them to its breast which opened into a widening vortex. Twinned screams echoed down, down a subterranean shaft.

H Shaw fled the scene.

"Never return," Polyphemus called.

Rak the Techmaster lazily aimed his rifle to zap the escaping Terran. Ordinator Vennen stayed his casual savagery with a sharp glance.

"Let her be." He rubbed his breast, which had quieted. "Her companions will provide ample material for forensic inquiry. Besides, we're dealing with temporal forces of unknown power, the consequences of causality. For all we know, she's the second coming of Eve."

Rak the Techmaster sighed.

"I suppose one doesn't screw with causality."

"Indeed. Shall we return to our mission, then? I seem to recall you were prepping to descend a certain pit..."

Rak the Techmaster smiled grimly and swung his plasma rifle to cover the Ordinator. Trigger finger tightening, tightening...

H Shaw ran until she reached the ship. It lay askew, dented and battered, but essentially intact, nestled like a silvery-white egg in a clutch of blackness. She clambered inside and sealed the hatch. Her assiduous study of the employee handbook and its comprehensive details proved useful. Guided by a fuzzy lamp in the collar of her suit, she flipped the requisite switches, snapped shut her harness buckles, and toggled the fake engine toggle. Cabin light strips fitfully illuminated.

She slowed her breathing, concentrating upon building an image, a material manifestation from quantum uncertainty. She swiftly conjured an image sequence: the ship was truly a ship, the fake toggle would fire real engines, and she'd hyperjump back to Odessa. Metal clashed under her seat — rotors whined; steam billowed. Out the starboard portal, a maelstrom of white light bloomed and incinerated the cavern—

She awakened in the Orbit One infirmary a week later. Left arm amputated. Burns, bruises, fractures, and mild radiation poisoning. Luckily, OmniPark staff included world-class physicians. They administered medicine and gave her clay to squeeze to strengthen her remaining hand. Engineers were readying a lifelike prosthetic. She'd be good as new. Shinier, perhaps.

The Operations Coordinator sat at her bedside while explaining the accident. The gyroscope had suffered unexpected stress and been shorn off its central housing, catapulting the ship through the floor and into a subbasement. Emergency Services personnel used blow torches and heavy-duty cutting tools to extricate the team from the wreckage of the ship. She was the lone survivor. In fact, she was the lone occupant. Emergency Services recovered no one else, alive or otherwise.

H Shaw, propped on pillows in a small, barren room, stared him down.

"Horseshit. I want to speak with your boss." She stoically waited until he wheeled in a phone and handed it over.

Radio Voice spoke into her ear: *You've a right to be angry. The intent was to achieve minor astral projection for your first experience, not achieve fully corporeal manifestation. The black hole is our conduit, but also an obstacle that warps results. As you can see.*

She gritted her teeth. The hospital room felt increasingly like a cell, the nurses her jailers.

"*First* experience?"

Radio Voice said, *Yes, my dear. Your father said you were a dreamer. He was eminently correct. Dreaming is the only way we'll escape our system and one day command the stars. You will be debriefed — we must learn the details of your odyssey. Then, perfect the procedure, replicate and amplify it—*

"Through the millions of patrons who will soon pour through the doors of the park. Warm-blooded batteries."

Radio Voice laughed, cold and indifferent as the void.

Take heart. You might locate your father, given time and resources. Develop your psychic weaponry, you might even punish those who abducted him. With a mind such as yours, anything is possible.

Imagination is a Power, not a plaything. Ace Pilot Shaw painted his youngest daughter's bedroom ceiling with constellations. He sculpted model star systems of red, yellow, and green clay. *Here is a dying star named Nemesis, and here are its dying planets. Here is your rocket ship, surveying the ruins of extinct civilizations. Sooner or later, a young astronaut from Alpha Centauri, or Hercules, or waaay farther off, will cruise past reddening Sol and dead baked Earth, and she will say into her flight recorder, This planet was blue once. There were plants and animals and little girls with big imaginations.*

Now, H Shaw lay abed, molding clay into a ball, imagining a distant star. She clenched the sun in her fist. Clay oozed between her fingers — redyellowgreen...

January 18, 1952

...and Georges Lemaitre agrees. If not for this, I would be happy to attend.

While it may seem like a vast and empty void, it is actually teeming with malicious ambition. The slightest miscalculation can lead to disaster. Any incursion should be approached with great caution. With each attempt the danger increases and increases rapidly.

There is knowledge and there is wisdom, Dalton. You pursue the former with little mitigation from the latter. I implore you to discontinue these endeavors.

In the vast expanse there is a dark melody. I have heard it. I feel it still, humming deep within my mind. The worst thing we can do is keep firing up flares, alerting the universe of man's intrusion into the dark.

Very sincerely yours,

Edwin Hubble

EPH:pg3

Page 3 of a letter from the astronomer Edwin Hubble to Dalton Teague, 1952. The letter's first two pages have been lost. Hubble appears to be declining some sort of invitation from Teague (who would found Omni Oil the following year), due to Teague's pursuit of dangerous scientific "attempts" of an unclear nature. The letter's tone indicates that Teague and Hubble were on familiar terms, though it's unknown how or when the two met.

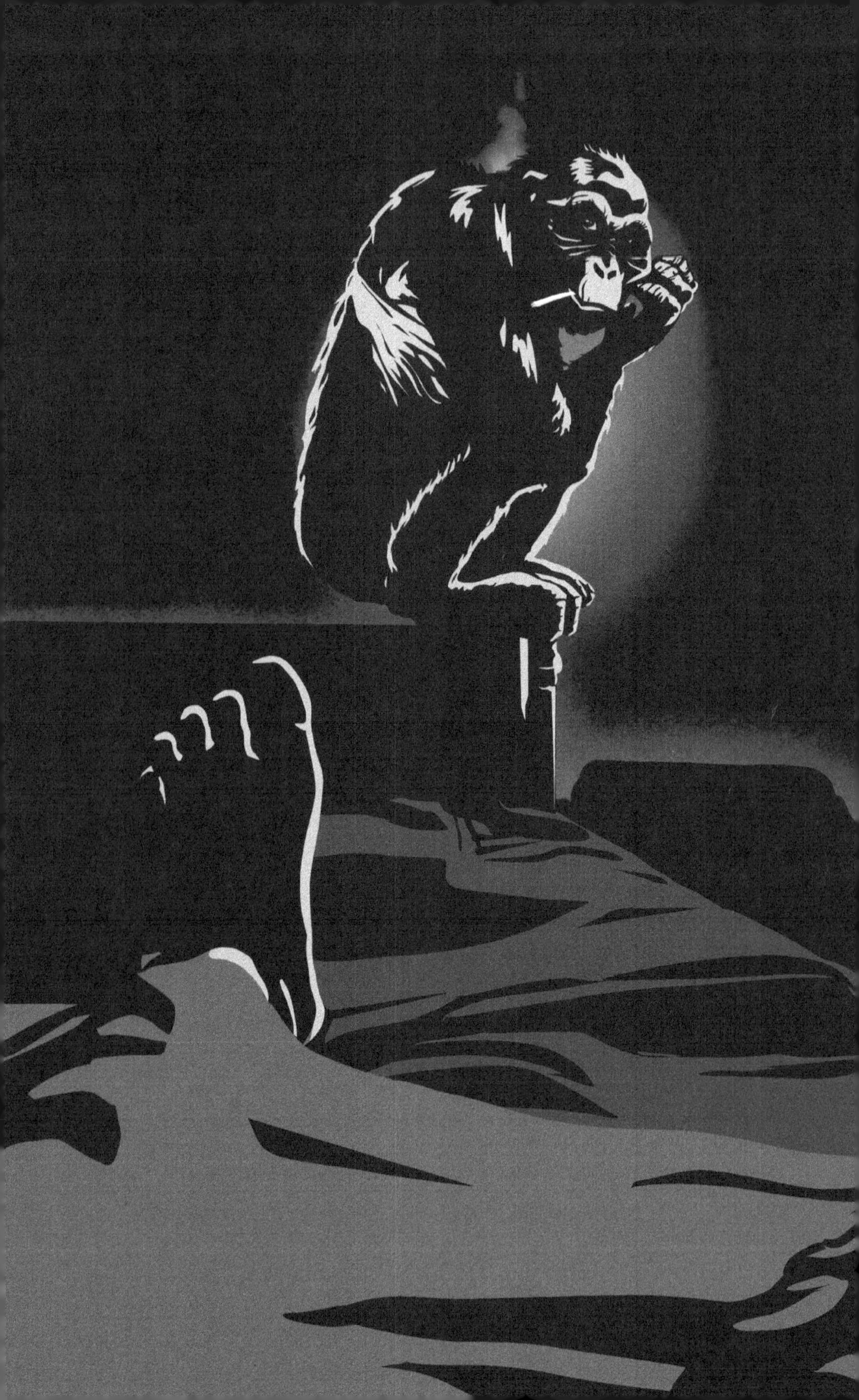

Fossils of Us

John Wiswell

You said I'd have control this time, Dalton. If I'm supposed to run this operation, then where on earth did *she* come from?

I didn't fly around the world to play second fiddle.

When the Chinese wanted a rollercoaster that flew through the fossils of a diplodicus's body and came corkscrewing out around its neck, they called me. I made it happen. And it was me and me alone who built the Tornado of Darwin in Australia when everyone else said it was unethical and unsafe. You know Shattuck and Masaru's rides wouldn't go twenty feet without me. I'm the guy who makes the gears turn — literally. I do it all.

But there's one thing I won't do, and that's fly halfway around the world to play second fiddle to a lunatic. You put somebody I've never heard of in charge of the Realm of Man? Tomorrow you'd better send me a sweetly worded wire explaining why I'm working under this Wilma person.

I touched down in this jungle so jetlagged it felt like a Tuesday and next weekend all at once. None of the other so-called Technosophers you hired had to trek out here, and they darned sure *are* allowed to talk about where they're going, unlike yours truly. I'm not even allowed to write the name of the country I'm in? Seriously? Do you think some rival company is going to catch the name off my paper via spy satellite and steal our secrets? There is no rival company. Nobody would even be able to put together what we're doing, let alone create a competing product.

I stepped off the plane and immediately sweat soaked through my shirt. I'd packed Egyptian cotton because it breathes better, but the climate here is still an assault on the senses. I've always been scrawny, but here I felt like I was just bones. Funny, right? Bones?

Anyway, I'd scarcely had time to wipe the sweat off my brow when that woman strode onto the tarmac. She was smiling and smug, almost as if she *liked* being covered in perspiration and bug bites. In that sleeveless top you could see what a meal the mosquitoes had made of her arms. Her black hair was bound up in small braids, pulled back into a bun behind her head, skewered in place by two steel pins.

She asked, "Erasmus Haymer?"

Didn't you say to be discreet? So why isn't she following protocol? She said my full name aloud, right in public. Doesn't that raise your paranoia, Dalton?

I asked, "They have lady chauffeurs here?"

"I'm not here to drive you, Mr. Haymer," was all she said. "I'm here to introduce you to the origins of humanity."

Now, I live down the street from a professional bodybuilder. He's a mountain chiseled out of muscle. They use his picture in ads in the back of comics and magazines to advertise miracle supplements he's never actually tried. The guy crushes my hand every time we shake.

This woman made that guy's handshake feel as gentle as a warm towel after a shave. She squeezed and looked me square in the eyes like she was enjoying watching me fight to keep my knees from buckling.

I said, "The Organization didn't mention you."

She smiled. "Then they're not as organized as they should be. I had to find your flight myself."

I groused about how neither of us has ever been fully informed by you, ever since we started this thing. Then I asked her, "So what do I call you?"

Her smile widened. "Do you watch much television, Mr. Haymer?"

I shrugged. "I watch the news when I want to be lied to. TV is a dying fad."

"So you don't watch cartoons?" She raised an eyebrow.

I scoffed. "Not since I got old enough to buy my own cigarettes."

"Well," she said. "With where we're going, you can call me Wilma."

That's what talking to her is like. She wouldn't even let me in the truck until I put out my cigarette. I half expected her to blindfold me like we were spies. Wilma spent most of the ride staring unblinkingly out the windows, lecturing me on microbiomes that could exist between any two passing trees, and how apartments were merely the illusion of solitude while actually sharing a space. I spent the ride scrutinizing her bug bites. She never scratched them once, like she was too focused to be bothered with itching.

The room was three stories underground, with concrete walls twice as thick as they needed to be. Wilma's unit had its own separate ventilation system, which meant that while it was a sweltering crotch rot of a summer up above, it could've been the first virgin touch of autumn down there. And it was dry as a rock. The samples resided in individual metal cabinets that she had to unlock using a physical key and a keypad simultaneously. I've never seen storage locked down this tightly, and I've been in that bunker in New Mexico that supposedly doesn't exist. Remember?

Wilma walked past me and gestured to the cabinets. She said, "Most of this is from my private collection."

I scanned the room appreciatively. "I'm sure the Technosophers would be impressed. You talk to them often?"

"You're the first one I've bothered contacting," she said. "So please behave yourself."

She placed a steel suitcase-looking thing on the table. The container was nearly as long as Wilma is tall. It hissed mechanically when she unfastened it.

Inside was a slice of earth that had been carefully peeled away, dust-layer-by-dust-layer. Trapped in that hard-packed earth was a skeleton that could've been a monkey or a man. I circled the case, craning my neck at different angles to try to figure out which it was. One of its legs was stretched out as far as it could go, the thigh and ankle bones more exposed from the dirt than the rest, while the other leg was drawn up to its chest. Whatever this thing was, it'd been trapped eternally in the last jump of its life, or so it looked to me. Its toothless mouth was wide open in a silent scream. And it was tiny — too small to be human.

This could've been the literal Missing Link. I envisioned something like this screaming at the riders at the entrance to the Realm of Man. Give them a good scare to start things off. We need these bones, Dalton. There's nothing else like them.

I couldn't keep the excitement out of my voice as I asked, "What am I looking at?"

She hummed fondly, like this skeleton was her own child. "Not what. *Who*. This is the oldest complete Australopithecus skeleton humanity has ever found. He was born almost a thousand miles from where humans discovered his remains; in his own way, he was one of the first great explorers. I'm proud to introduce you to each other. You can call him Fred."

I leaned in closer, scrutinizing the bones. For remains that old, his bones were remarkably well-preserved. I couldn't imagine what natural conditions had kept him like this across all those silent millennia beneath the ground. I asked, "Did you find him here?"

Wilma shook her head. "He wasn't found in this country. He was discovered by a shell company in another country, and I shipped him here for preservation purposes. Sometimes the local governments plant fake stories about the discovery of ancient human ancestors to cover up the theft. All they want are the dollars that international dig grants will inspire, and the kickbacks from the shell company. It's all quite complicated."

I contemplated all the international chess she'd had to run to get him this far. "I don't know how we're going to smuggle him to the United States. But it'll be worth it. Everyone who comes to the park will be terrified of him."

She placed her hands gently on the case, as if she might scoop little Fred out of the earth and into her arms. "He is not going to be displayed anywhere. I'll never let the world have him. He's been through enough. He's going to rest."

My brow furrowed. "You just brought me here to — what, look at him? I just spent twelve hours on a plane because Dalton Teague told me you had something worth bringing back."

"And I do, Mr. Haymer," she replied. "I do indeed. You'll see Fred's relatives today, and the Neanderthals, and humans from a hundred thousand years ago. What I'm going to show you this week is everything you and I no longer are, and what everyone who visits your park could be. This is far more significant than any animatronic prop you could ever build."

"Significant," I repeated, stepping back from Wilma and her petrified pet. "Dr. Teague likes to use that word too. But I'll tell you right now, I don't go in for mysticism. This park is going to be about the sciences. Humans evolved out of beings like Fred. He's a late model — obsolete. It's us who won evolution's war."

She shot me a stare that could've cut glass. "Evolution isn't the only way people change."

I rolled my eyes and patted my pocket for my cigarettes. "Spare me the pseudoscience. I don't believe in destiny or new-age astral projection or whatever you're going to try to sell me. I believe in bones. We're just the products of natural selection."

She chuckled softly. "You're the one building a ride about evolution in Texas, where they glue the pages of biology textbooks together." She placed her hand over mine, refusing to let me pull a cigarette out of the pack. "Smoking is forbidden in this room. This is your final warning."

When our hands touched, my stomach tightened. You know sneaking into a concert feels fine until the first cop looks your way? This was like that, but with the volume cranked all the way up. Like I suddenly belonged in the concert of her species.

Still holding my hand, she said, "You have to be careful with fire. The first primates to hold fire — to *own* fire? It seemed impossible. Yet there *was* a first fire. A first hammer. I have samples to show you of the first bags our ancestors ever made. You will respect every first thing we've created. And when you return to Texas, you had better build something that reminds people of everything we were before now. Remind them of when we had nothing but the bones of our dead. I had better want to ride your ride, Mr. Haymer."

What do you say to something like that? My pulse thundered in my ears, the way it's thundering now, remembering that moment.

I gave a nod that felt too small, avoiding eye contact with her. I asked, "So you don't smoke?"

She grinned. "Only when I'm angry."

So thanks, Dalton. This is who I'm working with. I'll get you for this.

You know what I woke up to last night, Dalton?

A monkey sitting at the foot of my bed, smoking a cigarette.

The smell of tobacco smoke woke me from a dream about bones in the desert. My first thought was that I'd left a butt burning in the ashtray. I groped in the dark and found all my cigarettes were stubbed out thoroughly, but my pack was missing.

Then I noticed the orange glow near my feet, the cigarette burning just bright enough to illuminate the thief's furry muzzle. Despite the light being near its face, its eyes were darker than the shadows. It was perched square on top of the right bed post. Its long fingers held the burning cigarette near its face. It was watching me.

This couldn't be happening. It was so absurd that I pinched myself to wake up.

The thing screeched like a trumpet having a heart attack. It leaped off the bed post right for me, and in that moment, I saw it was more than a monkey. Chimps or bonobos or whatever aren't this big. Its legs were too long; its face too broad. And its face — I've never seen an animal glare with such contempt. It wasn't spooked. It was furious, and it scampered across the bed with a long-fingered hand outstretched, grabbing for my hair.

I tried to run while still lying down. Its fingered feet kicked me in the stomach and the pain sent my whole body lurching. I writhed, trying to roll out of the bed, but it grabbed the sheets. The sheets trapped me like a net, and I wriggled against them, putting all my body weight against the seams. I had to be bigger than this thing, but I couldn't outmuscle it. Its rank breath fell on the back of my neck, and I squirmed further under the covers for escape. When it grabbed onto one end of the covers, I jumped out through the bottom and fell onto the floor.

Hearing that thing howling after me, I scrambled for the door. I jerked it open and threw myself outside, hoping to get clear. The last thing I saw, right as I slipped into the hall and slammed the door to lock the thing inside the room, was those long fingers flicking my own cigarette at me.

I ran downstairs and spent the rest of the night in the safety of the lobby while the hotel manager called the constables, all the while eyeing me as if I was a mental patient. Said nothing like this has ever happened, and that there aren't any giant monkeys around here. But I've still got ash burns on my neck. When the police finally arrived, they inspected the whole room and said they found no evidence of any such animal — just a cigarette stubbed out on the floor. They were laughing when they left.

I'm switching to another motel until I can get out of here — which I can't do for another three days, because that's when the next flight leaves. Of course, you could send a plane yourself. You've got the cash to spend. But you haven't even responded to a single one of my messages yet. What am I here for if you care so little that I can't get a word? After what I've been through, I'm starting to feel like I don't even exist anymore.

"How do you think the animal felt?" was all Wilma said when I told her.

I survived a nightmarish assault last night, didn't sleep a wink, and couldn't even smoke my own cigarettes because of God-only-knows what disease that animal might've left on them. After everything I'd been through, *this* is how that woman greeted me.

According to her, she'd come with me to make sure I was safe on my morning walk through the sweltering streets. I let her tag along, maybe as a security blanket, but mostly as a second pair of eyes as I went looking for a newsstand or tobacco shop. I was dying for a smoke.

She asked again, "Haven't you considered what the animal felt when it saw you?"

I snorted a laugh. "It probably felt great. That's got to be the most expensive cigarette it's ever had."

Then she had the gall to look at *me* like I was somehow out of line.

"This is an opportunity for you, Mr. Haymer," she said. "You can view the event in two ways. One: you can see that hotel room through the animal's eyes, and question what it would feel like to be alien to the modern world."

I asked, "Or I can realize I was nearly killed? Is that it?"

"Or two," she said without breaking stride, "you can reflect on how small you felt when you encountered another primate. You were surrounded by tools, and comforts, and society. One alien event in your civilized world took the feelings of civilization away. You can reflect on how that felt, and share that feeling. This can be your inspiration for your little theme park."

There went my patience. I'd just survived an attack that nearly left me dead, and Wilma was talking to me about OmniPark. I couldn't put up with her for another minute. I'd rather be lost in a foreign country than get rambled at by some crank who keeps bones in an underground vault.

I stormed my way down the street in search of any relief. I figured any city this size must have thousands of smoke shops, but I couldn't find one. With Wilma following me, asking about how going extinct might feel, I would've settled for finding a butt in the gutter. I quickened my stride just to get clear of her.

In hindsight, I should've kept her around. Then that nudist wacko would have attacked her instead.

I wove down several alleys trying to shake off Wilma and find a main street where more shops might be open. I heard the cry of roasted nut vendors not so far off. Maybe I'd find something to drink, too, along with that cigarette.

Instead I ran face-first into this nudist. Calling her a woman would be too kind. She crouched at the end of the alley, with the light from the street streaming in behind her. Not a stitch of clothing on — just brown fur.

Nudism is not common in this country; my first thought was that she must be on some mind-altering drug. She rose and revealed she was stark naked. I would've sworn I was looking into the face of one of those Neanderthal fossils in Wilma's collection, except this one was obviously alive in the flesh. The broad cheeks, the protruding brow, and even her ears were tucked back into her hair all funny. The skin around her eyes and lips was all pink and puffy, like she was allergic to the modern world.

I stopped in my tracks, and she breathed at me noisily, like the act of breathing itself hurt her.

And then she said, "Remember this feeling."

Her words didn't register right away. Part of me was surprised she was capable of speech at all. Some deep animal part of me expected her to grunt at me in a primeval proto-language. But I was the one grunting as I backed away from her, desperately looking up the street for Wilma.

The nudist said, "Are you afraid? Are you looking at someone strange? Or does seeing this make you the stranger?"

She advanced on me, closing the gap I made by backing away. Her broken fingernails and puffy pink fingers stretched out, trying to snatch my shirt. I banged into a wall and kicked out a bag of rotted vegetables, scrambling to keep her at bay.

No matter how fast I ran, I heard her bare feet slapping the dirt behind me. She was close enough that her breath touched the skin of my neck, making me shudder.

"This is what we were," she snarled. "Show them what we were."

As I neared the escape, I cast one more glimpse back at her. But she wasn't there. Down the alley, the darkness shattered into a flash of light. I've never seen something so pure and bright — so bright that it seared away my sight, and everything else, too. That's why I didn't hear the crowds of people as I ran right into them, and bounced off two burly men, falling into a wall. I shook my head and the roar of the city rushed over me, welcoming me back to reality. Yet in some way, ever since, it's like I can still see that queer light in the corners of my eyes.

I don't know what's happening here, Dalton. But you've got to get me the hell out of here. If I don't hear from you today, I swear I'm going to barricade myself in the airport until I can catch the next plane across the border.

Where are you, Dalton? I haven't gotten one reply from you since I landed here. How long has it even been since I landed in this miserable place? How long has it been since that nudist attacked me, and you didn't bother to respond? I've checked both the Western Union and the original hotel. Nothing from you or any of the Technosophers. What is going on?

Instead, I got a message from Wilma.

She offered to let me stay at her place tonight and wants to talk. She wonders if I want to apologize for anything. *If I want to apologize?*

I'll be dead and buried before I take shelter with that madwoman.

So I'm staying at the airport. If you want to reach me, forward something there. The next flight isn't for two days, and I won't set foot outside the terminal until then. If you want fossils from this godforsaken place, you can work with Wilma yourself.

What do you mean she doesn't work for you?

She met me at the airport. She brought me to her collection of pre-human fossils. She knows what we're building.

She must be part of the project, or else one of the other Technosophers must've brought her in. How does she know what we're working on if she isn't one of us? This can't be espionage. I've had spies trifle with me before, to get access to some oligarch or another. This has been nothing like that. Do you think she's part of some Neanderthal spy network?

Don't ask me who she is. *You tell me* who she is. You must know something.

That's your job, though. If you want to send me another message, put it on the plane you send for me. I'm done with this. Done with the park, the research, the destinations that don't officially exist — all of it. I quit.

All right, Dalton. This isn't easy for me to say, but I was wrong. I'm admitting it. I was completely wrong about this project, and I need to make amends.

You were wrong once, too, but now you know better, as I do. You and I will fix this. We'll make a ride that teaches everyone how to fix this.

In the hours before dawn, the airport was quiet as a graveyard with travel brochures instead of tombstones. Not even the one ticketing clerk was still there. My only company was the hum of power generators, which also perfumed the airport lounge like a diesel cigar. I was watching the sky out one window, counting the stars and willing any of them to start moving and turn out to be the lights of an oncoming plane. But the sky was empty of opportunities.

Then a light erupted in the dark terminal, bright and colorless. The hairs on my arms stood up, and I knew I wasn't alone anymore.

In that first split-second when I turned, I thought I saw the same animal that'd broken into my hotel room. The thing that had stolen my cigarettes and smoked one at the foot of my bed.

I screamed and fell into a rack of travel brochures, casting about wildly for anything that might serve as a defensive weapon.

But it wasn't the same animal standing with me at the window. Not unless you accept that humans are animals.

It was Wilma, standing there in a white dress that left her arms bare, showing off all the bug bites on her shoulders. She was pointing at me.

"This ride better show me something, Mr. Haymer," she said.

A chill went down my back and my whole body stiffened up. I hadn't felt this way since I was a kid in school, like when I'd get called on to explain a Math problem that I hadn't done yet. Humiliation churned in my guts. I couldn't look her in the face.

And yet, I stood and faced her. I had no choice.

"We're not that far from where we were," she said. "We tell ourselves stories of the heights we've ascended to. About how the animal kingdom is for everyone else in the food chain. These are untrue stories, Mr. Haymer. You're going to go back to Texas, and tell the people a truthful one."

She wasn't in the white dress anymore. It's not that she took it off, nor did I see her put anything else on. It's simply that she finished speaking and was suddenly a different person. She was that nudist — the Neanderthal from the alley, with the puffy pink flesh around her eyes, and the dark brown fur. She'd caught up to me after all.

We weren't in the alley. We were in the airport terminal. Alone, with our history.

I looked into this new version of her face, her Neanderthal broad brow and features expressing the same contempt her human face had worn. I imagined her going back to her climate-controlled basement every morning, and sleeping through the day in one of her metal suitcases. Like a vampire with her coffin.

I was wrong, Dalton. The truth is so much bigger, and we're a part of it too.

And the first step towards accepting the truth was asking her the only question that mattered.

"What are you?" I asked.

"I'm what we were. And what we could become if we face the truth of what we are."

Then she wasn't wearing fur or a dress. She was a light that didn't hurt my eyes. Every wall in the terminal lit up from her glow. Every crack in the floor was clear as the outlines of a maze. The windows flared so bright it was like everything outdoors was erased from existence.

The funny thing is, I couldn't describe what she looked like in that moment. I felt like a mosquito trying to describe a light bulb. Every feature of her face I tried to look at was a glow that slipped from my mind. I couldn't comprehend her, no matter how much I looked. Yet I couldn't look away from her light.

Wilma asked, "Do you see it now?"

I wiped a tear from my left eye. "I'm starting to."

"What do you see?" she asked.

Like now as I write to you, Dalton, I couldn't say. "I don't have the words," I told her. "I don't know."

She smiled. "You just know how intensely you feel it. You know what the people who come to your park should feel now. You know what they need from the ride you're going to build."

"You care about the park?" I asked. "With all that you can do? With what you are?"

She nodded. "Your ride needs to make them see it, Mr. Haymer. Remind people how small they were, so they can become something more. You will build something worth my time. Worth *our* time. Something that gives everyone the experience I've given you."

Now the tears were flowing too fast for me to wipe them away. I slumped against the nearest window. "I don't know how to do that."

That woman — the light — reached out for me. With infinite kindness she said, "I'll help you climb."

The plans I've attached aren't really my own. They're a collaboration. A beginning. They're completely different than our original plans for the Realm of Man, I know. They will pose engineering problems like nothing I've ever tackled. And I can't wait to try it. They might seem impossible, but you can see how they'll work, if you look carefully. If you look with an open mind. It'll show people where they came from and where they can go.

Don't you want to ride this ride, Dalton?

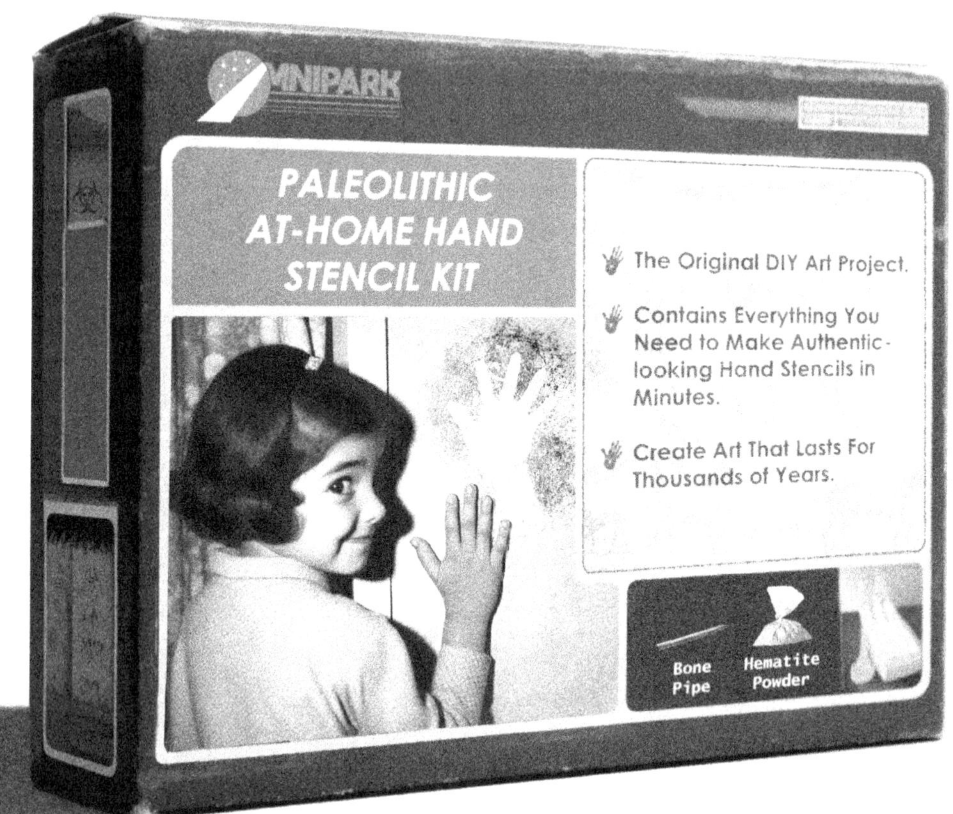

A home cave art kit sold in the Great Tent Gift Shop, in the Realm of Man, in the early 1980s. OmniPark withdrew this kit from shelves in 1985, after parents complained that its ochre paint was annoyingly resistant to conventional cleaning agents.

(Top, left) The Conservatory Parlour in the Realm of Time. (Top, right) The mansion's main library in the Realm of Time.

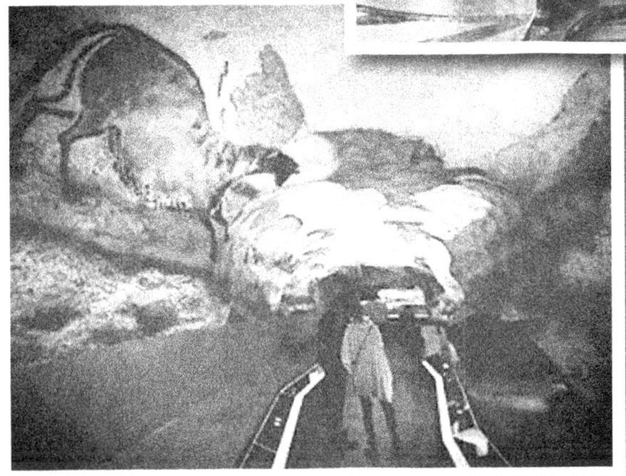

(Bottom, right) A contraption displayed in the Realm's mansion. (Bottom, left) Guests explore one of the painted caves in the Realm of Man, circa 1979.

Incarnate

Kristi DeMeester

The house was there long before Dalton Teague fell into his waking dream of what OmniPark could be. The turrets and gables and writhing ivy that contained whatever ghosts tread the halls exhaled whispers and sighs so that the local children pedaled their bikes faster when they crested the hill on Brentwood, the sight of that Victorian manor setting their skin crawling.

Every town worth its salt has a haunted house, and this was ours.

My husband hadn't known about the house when he bought the one next door. We weren't local to Odessa and hadn't known better. All he knew was it was a quick drive to the construction site where he would spend the next three years chasing after contractors who worked on the basis of a handshake and a wink instead of hard deadlines and legal, written agreements. Maybe that's how things worked in the big city, but Odessa had not yet managed to catch up with the fact it was 1972 rather than 1952 — a lesson that rankled me but that I learned nonetheless. Here, I was still Perry's "little lady" instead of his wife, and when the men came to deliver the furniture, they'd raise their brows at my slacks.

"Nothing ceases to amaze," one of them mused, eyeing me up and down, as Perry counted out their payment. "Next thing you know they'll be wearing ties, too."

Of course, Perry pretended he hadn't heard even as I gripped my mother's Tiffany vase so tightly I nearly sent a crack running down its center.

"Oh." The man paused at the front door, withdrew a yellowed handkerchief, and wiped his nose. "You'll be wanting to plant something between the houses. A privet or such. I have a guy who can do it for you for twenty-five."

"Between the houses?" Perry asked, and the man grinned back at him all while he kept his watery, red-rimmed eyes trained on me.

"Well, yessir. Wouldn't want to be staring at that eyesore day in and out if it was me. Besides, ain't no telling what you're liable to see. Wouldn't want the little lady getting spooked." He tossed a wink my way. "Or maybe ya would. Something about the scary stuff that gets the ladies wanting to cuddle up closer, if you catch my drift."

I turned away and rolled my eyes, the conversation drifting into murmurs as I made my way back to the kitchen. I didn't want to admit he was right. The house next door *was* unsettling. The picture window over our sink looked out onto its wraparound porch with two smudged windows looking back, the darkness within an unknowing, unfathomable emptiness. I could feel the absence of life those rooms held. How heavy. How like the holy dust of a cathedral as it invades the lungs and transforms the body into something alien and sanctified.

I shook my head. Stupid. It was only a house. A house that had once held light and sound and people.

"Alone. Finally," Perry said from the doorway behind me.

I watched Perry in the window's reflection as he picked his way past the hastily stacked boxes before wrapping his arms around my waist.

"You didn't want to take him for a beer? Get to know him a little better? Make friends?" He poked me in the side and buried his face in my neck.

"I can think of at least a thousand things I'd rather do, and all of them involve you."

"Thank God. I've been looking for a reason not to finish unpacking."

Later, after a cigarette and a plain cheese sandwich on Wonderbread, I stood alone again in the kitchen wishing I'd put on socks to ward off the chill from the hardwood floors. The picture window stood before me, a stark reminder of the house that slept beyond, and I turned away. If I didn't look, I would not see the cold, pale thing that must be creeping through the other house. How it would turn to look back at me without eyes, its mouth opening wide and then wider as it scraped its teeth along the glass.

I went to bed, but it was a fitful sleep. A tumble through dreams I couldn't remember on waking, and when Perry's alarm finally went off, I didn't know if I was grateful or if I wanted to smash the damn thing to bits.

"Up and at 'em. First day," I said, and Perry groaned.

It took three boxes to find my house coat, and then another four to find the percolator and coffee and filters. I waited at the window as it perked, the water from Perry's shower a pleasant sort of noise that settled me back into my bones. In the faded morning light, the house next door was just a dilapidated pile of paint and wood. A regal entity returning to dust as we all would in time.

I found the mugs after a bit more rummaging and was pouring just as Perry found his way downstairs, a fleck of shaving cream still on his chin.

"No milk. I'll have to find the closest market today," I said.

"Any sugar? You could at least stick your finger in. Sweeten it up a bit," he said, nuzzling into my neck. I swatted at him and gestured at the boxes.

"In those somewhere. Keep that up, and you'll be late."

Twenty minutes and a hurried kiss goodbye later, the house, for the first time, was silent. I had finished unpacking the kitchen, the picture window reflecting the cheery daylight only, and the boxes broken down and dutifully set by the side door, when the doorbell rang.

I was covered in a film of sweat and dust, but there was no time to do anything other than wipe my hands on a dish towel and pray I didn't look as filthy as I felt.

"I hope I'm not bothering you. Wanted to bring this by and welcome you to the neighborhood." The immaculately dressed woman on my porch lifted a pie and offered a coral-lipsticked smile. "It's buttermilk. Sort of a tradition round here."

"Not at all. Please, come in. I'm Jo," I said and stepped back.

"Robin. So glad to meet you." Her dress was a forest green gingham that skimmed her thighs. A pair of tan leather sandals wove over her ankles and up her calves. I instantly felt the part of a homely fuddy-duddy and tugged at the hem of my old, paint-stained sweater.

"Like *Little Women*," she said as she offered me the pie.

"My mother was a teacher. Retired a few years ago. I have an older brother who is a Byron, if you can believe it."

She laughed, and I relaxed a bit. "Better than being named after a *Winnie the Pooh* character."

"Or a bird," I said, and she laughed again. "Would you like some coffee? I could cut into this. It only seems fair since you were the one who made it."

"Oh, I've had my share already. Made two of them last night and already sneaked a few slices. But I wouldn't say no to coffee."

I led her toward the kitchen. "Excuse the mess. The movers only came yesterday, and it seems like I'll never be finished unpacking. How two people managed to accumulate so much stuff over six months, I'll never understand."

"Newlyweds!" She clapped her hands together. "I'm so glad y'all bought this house. It needs to be filled up with babies. The Thompsons were sweet, but their children were grown up with kids of their own, and it was too big for them."

I held myself back from rolling my eyes for the second time in less than twenty-four hours. Robin seemed nice enough, but once again, it was like I'd stepped backward in time. It was entirely possible that Odessa was permanently stuck in the 'fifties.

"We haven't really thought about children yet. Between the move and looking for a new position, things haven't been settled enough to even consider it."

"New position?" She raised an eyebrow. "But didn't you move here because your husband was offered a job?"

"Oh, I meant for me. I'm a librarian. At least I was. I suppose the apple doesn't fall too far from the tree."

"I see. Have you—" The clatter of Robin's heels stopped, and she drew in a sharp breath. "Oh, goodness. There it is. I didn't realize you were so close. You can practically see inside."

I turned to face her, but she was looking past me and out the picture window at the house next door.

Her voice dropped to a whisper. "I was terrified of that house when I was a little girl. The man that built it... his daughter died. And then a year later, his wife. A broken heart, I guess." She brought a hand to the simple gold chain at her neck and twisted a loop of it around her finger. "He went crazy in there. Said he was trying to find the gate to heaven. That it was somewhere in the house and that when he found it, he would see his wife and girl again. He stopped coming outside after a while." She drew in a shuddering breath. "And then the house was just empty. No one knew where he'd gone. Likely that he died, too, but everyone said the house had eaten him the same way it had eaten his wife and daughter. And then people said they started seeing things. Strange things. But they never saw him. No. Never him." She laughed then, a high-pitched and nervous sound. "But you know how kids are. Ready to believe any old thing so long as it scares the pants off 'em. Even now, my own thought I was crazy for coming here, but I told them it was the right thing to do. Hospitality ain't dead no matter how much people say it is."

I blinked back at her, trying to process what would be the right thing, the *polite* thing, to say. Ideally, something that wouldn't reveal how uncomfortable she was making me. How I was wondering if she wasn't just the tiniest bit unhinged and had come knocking just so she could see the house next door without standing in the street and staring at it, her obsession on full display for the neighbors.

"Oh, my Lord. I'm so sorry. You must think I'm crazy. Showing up here with a pie and then prattling on about something so ridiculous. It's like seeing a movie star or your childhood hero, you know? Dazzled for a moment before you realize how silly you're being."

Relief sank through me, and I set the pie on the counter and reached for the percolator. "Not at all. We don't have any milk, but do you take sugar?"

An hour and a half later, I'd learned where Robin met her husband (in line at the bank), where she'd gone to high school (Odessa High, go Bronchos!), and how poorly her last pregnancy had gone (sick as a dog the entire time). I might have spoken fifteen words in total, but it wasn't unpleasant, and by the time she'd given me her life story, I felt a certain warmth toward her.

"Why didn't the house ever sell? Seems like someone would have bought it. Some unfortunate out-of-towner?" I asked. I'd finished my slice of pie and practically licked the plate clean.

Robin shrugged. "It goes up for sale every now and then, but nothing ever seems to stick." She drained her coffee and placed the mug on the table. "There were rumors a while back that someone was looking to buy it only to tear it down and build something else, but it never happened. So the bank just lets it sit. I guess they think they'll eventually find some sucker to buy it, but until then..." She shivered. "I should head back. I left the baby napping, but those are getting shorter and shorter these days."

"I'll walk you out," I said, and she rose, smoothing her impossibly unwrinkled dress.

"A group of us get together to play cards every Thursday night. You should come by," Robin said as she descended the porch stairs.

"I will. Can I bring anything?"

"A bottle of bourbon," she giggled and threw a wave over her shoulder. "Bye, darlin'! Call me if you hear anything go bump in the night!"

I couldn't help but laugh with her as I closed the door. She was all fluff, but it never hurt to have a little fluff in your life after so many years shelving and reshelving dusty books in silence.

Not quite ready to resume my battle against the endless boxes, I wandered back into the kitchen with the intent of having another forkful of pie, but the picture window and the memory of what Robin had told me drew me to it. Locked there against the glass, staring out into that other house, I felt unbearably small. An insignificant heap of skin and organ and bone. Made of dust and unto it I would return as the house next door carried on until some final revelation brought it down. Even then, I wondered if it would carry on, oblivious to any sort of god that might wish it ended.

Around me, the light grew darker, the sun fading into its death, but I found I could not move from my place at the window. For there was something creeping over there. In the other house. Something pulling itself along on its belly. Back and forth. A pattern endlessly repeating. I was not imagining it. It had no face that I could see. Only a round, slick head that seemed to turn to look back at me as it offered a silent mewling. Even without eyes. Even without a mouth.

When I heard the sound of Perry's key in the lock and the door opening, I didn't jump. Didn't move. There was only that terrible, creeping thing and the hollow glint of my own eyes reflected in the glass. If I squinted hard enough, the creeping thing was me.

"Hon? What are you doing?" Perry's voice was quiet. He hadn't bothered to turn on the light.

I opened my mouth, and a thin line of drool escaped instead of the words I'd intended.

"Hey. Come on." He drew me away from the window. "There's a girl."

I wanted to scream. To throw myself against the glass until it broke. Until it was wet-slick with my blood. An offering for some darker god.

Upstairs, he wiped my face with a damp washcloth and tucked me into bed, the sheets pulled tight around my shoulders as if to restrain me. As if the wallpaper around me was going to shake and come alive to reveal the woman living behind it. Hadn't there been a story about that? I had the dim memory that my mother had read it to me once, long ago.

"You're burning up. We'll find a doctor for you in the morning. Sleep now." He pressed a kiss to my forehead and left me there in the dark.

I'd never told Perry about my baby sister. How my mother had left her sleeping in her little basket while she hung the laundry out to dry. How she'd dashed inside for more clothespins and to check that I was still playing with my dolls, secure in her knowledge that Meg was sleeping, and she would only be gone for two, maybe three, minutes. But when she'd come back outside, the basket was overturned, the lavender blanket my mother had crocheted while she was pregnant spilled on the dirt.

The police found her tiny, broken body in a shallow grave not even a full mile from the house three days later. Enough time for a resurrection if my mother had only believed hard enough. The police told my parents it could have been an animal that did it. Could have been a person in animal skin, monstrous in their capacity to harm a child. There was no way to tell for certain.

I was only four and didn't quite understand that she wouldn't come back. For months, I asked my mother when Meg was coming home and why couldn't the ground give her back? I'd seen her go in at the funeral. Wouldn't it be easy to take her out again? And then I'd wonder why my mother was crying. It became the sound I carried into sleep; my dreams formed around the hymn of her sobs.

I grew up, and my mother and father and brother never talked about Meg. Eventually, she faded into a distant memory. There'd been no reason to tell Perry when we first started dating, and eventually, there'd been no reason to tell him at all. Why bring such sadness into this new, shining thing?

But what I'd seen. The creeping, faceless creature dragging itself through the other house. I knew it as only a sister could. Our blood sang the same notes. It was calling out for me. Calling me home.

I waited for Perry to come up to bed. For him to settle in next to me, his breath deepening, and then the light sound of his snores washing through the room. I went slowly, careful to keep myself from waking him, my body creaking through the motions of standing and then shuffling out of the room. Taking the stairs one step at a time so I made no sound. It was important when you went creeping to be silent.

I went through the side door and out into the warm night, the grass cool beneath my feet as I crossed the yard to the house next door. If anyone were to peek out their window, they would have seen me, the blurred form of a woman become a ghost. At least that's what they would have believed. Ghost stories have a way of becoming truths.

There was no lock on the door. Of course there wasn't. Haunted houses want you to come inside. To swallow you whole.

A set of stairs led up, the balustrade's delicate carvings gleaming in the moonlight, and to the left, a sitting room with a fireplace large enough for a man to stand upright. On the right, another high-ceilinged room that had likely once been a formal dining room. A hallway stretched to the rear of the house where I imagined there was a kitchen, but I did not need to see the rooms at the back of the house.

I'd thought it would be warm inside. A damp, creeping fecundity that smelled of ancient earth. But the air was cold and smelled of something metallic. The floor slick beneath me instead of covered in the dust I'd anticipated. *Unnatural*, I thought and stood on my tiptoes, but it did nothing to quell the disgust roiling in my belly. My body was in a full act of rebellion, every muscle poised to flee. I bit down on my tongue and forced myself forward and stepped into the room with its fireplace and large bay window that looked back into my own picture window. The room where I'd seen the creature crawling back and forth.

I'd once read that a poltergeist was like a stain. A loop doubling back on itself; violence locked in time. That a haunting was little more than the imprint of the past made present again and again. Perhaps that was what drew Teague to the house. The knowledge that he could take that doorway and make it something else. What is time travel after all but a haunting made manifest? Our histories playing out over and over as we watch, unable to touch those shadows for the fear it might destroy the futures we've crafted for ourselves. It would only take the right sort of person to channel such power, to bend it until it became something you could build wonders around.

Slowly, slowly, I took another step inside and then paused to look at the impossibility that was that pale creature.

"Meg," I whispered. It did not stop its creeping, but I felt it look at me with that blank face. "Did they take your eyes? When they stole you from Momma? Or have you just forgotten what you were?"

She could not answer me. She wasn't really there in that house. She was a memory. A past I had not seen somehow carried with me to this new place. To this gate of heaven or, perhaps, hell that could take our ghosts and make them real. The past transported. Time travel in its most obscene form.

I sank to my knees, but there was no semblance of prayer on my lips. Only my trembling hands as I tried to keep them still so I would not touch this creature that had once been my sister.

Only when the sky began to lighten did she fade. I stood, my legs tingling as the blood rushed back into them, and quietly made my way back to our house. Perry still slept, and I climbed in beside him, my skin cool and dry. Whatever fever he'd felt had broken in the night, but I knew it had never been a fever. The heat in my blood had found its counterpart and called out to it. It was nothing more than my body responding to whatever strange portal existed in that house.

My mother had spent a lifetime pretending at normalcy after what happened to my sister. I could do the same. I could forget what I'd seen in that house. Forget the shadow screen cast among those abandoned rooms. The gate that somehow cracked open to reveal the space where our ghosts linger.

When Perry woke, I smiled at him and hoped it reached my eyes.

"Feeling better?"

I nodded but kept my lips pressed tight.

Perry went to work. I went out. Found the supermarket and wandered the aisles with my buggy filled with milk and bread and eggs and all the other things that belong in a home. The things that make a family. I went home and put them away and finished unpacking all the boxes downstairs. Books on bookshelves. Records in the cabinet. I did not look out the picture window. I made coffee and drank it and went into the backyard and thought about a little vegetable garden. I did not look out the picture window.

I made dinner and had a cocktail with Perry. The next day, I went to the local library and spoke to the head librarian, a Mrs. Whitney Trepel, who directed me to Odessa High (go Bronchos!) where they were looking for an assistant.

For the entirety of those three years, I did not look out the picture window. In the kitchen, I kept my eyes lowered like a supplicant at an altar, and if Perry ever saw anything, he kept it to himself. On Thursdays, I played cards at Robin's house.

We hosted no parties. No dinners. Perry never questioned me as to why. If anyone did happen to drop by, we entertained in the sitting room that featured a window that did not face the other house. And then Perry's job was finished, and the house was once again packed into boxes. Robin cried a bit when I hugged her goodbye, and I laughed and told her I would write once we got resettled back in Fort Worth, but I never did. Those moments of our lives were an infection I wanted desperately to forget.

We had two boys, and Perry wondered how I could not bear to be separated from them even as they grew older and sturdier.

I read about Teague and OmniPark later. How he'd bought up the land and razed all the houses except that old Victorian. How he made it the center of his theme park. The Realm of Time. The boys begged to go, and I crafted some excuse or another until they were too old to care about such things anymore.

Because I knew what it was that Teague had found in that house. Not a time machine but a portal. The gateway to a haunting. And whatever it was he'd done to make it obey him, well... I wonder if there's a hell that will greet him when he dies for twisting the natural order in such a way.

I have grown old, but my sister sleeps on in that house. I can only hope that whatever Teague unleashed upon the world remains only dimly aware of the people looking into it. That whatever is reflected back is only the shadow of the truth. And that, one day, it burns and burns until all that is left is ash.

The Supplier

Kaaron Warren

The Supplier
Odessa, Texas
May 17, 1974

Leon Strezlecki's motto was: Just Get it Done. With a sidebar of: No Questions Asked. He didn't have a billboard, or a business card, or even a registered business name. What he had was word of mouth.

"Leon can get you anything," Elijah Shattuck was fond of telling the other Technosophers. "And I mean *anything*."

Construction was nearing completion in the Realm of Time, which meant it was time to call on Leon. Because alongside the clocks, the watches, the pendulums, and hourglasses that graced most of the Victorian mansion that housed the Realm's Time Machine attraction, one small chamber, adjacent to the entrance of the queuing area, was set aside as the Amber Room.

Dalton Teague had spoken clearly of this room's significance: "Amber itself, with its soft permanence, its preservation of ancient insects, proves by its very existence the mutability of the cosmos. Within it are imprisoned times we cannot touch." He'd ordered one wall tiled in amber, the other covered with mirrors. The effect would be startling; no one argued with that. Dalton had heard tell of a stash of panels, years ago, and he'd never forgotten it.

The Creator
Marrakech, Morocco
November 14, 1951

Dalton Teague sipped his strong, bitter coffee.

He closed his eyes, savouring the flavors, spiced with ginger, cinnamon and nutmeg, but was interrupted by four men arguing about what sounded like sunken treasure: a missing, and from their descriptions, almost priceless series of amber panels.

Dalton unfolded a newspaper and pretended to read it while listening. This would be a good story to tell Evelyn, at the very least. The man who spoke the most, stabbing at the table with a stubby forefinger, was an astonishing looking fellow, with both ears missing their lobes and sprouting hair in tufts like the Mexican Feathergrass Dalton was so familiar with from home. Before long the men got up and left, throwing down coins onto the table, leaving their chairs disarrayed. Dalton shook his head disapprovingly.

Odessa American Headline, November 14, 1951:
Three Dead in Attempt to Retrieve Sunken Ship

The Supplier
Odessa, Texas
December 6, 1974

"I'm leaving this in your capable hands," Dalton told Shattuck. Shattuck thought it through while he smoked a cigarette down to the butt.. Then he called Leon Strezlecki.

"I'm on it," Leon said at the other end of the line. Then he paused. "I know I'm big on not asking questions, but I'm going to have to ask one or two if this job is going to work! You'll need to tell me everything Dalton remembers or has discovered about those tiles, the men who tried to find them, and what's happened since."

Leon started with the Odessa American archives in Ector County Library, trawling through piles of newspapers, his fingers becoming ink-stained, and his face, too, when he rubbed it tiredly. He traced forward and back the references to the sunken ship exhibition, and gave a shout of joy that earned him a "shush" from the librarian when he tracked down the name of the expedition leader. It was the snippet in the Real Estate News section, about an apparent wreck of a house purchased by this man that almost caused Leon to leap in the air, biting his fist with excitement. This led to his expulsion from the library.

"There's a certain amount of risk involved," Leon reported to Shattuck, in the Technosopher's office overlooking OmniPark's Entryway Pavilion. It wasn't a question, more a statement of negotiation. Leon was a large man who liked to discuss matters in person. His clear blue eyes could go without blinking for minutes at a time. He leaned forward, knuckles on a table or a desk, making everyone but Shattuck squirm.

"Money is no object," Shattuck told him. "You have clearance to offer them whatever's necessary to get them to sell."

Leon shook his head. "Money isn't the issue here, Shattuck," he said. "I'm saying there are risks. No one can tell me how this couple got their hands on the tiles; I don't know yet who I'm dealing with."

"I know one thing apart from more money that might make this worth your while," Shattuck said. "Park management can offer you an OmniVisa. Lifetime entry. Full access. All food and drink supplied at all dining establishments, once the place opens. For you only, of course. Not your family."

Shattuck poured coffee for the both of them.

Leon's mind worked overtime as he sipped the coffee. He thought about the room he had at his sister's house, how he had to sneak around so her night-shift husband didn't wake up. How he could live anywhere, really, but he'd have to negotiate people, no matter what. And how it would be nice to have a little hidey hole, a place to escape for a while, when he needed to. "Does this free pass include the maintenance tunnels?" Leon asked.

Shattuck shrugged. "Whatever floats your boat. But I make no guarantees about what you may run into down there."

"It's where the bodies are hidden, right?" Leon said.

Shattuck only grinned.

The amber house was in Portsmouth, New Hampshire, near the Sagamore Creek Headlands. Leon booked himself a room in the Aquaview Motel, on the water, and took a night to relax, clams and beer at a busy bar decorated with seashells, then back to his orange-walled, smoke-smelling room from where he watched *Happy Days* reruns until he fell asleep.

The next morning, he set out to work his way into the elderly couple's trust. He pulled on a pale blue shirt, combed his hair, slung a messenger bag across his chest. He put glasses on. In the car on the way there, he practiced keeping his voice soft and slightly high.

He parked on the street, picked up the box of chocolates he'd bought on the way, and picked his way up the cracked footpath to the front door. Signs of neglect were everywhere: the veranda needing a sweep, two broken chairs in the corner. Cobwebs on the door knocker. He pressed the doorbell and the chime played Swan Lake. He waited two minutes then played the song again, this time hearing a slow shuffling behind the door.

"Ah," said the old man who opened the door. "Have you come to fix the..." He stopped, struggling to recollect what needed fixing.

"I'm so sorry to bother you," Leon said. "But I wondered. The thing is. I used to live here! As a child! And now my mother has died, and I just wanted to see the old place. My name's Len." Close enough to the truth he wouldn't forget it.

"Ah," the old man said again. "I'm Graham." He stepped aside, letting Leon in. The house smelled fresher than expected, although the fake lemon scent told Leon this was a room spray rather than actual cleanliness. He wrinkled his nose, and would have held a handkerchief over his face if he wasn't concerned about offending Graham. No one had taken a cloth to any surface here in a long time. Dust and grime covered every surface. Used plates and half-opened mail covered the dining table. Dead flies stuck to the counters.

"My wife Gerta's having a nap," the old man said. She was, indeed, sitting up in an armchair in the lounge room, snoring gently. "Look at her," the old man said. "Like a dying pig."

Leon thought he'd misheard, but the man repeated it. "A dying pig." He poked her awake. He said, "We'll make you some hot chocolate," and without a word the woman rose and shuffled to the kitchen.

"She's well trained," the old man said. "Wish I could say the same for the cats."

"You've got a nice house, I mean, you've done nice things to it," Leon said, because it would've been impolite to say, *This is a dump, get me the hell out of here.*

"It's not looking its best," the old man said. "I know, boy. I know. We're tired old folks! We don't care anymore. There's a freedom in that, son." The old man caught his reflection in the mirror. He was mostly bald; what Leon thought might be hair was sprouting out of his ears — those ears without lobes.

"The things we've seen," the old man said. "What you see changes you. What you see when you look at your reflection changes you."

His wife walked in, carefully balancing the mugs of hot chocolate on a small tray. She handed one to Leon, her head slightly bowed. Leon took a sip; it was sweet, beyond sweet, but delicious.

"Melted chocolate, that's the secret," she said. "My husband worked in a chocolate factory, and we never got over the abundance!"

The old man said, "My room was the smallest one upstairs. A bit bigger than the bathroom but not much! That's what you get for being the youngest." Ten more minutes of this tedium, and he'd have the info about where the tiles were, and how to get in. Everything he needed.

"Poor love," the woman said. "We call that the Golden Room."

"Because of the sunlight that comes in?" Leon asked.

"Ah, you'll see. Go on," the old man said, gesturing upstairs. "We're proud of it. We went through a lot to make that the Golden Room. Mind you, it needs a bit of love. We glued those tiles on nearly thirty years ago!"

They held hands at that, but the side eye the man gave his wife sent a shiver down Leon's spine. He climbed upstairs, avoiding the piles of clothes, the stacks of papers, and opened the door to the Golden Room.

He almost fell backwards; the amber wall inside glowed with such brightness it nearly blinded him. He could see reflections, inflections, he could see *beauty* in there. Once his eyes adjusted, he saw perhaps forty tiles, imperfectly laid with discoloured putty between them. They were dotted with a random pattern of black specks; and, as Leon looked more closely, he discerned that these were tiny insects. Excitement fluttered in his gut; this was what he was being paid to find. The elderly couple stood at the door, Graham in front, Gerta hiding behind him.

"You wouldn't believe what people have offered us for those tiles," Graham said. "But never enough! For the right price, perhaps..."

But Leon only smiled, because he knew he wouldn't be paying a cent.

Off the coast of Morocco
November 14, 1951

"I won't be paying you a cent over what we've discussed, " Graham said. "The deal we did in Marrakesh is the deal we're sticking with. I've put everything I've got into this. I don't have a penny to spare." He'd hired the three men after meeting them at a cafe in the city, saying to Gerta, "It's hard to know who to trust in business, especially in the treasure-hunting business. You're the only person I can count on."

The men nodded. "The four of us will head down," Graham said, "with Gerta staying on the boat for safety reasons. Everything's planned to a T. Danger is minimal."

Graham steered the boat he'd hired under a false name to the coordinates he'd been given for the location of the amber panels. He didn't know for sure they were there, but sometimes a dying declaration — especially one in jail, with no one else to hear — was a surprisingly sound source of truth. In this case, Graham had faith his late cellmate was on the money.

The four men climbed into the submersible. It was a simple design, cigar shaped, enough room for four smallish men and nothing besides, with a hook and a rope for winching back up again, and a cage on the back for the amber panels.

At Graham's signal from inside, Gerta turned the crank to lower the submersible into the depths below. The water was dark but clear, with hundreds of tiny fishes flashing past, along with floating kelp and flakes of wood. The prow of the deck was clearly visible as they approached. The vessel itself was broken apart, its center exposed to the saltwater. Rust, seaweed, and shells clung to its surface, and cases, boxes and tins littered the deck and the ocean floor.

The four men emerged from the submersible, small air tanks on their backs, goggles and face masks in place. Graham checked all of the tanks, then his watch, nodding to himself. They explored, gathering coins, cigarette lighters, knives, and jewelry and tucking them into pouches strapped around their waists. Only Graham remained on track, seeking the amber panels he desperately hoped were there, tugging away broken sheets of metal, pushing aside disintegrated planks, digging through debris.

One of the other men identified the cracked crate that held the panels, waving his arms and pointing. Elated, Graham directed them with sweeping arm gestures, indicating they should load the cage, then pressing downward with his palms to say, *Take it easy. Take it slow.* He checked his air tank, then indicated they should make one more sweep of the wreck for treasure.

Ten more minutes passed before Graham signaled to Gerta, via the rope, to raise the submersible. All four of them clung to the cage. It was slower going up than it had been going down, because of their heavy load. Graham watched impassively as, one by one, the men ran out of oxygen. He watched as they clutched at their throats before letting go of the cage and frantically trying to swim to the surface. He watched as the bodies sank, breathing deeply of the oxygen he'd made sure he had enough of in his tank.

As the submersible broke the water's surface, Graham emerged from the hatch and tore the mask from his face. Gerta leaned over the side and helped him in, then the two of them worked to winch the cage aboard. She didn't ask him where the men were — but when at last the silence became almost painful, he simply said, "Something came over me."

"You were always going to leave them," Gerta said.

Over the next twenty-three years, Graham tried to sell the amber through black markets, upper-class collectors, jail connections and government officials. But the answer was always the same: "This stuff is too hot. Always will be. Too many questions will be asked!" So he and Gerta settled in Portsmouth, converted the panels to tiles, and decorated one small bedroom.

Gerta shuddered as she said, "I don't like to think about those walls." But Graham winked at Leon. "You gotta do what you do to get ahead in life," he said.

"It's been a curse," Gerta whispered. "A rotting, festering corpse around our necks."

The Supplier
Portsmouth, New Hampshire
December 14, 1974

As the three of them walked back down the stairs, Leon noticed a number of holes. "Not too safe!" he said. "I can fix those." An easy excuse for him to come and go for a few days.

"Our son will do it," Gerta said.

Graham shook his head. "Dumbo. Dummy dummy dummy." He spun his finger around: *She's cuckoo.* "We've got no son."

"We do have a son, you just don't like him," Gerta said.

"My father doesn't like me either," Leon said. He instinctively touched the small of his back, where his father had once kicked him so hard he'd fractured a rib.

"Ours slept in the Golden Room, like you did," said Gerta. "Do you see your father often?"

"Twice a year, Christmas and his birthday," Leon lied.

"Any children for you?" Gerta asked him.

"Two boys, two girls," Leon said, and for a moment he believed it.

Leon returned that night, parking his truck a street over from their house. It was quiet. Most people were tucked up safely in their houses, and he didn't think he'd been noticed. Lights glowed in some rooms, the smell of dinner cooking — onions frying, meat roasting — drifted over to him, making him hungry. The street lights were bright here and he jumped between them, not wanting to be seen. For all his size, he often felt invisible but here he was highlighted in the otherwise empty street. He let himself in through the back door, which entered into the laundry room. They'd left a load of wet laundry in the machine too long; he could smell that old-water stench. A TV roared. They'd hear nothing. He crept along the hallway and upstairs, to the Golden Room. He'd seen an offer for these walls turned down, *oh we couldn't sell.* It was worth a literal fortune.

Pulling a chisel from his tool bag, he knelt down and pried up one edge of an amber tile. Luckily, it had been installed many years earlier and the glue was starting to disintegrate. He levered one off, carefully, slowly, and then another. The wall underneath was damaged, but the tiles themselves were in very good condition. He wrapped three of them in a towel he'd brought with him, and carried them to the car.

He figured it would take three days. He arrived each evening, once he could see the glow of the television and hear its dull roar. Even in the low light the tiles seemed to glow. Time and time again he jumped, thinking the couple had snuck up on him, because he could see them reflected in the amber surfaces. But when he turned, the room was empty."

They caught him on the third night.

"What are you doing?" Graham said. He was far less distressed than Leon had imagined, but he carried a gun, held loosely in his weak hand.

Gerta pushed forward, her hand over her mouth.

Leon panicked. It was easier than anything he'd done in a while; one whack, then two, and both of them were down, but still conscious. He had to decide whether to finish them off or not. His mind oscillated: Leave them there? Call for help?

The old woman said, "Yours now."

The old man said, "Thank you."

Leon took pity and finished them off.

He dragged them into their bedroom. The bed was layered with a dozen quilts; he heaved them onto the mattress and covered them both.

For the next twelve hours, he removed tiles and fed the cats. Twelve hours of solid work and he was done. He felt a kind of affinity for the old couple and their cats. No one would know if they were dead or alive. Just like him. He liked that in a way. Anonymity brought freedom. It was a very different thing than the immortality, the fame, the theme park would, in theory, bring to the Teagues.

He collected books and treasures as well, but on the third day, the car smelled like death on the way back to the motel and he knew he would go inside the house only once more.

He packed up, let the cats out and set fire to the house to cover up evidence, laughing at his own unoriginality.

He loaded the car with the last of the tiles and other treasures, and undertook the long journey back to Odessa. He delivered the tiles, took payment in cash along with his OmniVisa, and headed into the tunnels to make his hideaway under the Realm of Time.

The Installer

Odessa, Texas

December 20, 1974

The installer sat in his car, eyes closed. He rubbed at his face then slapped his cheeks, trying to wake himself up. His assistant tapped at the window, grinning.

"Big night?" the assistant asked.

"Big life," said the installer. He climbed out of his car. "Wait'll you see what we're laying today. Beautiful. You've never seen anything like it."

The assistant shook his head. "I doubt it." But when he saw the amber tiles, piled carefully in place inside the Realm of Time, he stumbled. He reached out a hand to touch them; they were almost soft, malleable, he thought, but with a look of bright hardness about them that made him catch his breath.

"Wouldn't mind a couple of these at home," he said to the installer. "If one breaks, we shouldn't let it go to waste."

The space was very small, a walkway, really, and the installer had to twist himself to reach into difficult corners. His assistant held the adhesive, eyes closed.

"Open your eyes, idiot," the installer said.

"I don't want to see myself in them," said the assistant. "I look weird. I look like someone else."

"Idiot," the installer said again. But he thought, *Strange what an ancient material will reflect.*

The two men worked hard, barely speaking, laying the tiles carefully, ensuring that no adhesive leaked between the cracks.

"Look at this one!" the assistant said, holding up a tile in which was encased an ancient dragonfly, wings and all.

The installer sent his assistant to fetch them some coffee and, unable to resist the urge, hid one tile — slightly damaged, he told himself — under the coat he'd laid in the corner.

They finished the job, cleaned up, and left.

"I'm glad that's over," the assistant said. "Hope we never have to see tiles like that again."

"I could work with those tiles forever," the installer said. "They make me feel... I don't know. Like I matter, somehow."

He pulled on his jacket and laid the tile on the passenger seat of his car before starting the engine and peeling out of the parking lot. It was the reflection of the sun, perhaps. Golden, bright, blinding in his rear-view mirror (but how?) blinding, and not the utter uncontrollable rage he felt at the sight of a pedestrian jaywalking that made him veer off his side of the road and slam with great force into the pedestrians.

They never had a chance to dodge the car that sped toward them.

Three of the children lay crumpled, almost unrecognizable as children, blood pooling around them, arms at broken angles. A woman lay across them, arms splayed. The other two children stood in shock, shaking uncontrollably. Nearby, a teenaged girl screamed, a guttural sound that summoned help.

"They're dead! They're *dead!*" she screamed.

The installer's car, meanwhile, had crashed through the plateglass front window of an independent bookstore, its front end crumpling as it collided with a concrete support pillar. The car had no air bags, so he was flung forward and back, his seat belt breaking his collarbone as an unsecured hammer flew forward to slam into the back of his head, rendering him unconscious. He was soon surrounded by horrified witnesses, who pried open the driver's-side door and tried to pull him out. But his legs were trapped; the more the bystanders pulled, the more he screamed — and the more they wanted to kill him for what he'd done.

Ambulances arrived, sirens wailing. Paramedics leaped out, rushing toward the surviving children, and to the installer's car.

But the bystanders crowded together, preventing the paramedics from reaching the installer. The bookstore owner leaned in the passenger side, asking the installer for his name. But he was utterly distracted by the square tile on the passenger seat. Amber colored, flecked with black (insects? How old?). He gazed into its depths, watching a story unfold that he didn't understand.

The installer blinked into consciousness. "I got bit by a rat," he said, extending a bloodied arm as evidence. "That's why. I got bit."

He seemed to have lesions, sure. Enough to start a panic, which made the nightly news, and made its way back to OmniPark, where a furious Dalton Teague ordered the sanitation manager to call in an exterminator to clean out the access tunnels.

As for the bookstore owner, he kept that amber tile displayed by his register, accompanied by a sign saying "Don't shoplift. The Amber knows." He was astonished by how well this worked.

The Supplier
Odessa, Texas
February 3, 1975

Leon took another job, recommended highly by Elijah Shattuck. The house was empty during the week, so he broke in on a Monday morning, found the requested artwork, wrapped it in a sheet and headed for the front door.

He noticed a doorway under the stairs and decided to take a look, in case there were some unaccounted for goods down there he could sell on the sound. Instead, he found the basement full of cages holding rare snakes, neglected, barely alive. He was glad no one was there to see him squeal and run upstairs. He didn't set them free, as was his habit with abandoned pets, but called authorities and left an anonymous tip.

Still, the discovery of those half-dead creatures left him feeling anxious and saddened. He looked forward to heading underground, to the place he was gradually making his own. He needed to gather some of his things, though. His basement home under the Realm of Time was comfortable enough, but could do with a few more personal touches. It was light and surprisingly airy, and he'd settled in there nicely.

He'd just stopped into his sister's place one last time — the place he'd stayed for years because she'd let him keep a room without putting his name on the lease, or on any bills. And because he didn't have to deal with people much.

But now his sister had moved away. Upstairs in his small room they'd allocated lay a pile of letters and magazines, none of them important; and a note saying, "Don't forget Dad's birthday."

The kitchen showed evidence of family dinners he was glad to have missed: vegetable curries, lentil burgers, meatless casseroles. He liked his diet of fried food from truck vendors at OmniPark's construction sites. No one questioned him about his food choices. No one questioned him at all.

He left the door key on the kitchen table and headed back to OmniPark. He felt elated by this, in stark contrast to his mood a few hours earlier, when he'd pushed open the basement door and found those neglected snakes.

He was hungry, so he gathered his dinner from the food-truck vendors: large Coke, no ice. A hot dog, no cheese. Tater tots, with chicken gravy. These he gave to a street kid who was hanging around by the back fence; he often did this. Why not? He thought. He'd feed the stray dogs, too. He ordered another round — Coke, hotdog, tater tots — and these he carried to his place beneath the Realm of Time. He'd lined it with tiles (not amber!) that he'd scavenged, and with the things he'd brought from his sister's place. It really felt like his sanctuary now. The faint tick-tocking he could hear from above gave him a sense of comfort, as did the bottles of rum he drank from to get to sleep. He felt safe. Comfortable. The ticking lulled him. A strange smell entered his deep dream; he imagined it was the amber tiles, leaking, dripping down through the cracks into his small home.

The Exterminator

    Assignment: final removal of rodents from the
network of access tunnels under the Seven Realms
of OmniPark

    Method: chlorine gas pumped through all tunnels,
with exits blocked. Additional methodology: chemical
additive to allow for productive removal of remains
(bones only). Said tunnels to be cleaned out within
four weeks.

The Supplier

> **OMNIPARK THANKS THE ANONYMOUS SUPPLIER
> OF THIS LARGE HUMAN SKELETON.**

—Plaque in the Great Tent, in OmniPark's Realm of Man

Blurred Omnipotence

Maxwell I. Gold

i. The Gate

O'er the ruined gates which sought to keep my imagination closed off from dark and innovative dreams, I wondered at the dreadful possibilities which lurked in flame and stars;

That'd become mine, embraced by Tomorrow's Hand, swallowed, and forgotten was my fate, a toy of mediocrity unless the gates were forever shattered. Forever torn asunder, rebuilt into a radiant hereafter;

To break barriers without cost, without dogmatic constraints nor boilerplate justifications like chains of pragmatic folly pulling harder at the Future that flashed across my eyes as if the universe was mine to hold, to explore;

ii. Possibilities

Seven gates,
    One at a time.
Seven colors
    One at a time.
Seven deaths,
    One at a time;
Seven universes,
    One at a time
the gates collapsed upon themselves

iii. A New City

One at a time, and then no more,
Only my dark, unfurling dreams and the gaping ruin of a universe that
twisted into the absolute mystery that was my soul; a new city to rise
out of the ashes of sea, time, light, and space to condemn the treason of
Expectation for the love of Possibility;

Seven truths,
    Mine to behold,
Seven infinities,
    Mine to behold,
Seven stars,
    Mine to behold.
And seven gates,
    Mine to open.

iv. My Universe

No longer caged by omnipotence, I buried Yesterday in the graveyard of
my wretched fleshy machinations beneath the foundations of a world
constructed in stars and lights;

    The universe has seven Realms,

No longer confined by the labyrinths of books and desks and gods, the
hands of my imagination like tentacles from some leviathan, reached
furiously across the unending horizon where I heard the last sweet plea
from a familiar voice:

    The universe has seven Realms,

And I sealed the ruined gates which sought to keep my imagination closed
off from dark and innovative dreams, never again was I consumed by the
dreadful prospects that lurked in flame and stars.

    My universe has seven Realms.

$H_n(x)=(-1)^n e^{x^2} \frac{d}{dx^n}(e^{-x^2})$
$\psi(x)=Ae^{ikx}+Be^{-ikx}$
$V(x)=\begin{cases} V_0, & x<0 \\ 0, & x\geq 0 \end{cases}$
$\psi(x)=\frac{1}{\sqrt{k_1}}(A_+e^{ik_1x}+A_-e^{-ik_1x})$
$\psi(x)=\frac{1}{\sqrt{k_2}}(B_+e^{ik_2x}+B_-e^{-ik_2x})$

Above and Beyond

John Palisano

December 7, 1974

Gold embers floated over Forest Road, suspended like glowing fireflies in the night. Cars on Interstate 20 slowed, their drivers and riders marveling at the display, wondering where it was coming from. As beautiful and trancelike as the scene was, it came in contrast to the burning tragedy on the other side of the hill.

Odessa, Texas would not soon forget.

△▽△

"Intriguing. This'll work." Dalton Teague nodded, carefully surveying the blueprints laid out across the meeting room's huge drafting table. The plans showed a suspended transportation roadway above the half-finished OmniPark, its shape a figure eight pattern. "It flows well. It's a world all its own, yet it fits in with the rest of the park, as well — particularly with the Realm of the Stars. I see you've worked in elements of a gravity ride and a dark ride near the end, with the plunge through the galaxy. And it interweaves with what we're already building here. Fits neatly into the existing Realms, like a puzzle piece. And it adds to our skyline without overwhelming it." Dr. Teague stroked his chin, deep in thought. "Not bad. Not bad at all. You've served OmniPark well."

Kate Kelly felt her face grow hot. "Well, all in service of the park, right?" she said, trying to keep the sarcasm out of her voice, hoping Teague wouldn't notice.

"That's what we aim for," Teague said. "Name's good, too: 'Above and Beyond.' Simple yet effective."

"With our acreage running low, we can't really expand out," Kate said. "So, why can't we go up?"

"Indeed," Teague said. He gestured toward the others — a trio Kate'd never seen before — and the other person making up the secretive inner circle who accompanied him everywhere these days. *Another clandestine group of Technosophers?* Kate wondered. She'd met *the* Cary Egger just once... one of the biggest names behind OmniPark's development, and supposedly the manager of what happened at the Barn. She'd not seen or heard from him since. For some reason, Teague decided to take a hands-on approach to the Barn and its duo.

Anthony Bingham didn't smile so much as sneer. "Unfortunately, it's not very practical, is it?" he asked, glaring at Kate.

She knew this would happen. Of course he'd be negative. Her throat went dry and she balled her hands into fists. *I could just wring his little neck until his rat eyes popped out of his head, couldn't I? And no one would be able to stop me.*

Visions of Annie and Joannie and Christine flashed through her mind. She wouldn't risk being taken from her children or losing her job — not over rodent-faced Anthony Bingham. She swore his eyes even looked rimmed with red.

Teague looked over at her and smile-frowned. "There's just a natural intuition with design here that can't be learned." He stepped toward her and nodded. "As far as your concerns, Anthony..." Teague addressed him while keeping his eyes locked on Kate. "We were made from making the impractical not only plausible, but possible." He turned to Anthony. "A fact worth remembering when you hand in your proposal for a new attraction next week."

Anthony looked like he'd seen his own ghost. He froze, motionless as a startled possum.

Teague moved toward the door. His shady trio followed. Kate could never remember their names. "Above and Beyond is moving into phase two. Concept designs in seven days, all right, Katherine?"

"Yes," she said, her throat tight enough to turn a grain of sand into a pearl. "Absolutely."

"That'll work," Teague said again, clamping a hand on one of Anthony's shoulders on the way out. "Get some water, fella. You look like you're going to tip over."

As soon as Teague and his trio left, Anthony glowered.

Don't look at him. Don't engage. That's what bullies want. She hustled the blueprints into a roll, her back to him.

"Well, congratulations, I guess," he said. He was so close she could smell his breath. He smelled... sweet. Phoenix berries, she knew.

He's using that stuff at work?

"T-thanks," she said and rushed out of the room. "Thanks, Anthony." She hated herself for stuttering and allowing herself to show she'd been rattled.

"Pleasure's all..."

Kate was out of the room before his rat voice finished.

What else could she do, she wondered, when it came to rat-faced bully Anthony? How would she know what he was doing, anyway? She wouldn't, of course.

△▽△

Anthony studied Kate's plans. A clean canopy stretched across the park's rapidly expanding perimeter. Beneath the canopy, a track wound its way around the park 100 feet above the busy park streets and 50 feet below the artificial clouds. Riders would enter the four-person round capsule-shaped cars near the front of the park. In addition to getting an aerial view of the entire park, riders would experience the science behind flight. The capsules would simulate the lift of small aircraft, then helicopters, and, near the end — interstellar space flight.

Somehow, Kate had made it all work. It wouldn't require the demolition of any existing attractions already built or planned for OmniPark. It'd be cost-effective. Her plan hit all the marks. She always made everything look so easy. Anthony kept thinking about it, the details racing around his head. He had to come up with something equally grand. Better, though. Smarter. Undeniably the right choice. Now that he knew what Dalton Teague wanted, he'd adapt.

"I bet they're never going to go with something of mine," he said. "Teague's got a thing for Kate. Probably in love with her. Maybe they're secretly an item. She's his golden child. Time to prove him wrong."

Alone in the design lab, he went to his desk, withdrew his keys from his pocket, and unlocked the top drawer. Inside, he found his pouch of dried Phoenix berries and took it out. No sense in being coy. He was going to use again.

Dropping several small berries into a bottle of Coke, he knew they'd dissolve and be untraceable. He also knew that by the time he finished the bottle, his mind would be elevated to a different place. Likely, the work would keep him up all night. Riding on the fuel the Phoenix berries provided. If he had to sleep, there was the leather couch, or better yet? The dentist's chair. That was his favorite throne, anyway. He didn't mind. Collette wouldn't mind, either. She and the girls were usually fast asleep by the time he got home, anyway. He'd call to tell her just as soon as the Coke and berries kicked in.

Pushing back in the chair, he leaned his head and closed his eyes. He stretched his neck upward and to the left, then swiveled right. The creak in his neck bones produced a satisfying clicking sound as it released some pressure. Anthony took a deep breath. The edges of his eyes felt tingly. The warmth spread from his eyes to his cheeks, and down to his neck. At the same time, it bloomed just behind his temples, deeper inside, and filled him to his skull's crown. Moments later, his hands and fingers tingled.

He saw every color behind his eyelids. It was like looking at electrical currents, each a different color, pulsing and changing. After a few moments, the colors subsided and there was only a glittering image made of countless soft white pinpoints.

The berries had done their job.

Anthony replayed the conflict between Teague and Kate Kelly. His praise of her stung. *What can I do that's better? Something irresistible? Something that will work and win him over? There's got to be a flaw in her idea I can take advantage of.*

He knew in a blink what he'd pitch. Saw the attraction clearly in his mind's eye. Hopping off the dentist's chair, Anthony raced to the drafting tables and transcribed his vision as best as he could.

He leaned over his blueprints. Mechanics of a volcano. Anthony stared at the plan — a basic bisection of a volcano, with floors guests could explore. It'd vibrate in a mock eruption every half hour. "Ring of Fire. I love it. They're going to love it."

It wasn't until the middle of the night that he stumbled into his car, somehow making it home.

△▽△

Jim almost dropped the casserole. The oven mitts were much too large for his hands, but he managed to get the Pyrex up and onto the stove's burners.

"I don't believe you made dinner," Kate said to her husband. "Again."

He laughed. "You still don't believe my mother taught me how to cook, and that I love it, do you?"

"Men aren't supposed to cook," she said, tilting the pitch of her voice upward, trying to sound mock-snobbish.

"Oh, please," he said. "It's going to be 1975 in less than two weeks. We all know that way of thinking went the way of the dodo bird years ago."

"Wish that was the case at work."

Jim slipped off the oven mitts. "Not that rat-hole again?" He slammed them on the counter.

"Who else?"

Jim shook his head. "Teague needs to fire him." He grabbed a serving knife and waved it over the dish.

Kate put her hands on her hips. "Can't. There's that weird connection he has because of family. Nepotism at its finest. Dr. Teauge's hands are tied, but he knows he's trouble. That's why he put me with him out at the Barn facility, way out by the meteor crater, far away from the guest areas."

"There's got to be something someone can do."

"We can leave the work there and enjoy our family here on our little ranch," Kelly said.

"That we can."

"And that we will."

Loud footsteps echoed as loud and as sudden as thunder. "Girls!" Kate said just as their daughters Annie, Christine, and Joannie hurried into the kitchen. "You're just in time for dinner."

Annie, the oldest at 13, was first to squeak into a wooden chair and pull it up to the dining table. "We heard the oven open and the sound of Dad putting the food down."

"I tried to be quiet." Jim laughed.

"Doesn't matter. The smell gave it away," Joannie, the youngest, said.

Christine sat last. "I'm just starved and can't wait."

"Me, too," Kate said, beaming. They all reminded her or herself when she was their ages. "Just hold on, my little mirrors." That's what she always referred to them as: the Little Mirrors.

Jim already had two meals plated and ready. "Here we go." He rushed them over, winking to Kate. "Don't worry. I saved you the end pieces."

"You're just a peach, darling," she said.

△▽△

In bed, long after dinner, Kate's thoughts wouldn't settle. Try as she might, the events from work circled around on replay. So much for taking her own advice, she thought.

She heard Jim snoring next to her, and felt a sudden wave of disdain wash over her. So lucky to have the biggest worry be what to make your spouse and family for dinner and getting the kids to David Crockett Middle School. It was up to her to make the money and keep the family afloat. Her talent. She fought against shoe dirt like Anthony on a daily basis — just because she wasn't a man. *Maybe I should dress like a guy and change my name to Kenneth. Then maybe they'd respect me.*

Jim turned on his side and his floppy bangs covered one of his eyes just so as to make him look like a matinee heartthrob from the '40s. He could go back to acting and land a hundred roles in a hundred days, she swore. *But he gave it all up for the girls and me. He loves us more than anything. And I love him more.*

She shut her eyes and thought of a thousand witty comebacks she could have fired back at Anthony. Eventually, though, sleep came. With it? A vision.

△▽△

A centrifuge spun. It transformed into OmniPark. Time took shape. The control room that guided all the rides manifested. At the helm? Anthony pulled levers and bossed others around in indistinct language. Her stomach sank. All she made out was him saying, "More" over and over. There were feeds on monitors at key points of each ride. Everyone zeroed in on the Flight area. A vehicle in distress tried to right itself. Kelly made it out to be a helicopter. *Oh, no, they're in trouble.* High-pitched engine sounds made her cringe. She heard the sound of scraping metal. Within seconds, the helicopter broke away from the tracks, while some of its pieces broke apart from the force. She watched Mary Toussaint wave frantically from the capsule as it shattered. She's lost in an explosion of rubble. The tracks melted beneath. There was no escape.

Anthony's reckless drive killed her, and perhaps others.

Kate awoke in bed, frozen in fear. Her heartbeat was so fast she was sure she could feel it pounding right through her ribs. *Go back to sleep. You just had a nightmare. Anxiety over everything. That's all.* She sighed and looked over at her husband, still asleep. *Even my dreams aren't safe anymore.*

△▽△

"Fire! Brimstone! Volcanoes!" Anthony was on a tear, waving his arms as if they were on fire. "It's the primordial Earth!" He pointed toward the pulldown screen where his overhead projector showed his wax marker scribbles. He read what it said. "Ring of Fire will be an amazing new attraction for OmniPark. And the best part is that it will be dug underneath the park and not exposed to the elements." He stole a moment to look at Kate and wink. "We can even repurpose some of the service tunnels to make this work. It won't change the look of our park. It won't be as expensive as trying to shoehorn it somewhere else. It will be a great complement to what we already have."

He took a breath. Shut his eyes for a second. Crossed his arms, displaying his triumph.

Kate looked over to Dr. Teague, but he gave her nothing but a closed-mouth look that was more a *hurumph* than a smile or a frown.

"So, what do you think?" Anthony asked as soon as he opened his eyes. "Are we good to go, Dr. Teague?"

Teague took in a dramatic breath and released it. "What you've just pitched is the polar opposite of Mrs. Kelly's."

"Yes," Anthony said. "Exactly."

Shaking his head, Teague stared Anthony down. "That's not an endorsement. I'm illustrating what's wrong with your idea. Mainly the fact it's simply Mrs. Kelly's idea, only transferred underground."

Anthony's mouth moved up and down, but no sound came out. Kate thought he looked like a fish out of water. "But... but..." he started.

"No," Teague said. "I'm disappointed with this." He stood and gestured for his staff to do the same. "We're going to go ahead with Above and Beyond, then." Nodding to Kate, he said, "Good afternoon," and left.

Kate was left in the Barn's main room alone with Anthony staring her down. She gathered her things and stood, "Well, then," she said, breaking eye contact, "I've got to get back to my station, Anthony." She rushed to the door and slipped out and through as fast as possible.

Right as the door shut she heard him say, "Bitch."

Outside, in the front room, she paused for a second, processing what'd just happened. Every part of her felt on fire and cold at once. How dare he? *Do I tell anyone what he just did? Do I tell Teague? Jim? They'll both want to do something. Jim might break and track him down and beat him. That'd end my career, as right as it'd be for him to do so.*

Kate heard the door squeak behind her. Her blood went cold. *Move.* She hurried away from the front room and toward the porch. No way would she want to be confronted by him in the Barn's studio. Kate wasn't sure she wouldn't be alone with him there and at least in the front room, there'd be the receptionist and maybe even Teague and some others.

"Yeah. That's right. Run away," Anthony said, raising his voice. "You look better from behind, anyway."

One more fucking thing. She was ready to turn round, scream, and rip his eyes and tongue out. Instead, she walked faster. *Don't let him win. He's already lost.*

She made it outside and onto the large porch. Teague and the others were huddled around their car, chatting. He saw her and looked up. Smiled from afar, but then put his head down.

Tell him. Tell them. Don't let Anthony get away with this.

One of Teague's trio opened a car door.

Do it. Don't wait.

No.

Teague and his mysterious trio stepped inside the car. The doors shut.

Why am I so weak? Why can't I stand up for myself? She shook her head. *No. You know why. Blowing the whistle will ruin you. Even though you're right. Even though you'd likely prevail. The way the industry... the way the world looks at you. It'll be an invisible black list. It happened to Martha Church. Almost the same patterns of abuse. The work for her dried up. Where is she? If I drag Dalton Teague into this, that'll be my legacy. The woman who was harassed and won, not the person who created Above and Beyond and won even more.*

That won't be me. Can't be me. I won't let him win.

△▽△

She spotted the lights of the Magneto chamber and quickened her pace. She hoped Anthony wasn't inside. If he'd beaten her to the room, she'd have to wait another day to make the big printouts of that day's plans, which would put her back at least an hour before she could leave. "Shit," she hissed, under her breath, as she spotted his light blue dress shirt, complete with the ever-present dark spots under his pits. What would she do? What would she say to him after all of this came down, after all? Kate wasn't so sure anymore. *Just take a deep breath. Get through this moment.*

Anthony must have sensed her lingering because he turned around. "Oh, hey," he said. "You have great timing. I was just finishing up in here for the night." He used the long metal filament tool, rolling it across the back of his plans to solidify the silver nitrate.

"Oh," she said, surprised. "That's great. I was hoping to get home relatively on time tonight."

He got up and slid the filament into its sheath attached to the side of the table. Its end leaked a few drops of the blue fluid. He slid his plans to the edge, folded them twice in such a way as to keep the drawings concealed, and put it under his arm. "Well, same here. But not like I have anyone to go home to. My life's this job."

She nodded. "I understand," she said, knowing he was attempting some sort of putdown.

"Sure you do," he said. "You've got it all figured out, don't you?"

"N-no," she said, "Hardly." She eyed the folded plans under his arm and wondered what he had printed if his idea for an attraction was nixed. Surely he didn't have something cooked up again so soon.

He brushed past. "M-hmm. Sure. Have a good night. Thanks for destroying mine."

"I've done no such thing." Kate shook her head.

"We'll see about that." He was gone in a blink, leaving behind only a trace of his English Leather cologne in the air.

Kate waved the bad air away, hurried inside toward the Magneto printer, and went to work.

There was no time to waste. To hell with him and his jealous threats.

She started the Magneto printer and, knowing it'd be several minutes, made her way across the room to the Revo film chamber. It reminded her of a phone booth, only larger, and much more modern. Inside, she flipped on several toggles. The Revo chamber's lights came on, as did the several white orbs used to capture her. Those reminded her of big, soft white light bulbs. Somehow, the Revo film captured her voice, but also her image in three dimensions. There was another layer, too, that Teague explained as "...going a little bit under the skin... to capture the vital essence of who you are... like taking a photograph of your aura, as it were."

She didn't quite understand the 'how' of it all, but agreed to participate in the new technology so they could test it and see if it were applicable.

Pressing the red *record* button, Kate cleared her throat. "All right. It's December 7th, 1974. I'm Kate Kelly, recording what I've done today. Made some big headway into the physics of my design, Above and Beyond, as far as the inclines and natural declines speeding up along the tracks. Also, identified some key points where cameras might be placed, especially at the final descent that gives the final, largest drop and the best auto-photo drop for guests. It should make for some great pictures for folks to buy, I'll bet." She looked straight at one of the white orbs and felt energy flow from it right into the back of her eyes: the device's piece de resistance. "And I sense my internal vision has been captured now and will check the replay. Signing off for tonight. Thank you."

She pressed the *record* button to stop the process. "Hope that took." She pressed *play* and saw an image hovering within a glass pane in front of her. An eerily lifelike, smaller version of herself appeared and spoke, saying what she'd said. When the apparition stopped and looked right at her, an orb-like shape projected closer and she saw a glimpse of a ride vehicle just about to go down a big incline, a swirling galaxy looming just ahead. Kate flinched. "Just how I see it in my mind. Never gets old, seeing what's in my imagination like this."

Turning it off, she wished she could access Anthony's Revo films, that way she'd know what he'd been up to. Of course, the same security for hers had been applied to his. She shrugged. *Think about something nice.* She pictured Jim and the girls. Her heart lifted. *Yes. Time to go home.*

Printing her plans out, she took them, folded them, and locked up.

She made it home for dinner. Kate didn't tell Jim what had happened. Didn't want to worry him, or the kids. She played the dutiful working wife, happy to come home to her house-husband's home-cooked meal, and daughters, glad he'd wrestled to get their homework finished, while also managing to wash and fold almost all of their laundry.

He was still working on cleaning their bathroom sink when she slipped under the covers. "You should come to bed. You work so hard, darling," she said.

"Almost there. I'll just be a few more minutes. Can't sleep unless it's all done." Jim's back was to her. A strong, sexy back. She admired the way his shoulder blades moved under his tight, white button-up shirt. Loved the way his tight muscles traveled in a nice, slightly curved line stretching down to the tops of his butt. She imagined his dimples there and smiled. He shut the door so he could get to the area of the sink closest; he did so each night.

Kate took the opportunity to reach into the drawer of her bedside table, slip her fingers inside a jewelry box, and take out two dried Phoenix berries. She slipped them in her mouth and shut the door, as gracefully and as quietly as possible. *They'll take all the stress of the day away. Let me dream. Let me connect so I can see. Let me travel to where I need to go.*

She shut her eyes and let the earthy, sweet flavor fill her mouth. She felt her tongue tingle as the berries dissolved. *What a hypocrite am I? Anthony's on them, too, and I judge him. But I'm different. I won't get hooked. Only use them now and then. And they leave no trace. I'll be fine. No one has to know.*

By the time she sensed Jim slide in next to her, his hands still smelling of Pine-Sol, she was a million miles away.

She woke a few hours later, her mouth and throat as dry and as scratchy as she'd ever felt. Jim slept soundly. Making her way to the bathroom, she caught her face in the mirror. *I look half-dead.* Dark circles ringed her eyes and her cheeks and nose were bright red. She felt tingly all over. The berries' effects had reached their apex. She hadn't dreamt anything, she realized; just lain there, blacked out.

Filling a little Dixie cup from the tap, she looked at the water inside. It looked gold and she smelled the cleaning products. Made her gag. She poured it out, crumpled the cup, and tossed it. She turned off the light and slipped out, ensuring Jim remained asleep.

Creeping downstairs, she pulled her robe around her middle to stay warm. *Hope none of the kids hears me.* She'd forgotten to look at the clock on her midnight sojourn. *They all must've been asleep for a while now.* Once she reached the kitchen, she took out a bottle of water and sipped. She tasted the plastic it came in. Tasting some recipe of chemicals within, she swore, even though its label insisted it contained no such things.

There were no lights on, but she could see clearly. Usually, in the dark, everything would be fuzzy and pixelated like the white noise on the TV sets when they were tuned to empty channels. But she had no such distortions that night. She made out the sharp edges of their fridge. Saw every gradation of moonlight as it beamed in and seemed to paint a triangular shape on their sink and countertops.

The house creaked, sounding as loud as a gunshot. She covered her ears. As she did, her fingertips felt super sensitive. She felt every strand of hair over her ears. Felt the skin beneath. Felt the beating pulse of her temple under her pinky.

"You are high as hell," she said, her voice deeper than she'd believed possible.

She looked up and out the window, taking another sip. How was she almost done with the bottle? Spotted the white wooden fence near the top of their main yard. Saw the hill beyond. Grass stretched beyond for quite a bit until it hit the line where the yard turned into what they called Signing Valley.

Need to go out there. Look at the stars. Talk to them.

"Yeah. You're really stoned, honey," she said. "It's the middle of winter. You'll freeze."

But she knew she had to and so, she did.

△▽△

"Talk to me, heaven," she said. Looking up at the overcast gray sky in the middle of the night, freezing rain interspersed with snowflakes. She shut her eyes and felt them fall on her eyelids. Cheeks. Nose. She put out her palms to catch them.

The heavens opened. Gray clouds swirled. She heard whispers on the wind. Kelly put her hands up and touched the energy. Heard voices in strange, unfamiliar tongues. She believed she deciphered them, but it reminded her of when her aunt's cockatiel used to talk. Almost like something familiar, but far enough from the center to not be sure. She envisioned geometric shapes, intertwining. Algebraic forms so advanced — yet somehow, she understood them instantly.

Is this coming from deep inside of me? Or is this from some other world, deep in the recesses of the universe?

She saw how the tracks of the ride would echo the geometric forms she perceived. They're overlayed and blended. It was all so clear. But how might the shapes and forms be captured? *It's scrolling too fast, like countless pages in an encyclopedia.*

Her vision transformed into a spiral, then turned into a figure eight. *It's the tracks. The outline of the tracks. Somehow, that's the key. It's going to take energy. Tons of psychic energy to take all of this in and bring it to us.*

She pictured the ocean and its inhabitants. *Some believe there's a vast neural network shared between many sea creatures where they keep the history of the waters between them... Each holding a small piece; each able to access the network like a library. Which is how they warn one another. How they share the rules and what has happened and who are threats and who are allies. That's what this language I'm seeing must be. A vast library-like neural network. The history of another world. And with it? A kind of alphabet and grammar. Different than ours but compatible enough. If we can just copy it or print it out as we do with our blueprints.*

It came to her. Clear as could be. *Small pieces can be transmitted through the rider's mind when they hit the photo op point on the ride. We can put a Revo film sensor there. When it's intense and they are almost out of their bodies. We can capture the visions. Bit by bit. It might take several years. But we can get the cipher and discover the key connecting us to others beyond our world.*

Kate felt like she was falling upward into the sky. Something grabbed her and puller her. Everything distorted and flowed. Time bent. She floated through clouds of energy. *Like auras. Impossibly large. Bigger than Earth — than Jupiter — or anything.*

Millions of voices. Billions. Energy of lost souls coming and going.

Did I die? Is this heaven?

Energies intermingled. The forms weren't all human.

There are others. We are not alone.

A long flare shot outward and encompassed her. She was inside, traveling, somewhere so fast. Her flesh coalesced around her. Hurts bad.

Make the path here for those who seek us.

The path.

She saw the geometric shapes.

I thought math was something mankind created to try and make sense of the universe. Is it indeed something from the cosmos?

She realized its truth. *It's a cipher. A code for language.*

Pain blinded her. All turned white. Then black. She blinked and saw gray.

Felt snowflakes on her face, tingling. She made it back to her small ranch on Maple Drive, lying on the dirt, looking up.

Her fingers ached. She brought them up to look at them. They weren't split. *Oh, God. What's happened to me? That was some trip.*

She sat up and went back inside. Her husband was still in their bed, dead asleep. Creeping along as quietly as possible, she checked on the kids. Opening the doors just a crack to peer in, she spotted Annie asleep, her hands folded on her chest as in prayer. Kate saw their outlines in the dark, both on their sides on their own beds. She watched each and waited until she caught them move ever so slightly. Satisfied they were all okay, she tiptoed out and headed toward her office at the far end of the hall. It was 4:14 am. She hurried to her drafting table and drew as many details as she remembered. She made notes along the side of her drawings for things she couldn't easily put into pictures, such as how she felt — along with more complex ideas:

I've seen something spectacular, and it's anointed me. I feel it in every cell. I'm changed.

△▽△

Anthony wore his headphones all day. He kept his back to her, she noticed. Didn't greet her. She went right to work on her blueprints, etching out a design for support scaffolding for the track areas right after the load-in zone.

She tried to spy on what Anthony worked on. With Teague's rejection, was he working on another pitch? He was sweating. Likely the effects of coming off a day high as a weather balloon from the Phoenix berries. No wonder he didn't want to deal with anyone.

△▽△

The phone on Kate's desk rang. Kate's mind raced, but it was just Jim. "Just checking on you, sweetheart. Seeing if you'll be home on time tonight. The kids cannot wait to dive into my lasagna. Not sure I'll be able to hold them back for too long."

She laughed. "Oh, lasagna? I think I feel a headache coming on. I may need to leave work early."

Jim laughed. "Not sure it can live up to that."

"I'm hungry just thinking about it. I can smell it already." She wasn't exaggerating. He had a family recipe that added some novel ingredients such as cinnamon that really pushed it into the stratosphere.

"Well, it won't break any of our hearts to have you home at suppertime, that's for sure."

"I can," she said and looked over to Anthony, still lost in his headphones. "I know I can."

"Great, then," he said. "Love you, sweets."

"Love you, *sweeter.*"

No sooner had she hung up than Anthony was behind her. "Hey. I have something to show you."

She turned. "Okay."

"It's in the Magneto room. C'mon." He smiled, but she didn't trust it.

Kate followed him across the small hall. "What is it? I'm almost done for the day and would really like to wrap things up as soon as..."

Anthony was already in the Barn's Magneto room and stood near an open closet door. She saw the TV screen inside. Their security cameras. "What is this?" How did he have access to the equipment? Neither of them should have.

"I have something I want to show you." He pulled a large plastic cassette from the side of the Revo recorder.

"Anthony..."

He grinned. "All the recordings from the last six months are on here. Pretty precious," he said.

Her heart raced and she felt cold. *What the hell was he up to?*

"What are you doing?" she asked.

Anthony held up the tape. "I'm destroying this and you're going to call Dr. Teague and tell him I came up with Above and Beyond with you. It's half my idea."

"No. It's not."

"It is now," he said.

"This is wrong. You can't do this.."

"There will be no more proof." He walked away from the closet, toward the Revo chamber. "They'll just have our word. Your word."

"All they'll need to do is..."

"What?"

"Take a look at the correspondence. There's a paper trail."

"It won't matter if you admit you lied about everything and purposely left me out because you'd do anything to advance your career. Even sleep with me."

She wanted to rip his face off. "That's ridiculous. I'd never! And it will ruin both of us."

"Not me," he said. "They'll put me somewhere else in the company. But you? They'll send you out on your ass. Because I'm a man and you're not."

Her face flushed. *No wonder the worm was pretending not to see or hear me earlier.* She opened her mouth but clamped it shut. *If the accusations get out... hits the press I'm ruined. No. There's got to be another way.*

She rushed toward the door. "This is blackmail and I am not accepting this."

"Fine. Have it your way." In a blink, he came from behind and pushed a cloth over her nose and mouth. She knew who it was — Anthony — and what it was — chloroform. She smelled his awful cologne and felt his fuzzy forearms on her neck.

Kate pushed up and shoved his arm away. Saw the rag fall to the floor. "What the hell do you think you're doing? You had this ready?"

She went for the door, but it shut with a loud clanging. She grabbed the handle and tried it. Locked solid. Turning to him, she spotted a small device in his palm.

"Remote control lock," he said. "My secret project. Testing it here. Keep everything nice and secure."

"No," she said. "Open it. Let me out. You can't."

He lunged at her, his free fist flying toward her. She ducked but he still connected. He hit again. And again.

She fell. Hit the floor on her side. As fast as she could, she came to. Spotted him at the security closet pocketing the tape. It was hard to move and she staggered, but she made it to the Magneto table. Grabbed the filament and charged him.

He spun round in time to see her and dodge, but not enough that he wasn't stuck.

The tip of the filament pierced his side and he screamed.

"Take that, you little bitch," she yelled. The fluid inside was highly toxic, she knew, and if it didn't kill him, he would have a heck of a hospital stay.

"...the hell." He slid off and against the wall, the filament coming out. Blood drooled from the puncture site. He put a hand on it for a moment, then hustled away.

"You're not going..."

Kate swiped at him again, but he was out of range. The front door opened; he'd clicked the remote.

She followed, but he was outside the room in a blink. The door opened and he was out, not even looking back before it shut again. She screamed his name. Several times.

Kate hurried to the door. "Shit. Shit. Shit." She tried the handle. Locked. Her head spun, dizzy and sore. "Fucking asshole." Scanning the room, she knew there was no other way out.

△▽△

Heading to the Revo chamber, she stepped inside. Recorded herself. "I was just assaulted by Anthony Bingham, my co-worker, after his attempt to blackmail me into falsely stating he had half of the idea for my ride, Above and Beyond. He also stated we had an affair, which is a total fabrication. He punched me several times in the head and attempted to subdue me with chloroform because I wouldn't agree to his demands. I think it's important to document this event. In addition? I'd like to state my final update for the attraction." She sighed.

Orange dots caught her eye. It took her a moment, but she tracked them to the door. Sparks.

"Listen to me." It was Anthony. "This is it for you, Kate. You should've taken the deal. You shouldn't have stabbed me. You left me no choice."

"What are you doing?"

"Getting rid of the evidence. The whole wing will lock down in case of fire. That's the new project I've been working on. Auto-emergency locks keep it contained to one area. Time to test it."

She smelled smoke.

"Don't do this!" she cried, then called out to him. He never answered.

The Revo recorded what he said and what he was doing, she knew. Even though he'd taken the tape, he must have forgotten or didn't know the Revo had a memory that one couldn't remove or tamper with. The tapes were just backups. *Maybe someone will make it here in time to get me out of here. If not? I better record the final piece in case the papers are destroyed.* "I did the math. The pitch of the track needs to be 72 degrees, which will give a descent speed of 20 mph. The flashing lights will open the irises enough like in the Revo chamber. Some will glimpse the cipher, even for a split second, even if they don't realize it. We'll need to scan the Revo films for images captured of those who might."

She coughed. Regained herself. "And that should do it. The unit is on fire as we speak. I can see sparks and flames under the door. You heard him admit to this. I hope this recording survives this. I hope I survive this. Godspeed."

The smoke and fumes overwhelmed the chamber. She pressed *record* to stop and turned the machine off.

Coming out, her head felt light.

The electricity went out. "Just in time."

The only light she had were the flames reaching under the door.

Soon, her head was too light and she was too dizzy to stand, so she sat. She felt so tired. *They're going to come any second and break down the door and get me out of here. Just have to wait it out.* Her head hurt worse than she'd ever imagined possible. Her throat was so dry. Sitting upright felt like too much. She slipped off the chair and curled up on the floor, pulling her shirt up and over her nose and mouth.

Kate shut her eyes and blacked out, her head filled with visions of the cipher.

△▽△

May 19, 1977
Opening Day. OmniPark.

K1954 sprung to life as people approached. Its eyes scanned Teague. The greeter moved with a familiar gentle elegance. Its eyes blinked and followed him as he shifted. Teague nodded. "It really captures her," he said. Even though the greeter was made from plastic and metal, it looked strikingly human. Its eyes... her eyes... locked in and followed Doctor Teague's gaze. It was an eerie simulation. Its gestures were smooth and lifelike.

"The Revo films helped a lot with humanizing the animatronic." One of his engineers nodded. The Revo's recordings had survived the fire.

"Indeed," Dr. Teague said. "And here we are, minutes away from letting people in to experience her grand vision. Who will know a part of her is here to usher them in?"

He looked up at the steps leading up to the loading ramp for Above and Beyond. Saw the round buggies prepped and ready, their doors open for riders. "And if it takes years, we'll see her other visions bear fruit, too."

"Indeed, we shall," the engineer said.

Teague thought about Kate and her family, and what she'd sacrificed. Remembered the inferno that had taken the Barn and her. Pictured Anthony in the hospital, his body riddled with poison, his suffering long before he died. Still? Not justice enough. The best he knew to do would be to let people know her legacy in detail, and soon they would. But first?

He waved at K1954. "All right. We are ready to open for the day. Do your magic."

They stepped away and sat on a bench across from the greeter. Within minutes he watched the greeter raise her arms and blink her eyes at the first guests who approached and stopped in front of her. "Good morning, my adventurous friends, and welcome to Above and Beyond."

Poster advertising the popular "OmniGlobe" souvenirs sold in (from left to right) the Realm of the Stars, the Realm of the Deep, and the Realm of the Cell.

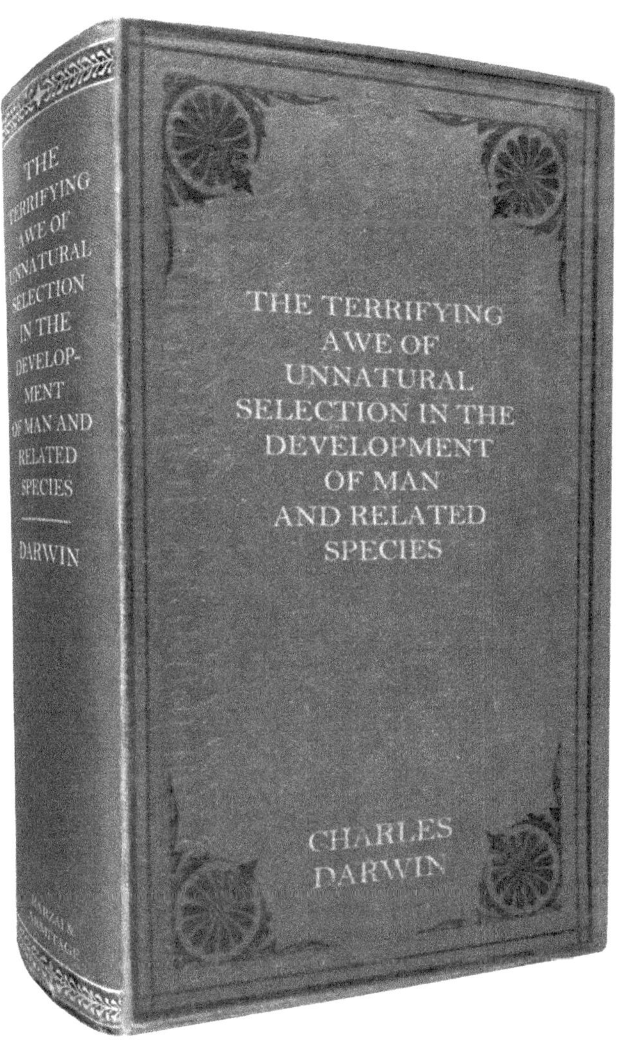

An imitation-antique book sold in the Great Tent Gift Shop, in the Realm of Man, throughout the 1980s. Although the book appears to be an obvious fake, OmniPark's official marketing insisted it was a reprint of a genuine Charles Darwin text, which was banned and burned in Darwin's own lifetime, save for a sole surviving copy discovered by Dalton Teague in an obscure Paris bookshop.

The Realm Between the Realms

Brian Evenson

Nearly a month ago, I was asked by Dr. Teague to investigate what has occurred in recent weeks in that portion of the park known as the Realm Between the Realms. He would, he told me, give me entirely free rein. I could interview anyone on staff, Teague himself included. Any expenses I deemed necessary and that he deemed reasonable he would cover. I could even, he told me, reach out to those VIPs (and here he provided me with a list of names and addresses) who had entered the Realm Between the Realms and claimed to have a family member who had returned from the experience to a greater or lesser degree transformed. "With these VIPs," said Dr. Teague, "ask what you will, but be discreet. Be careful not to give too much away, and certainly do not admit to any liability."

Ask what you will? Did Teague really mean it? I thought so at the time. The man is often surprising, and there was every chance that he had surprised me here. Later, however, I began to suspect that his motives were somewhat less straightforward.

___◯___

I began, as seemed most proper to me, with the Realm Ambassadors, attempting to compile the stories and rumors I had heard whispered. Some were reticent, but most, when I assured them that whatever they said would be held in strict confidence, began to speak — at first perhaps reluctantly, but then relaxing into it. A few remained silent and vague until I bought them a drink or two to loosen their tongues. One, Snyder by name, refused to give me anything at all. When I informed Dr. Teague of this, he immediately had a letter drawn up that gave me authorization to terminate the contract of anyone whom I deemed uncooperative with my investigation.

Snyder seemed surprised when I told him (in front of others, of course, so word would spread) that his services would no longer be required. Indignant, he informed me that I did not have the *authority* to fire him, that only his direct supervisor or Dr. Teague did. When I showed him the authorization signed by Teague he blanched and attempted to backtrack. He would, he quickly promised, tell me all he knew. Smiling sweetly, I inclined my head slightly and encouraged him to do so. Once he was finished, I thanked him and told him to pack his things and go.

"But I told you what you wanted to know!" he said.

"Not immediately," I said. "Not quickly enough. I'll arrange for you to have a month's salary," I said, "as a thank you for your discretion. If you choose to forgo that discretion, trust me, it will not go well for you."

It is true that at first their stories struck me as fantastical. The fact that they did not contradict one another, that they were insistent and consistent on several basic levels, I at first attributed to the employees gossiping among themselves: they had, I thought — just as criminals who had been apprehended but not separated — agreed on a story and held to it.

However, as time has gone on, I have substantially revised that opinion.

The stories all insisted on one thing: if you were in the Realm Between the Realms while the proprietary generator was going strong, buzzing, you must never step outside of the park-designated safe areas or, if traveling in or out of the staff areas used by the Realm Ambassadors or entering or exiting the Realm, step off the pathway clearly marked by the lights that would appear in the floor. If these lights disappeared or a portion of the line of them was extinguished, you should wait just where you were, not moving, hands to your sides. You should not extend an arm out past the row of lights that marked the edge of the path, even in play, and you should certainly not stick your head past it. In any case, no matter what was said or no matter how you were encouraged, you should not leave the safe areas or the pathway. Until the generator had been shut down and the lights had come fully on, and everything that made the Realm Between the Realms feel strange and *between* had been revealed to be dead cardboard and plaster, a simple albeit eccentric VIP welcome area, nothing more.

One employee, after he had spoken to me, showed me his hand. At first I didn't understand why, and then he showed me his other hand. Simply put, they were not hands from the same body. One was larger than the other, the fingers thicker, hairier. Even the nails were substantially different, thicker and yellowish in one case, delicate and paper thin in the other. And the color too: what he called his "normal hand" was well tanned, but the other one was a ghostly, ghastly white.

"What happened?" I asked.

"The Realm Between the Realms happened," he said. "I was walking when the generator came on. I kept to the path as instructed, but made the mistake of letting my hand drift over to the other side."

His hand seemed, the longer I looked at it, more and more wrong.

"It doesn't look like it belongs to you," I said.

He stared at it, mild disgust gathering in the corners of his mouth. "It *doesn't* belong to me," he said. "I've wondered sometimes what would happen if I hung it over the edge of the path once more while the generator was on. After that, would I get my real hand back?"

"Have you never been tempted to try?"

"Of course I've been tempted," he said. "But at least this works as a hand. Maybe next time I'll end up with something far worse."

— ჿ

Worse indeed was what another employee felt he had received. Again, a simple enough trip back and forth from the staff area to one of the park-designated areas, the kind of thing performed multiple times an hour just to be certain that everything was well and that none of the VIPs needed anything..

"I'd already heard the stories," this employee told me. "But, even so, when the generator suddenly kicked on this time, I was caught off guard. Halfway down the path I thought I glimpsed something, I couldn't help but turn my head and crane my neck to look back, and then lean to one side to get a better look." When he did so, his ear — just his ear! — must have passed outside the line of lights that marked the path. He felt exceptionally strange, and the ear tingled, and when he jerked his head back the ear was no longer his ear.

"How did you know it was no longer your ear?" I asked.

He hesitated, seemed to be searching for something on the floor. "You're going to think I'm crazy," he said, not meeting my eyes. I assured him I wouldn't. "It wasn't hearing the same thing as the other ear." When I asked what he meant by that, he informed me his ear was hearing things that weren't there. Or, maybe, things that were in another place. "It was like the shell of it was capturing sounds from a different reality. It was making me crazy, to always be hearing different things through each ear."

"Is that why you cut it off?"

He nodded. "Only thing I could think to do."

"Did it help?"

"I thought I might have to destroy the eardrum too. But as soon as the flesh and cartilage of the ear was gone, the noises stopped."

I could tell by the way he shut his mouth and then opened it again after finishing that he had more to say, and so I nodded and waited him out.

"Weirdest thing," he said at last, and this time he finally met my gaze. "Once I cut it off the ear just dissolved. I watched it melt away."

I nodded. I began to turn away, then realized there was something more I wanted to ask. "What was it you thought you saw? What were you looking for?"

"Myself. I thought I saw myself. Only not exactly me."

⟞ꝺ

There were a few more stories like this, though it became clear that before long word had spread that the Realm Between the Realms was dangerous. Some employees outright refused to work as Realm Ambassadors in the Realm Between the Realms. Others were merely extremely careful about following protocol. "It's like handling nuclear waste," one told me. "As long as you're meticulous, as long as you make sure to be careful and exacting and always stick to the proper procedures, you'll be okay. Never leave the path or the designated VIP areas ever if you can help it, and certainly never leave them while the generator is on. Follow those rules and you'll be just fine."

⟞ꝺ

One employee's name kept cropping up: a maintenance man named Barton Baines. Baines was, if rumor was to be believed, the first to have walked, late one night, into the Realm Between the Realms while the generator was going, back before anyone knew this was a problem. He'd heard the rattle of the generator but hadn't thought twice about it. He'd wandered around, checking that everything was in order, noticed that an access panel was a little skew. He'd opened it, tightened the latch with the screwdriver he always carried on his belt, and then walked out. Probably a minute and a half, all told. No more than that.

I talked to the woman who had been working with him that day, but had been inspecting another realm at the time. "He went in one person and came out someone else," she claimed. He looked almost the same as before, but not quite. His eyes were still blue, but a lighter shade of blue. His hair, when he had gone in, had been streaked with gray, hardly noticeable but still there, and when he came out the gray was utterly gone. There were other, subtler things: a different way of holding himself, a shift in his manner, the way that he no longer seemed to know things he had known before. She remembered him, as they sat on break shortly after, surreptitiously removing his driver's license and staring at it. Out of the corner of her eye she saw him mouthing something to himself, as if memorizing.

"What was he mouthing?" I asked.

She shrugged. "At the time I thought it was his name, maybe, or his address."

Other employees agreed: Barton Baines was no longer the person he had been before he went in. They began to avoid him, rumors quickly spreading about what the Realm Between the Realms could do to a person.

I spoke to Baines. His eyes were indeed an uncanny shade of blue. It is true that he is odd, his responses slow and slightly off in a way that made me wonder if he had suffered a minor stroke. But not having met him before, I had nothing to which to compare his current state.

I asked him about his experiences in the Realm Between the Realms.

"What do you mean?" he asked.

"Did anything strange ever happen to you in there?"

He shrugged. "Strange, how?"

"Just anything at all."

He seemed to be genuinely considering the question. "No," he finally said. "No. Don't believe so." He had, it became clear in the conversation that followed, gone in many times since while the generator was still on. Sometimes he stayed in the VIP areas or on the path, sometimes not — he didn't seem to care. He was the only employee I met for whom this was the case.. Only that first time had he come back changed. As one employee suggested: "It took the first time to switch him. Each new time was just pounding another nail into our reality to keep this other self firmly in our world."

ɔ

I telephoned the eleven groups on the VIP list that Teague had given me, spoke to them in vague terms about what they felt had happened in the Realm Between the Realms. Of these, there were three groups whose situation was such that I took the liberty of interviewing them in person. With the first one I pretended to be a reporter, but that raised enough other questions — What newspaper? When would the story run? Would they have a chance to correct my draft before it did? — that I abandoned that tactic for the last two and instead played the role of "concerned scientist" making initial inquiries to see if a formal study of the phenomena within the Realm Between the Realms might be merited.

With all three groups, the basics were the same. They told me that one individual in their party had gone into the Realm and come out "different." In one case, a boy's arm was completely transformed, "almost as if it had been taken from another person and glued on." I was shown an earlier photograph taken at the beach in which their boy clearly had two similar arms, and then they called the boy into the room and had him remove his shirt. One arm was noticeably more muscled than the other, several inches longer, and also freckled where the other was smooth and pale. But when I asked the boy about this he shrugged and claimed that the arm felt the same as it always had. He attributed the difference to the fact that the muscled arm was his dominant arm and so he used it more. As for the freckles, he said he often dangled the arm out the passenger side window when driving and so it got more sun. But it was clear to me, and in fact to everyone but him, that it was more than that.

With the second individual it was much the same: a portion of his body had passed outside of the path, his nose only, and perhaps his cheek and one eye. His face looked different than he had even in the picture his family had taken at the gates of the park moments before entering. And his sense of smell had shifted: he now smelled things that the rest of his family could not. But he insisted that he was smelling what was really there and they, for reasons he could not explain, were not. Nevertheless, a part of him seemed vaguely aware that something was severely wrong with him.

Perhaps, I began to think, there were even those among our staff who had been transformed but who, since they lived alone and their particular transformation was subtle, had never been identified. And surely there were other VIPs out there who had been in the Realm on their own and who had been affected without anyone else being aware, no? Were they all transformed too and simply hadn't been reported? Or were there only certain moments, brief ones, where you risked being transformed?

The last group of VIPs I visited were the most curious and, because of this, the most alarming. They all belonged to the same family: they had won their VIP experience through an AM radio contest. We all sat together in their dusty wood-paneled front parlor (which the mother made a point of telling me was only used for distinguished guests) sipping oversugared iced tea. The parents were both dressed in Bermuda shorts and worn t-shirts, and the husband wore calf-high athletic socks under a pair of cheap orthotic sandals. Between sips they told me about their daughter, Bella, as Bella herself sat demurely on the couch between them. They talked about her as if she wasn't there.

She had changed, they said — look at her: she hardly resembles us! Indeed, where they appeared thick and bovine, she was sleek and at least relatively attractive. Her eyes, too, were a different color from theirs, hazel to their blue — that was something they claimed was new too.

"Generator flipped on," the mother said. "Loud and noisy. Wan't no reason for it."

"Electrical cut," said the father, shrugging. "That's what a generator's for."

"'lectrical cut," nodded the mother, "maybe. But if it's that, normal power's gonna start up again soon. One of those guys, what were they? Realm Deputies?"

"'Bassadors," said her husband.

"Sure," she said. "Ambassadors. Before that generator even kicked on, he hustled us onto this path outlined in the floor by lights. When the generator went, he told us stay put, just stay on the path and wait. But she"—jabbing her finger at her daughter, Bella—"she never were one for waiting. Always been too impatient for her own good. She just goes off—"

"Leaves the path," said her husband.

"That's what I said," said the mother, irritation briefly tightening her round face. "Anyway, she's out and goes walking off, and then a few minutes later that generator clunks off and the normal lights are on again. So we call her back and go back to our VIP experience."

"Electrical back up," said her husband laconically.

She glared at her husband. "Who's telling this story?"

Her husband didn't even acknowledge this. "Only it wasn't her," he said to me.

"Not her?" I said, and couldn't help casting a sidelong glance at the girl herself. She still sat there, eyes downcast, still demure.

"Look at her. Does she look like she's our child?"

To be honest, she did not.

"Bella," I said. I had to repeat her name before she looked up and met my gaze.

"Sorry," she said. "I didn't know you were talking to me."

"What do you think of all this?" I asked. I fully expected her, as the other transformed visitors had done, to claim her family was wrong, that they were confused. Instead, she said, "They make a good point."

"Excuse me?"

"I'm not Bella," she said. "These are not my parents."

The shocked looks on the husband's and wife's faces made me realize that they had not expected this, that she had never said this in front of them before. They seemed dumbstruck.

"I knowed it," her father who was not her father said. "I goddam knowed it!"

ᴖ

With a little wheedling, I managed to coax the husband and wife out of the room, and then I began to question the girl in earnest.

"Who are you?" I began.

"Not Bella," she said.

"But who?"

She shrugged.

"It was the Realm that made you this way?"

Again she shrugged. "I was always this way. It just took the Realm to bring me out."

"What's happened to the real Bella?"

"The opposite of what happened to me."

I prodded her about what she meant by this, but she was either unwilling or unable to explain. For a while we just stared at one another, silent. Her eyes, I noticed, blinked considerably less than I expected a human's eyes to blink.

"What do you want?" I asked.

She smiled. "I want to see Mr. Teague."

ᴖ

And so, not knowing what else to do, I took her to Teague. We spoke hardly at all on the car ride there: she volunteered nothing and neither did I. When we crossed into the county, I pulled in at the first gas station. I called Teague from a payphone as the girl who was not Bella waited primly in my car. It took a good chunk of my change to convince the secretary to put me through, but when she finally did I briefly explained the situation to Teague, told him I could take the girl back if he preferred.

"No," he said. "You made the right choice. Bring her to me."

By the time we arrived Teague was waiting anxiously in his open office doorway. Immediately he grasped her by the elbow and steered her inside. When I made to follow, I found the door had begun to shut in my face.

"Ah," he said. "Thank you for all you've done. Truly. Wait here. Depending on how this goes, I might call for you."

—ᴑ—

I waited one hour, then two. I could hear the rumble of their voices, rising and falling irregularly. In the middle of the third hour Dr. Teague came out rubbing his hands together and smiling.

"Go clear the Realm Between the Realms of all Ambassadors and VIPs," he said. "Cordon it off, turn off the power, shut down the generator when it comes on, then return here." And then he went back inside.

And so I did. I let the employees know they should cordon the Realm off and turn away any VIPs desiring to get in. Once that was done, I ushered the employees themselves out, turned off the power, shut down the generator, closed off the Realm, then returned to Teague's office.

"Splendid," he said, and then hustled the girl out of the office and past me. She looked as serene and unruffled as ever.

I watched them go. "I'll need you to come as well," said Teague, when he realized I wasn't following. And so I came along as well.

He led us down from his office and through the park, until we reached the main entrance to the Realm Between the Realms. He reached into his pocket and removed a penlight. We entered.

Teague peered in. He turned on the flashlight. "I want you to wait three minutes," he said. "At three minutes precisely, you are to turn on the generator for ten seconds and then turn it off again, and leave it off. Do you understand?"

I nodded.

"Good man," he said. He moved farther in, pulling the girl who was not Bella along with him. Together, they followed the now extinguished path, and then after a moment he and she stepped off of it, standing outside the path.

"Starting now," he said.

—ᴑ—

And what happened next? Very little, and also far too much. I stared at my watch. When it reached three minutes, I turned on the generator and heard it begin to whine. After ten seconds had passed, I turned the generator off again. Everything fell dark and silent.

I waited in that darkness and silence for whatever would happen next. Eventually, I saw a distant glow of Teague's penlight. Slowly, it grew brighter. They had come back. Or rather *he* had come back. The girl was nowhere to be seen.

Teague smiled, nodded at me.

"Where's the girl?" I asked him.

"Girl?" he asked.

He came closer: I was, I realized blocking the doorway. For a moment he was very close to my face. I could feel the warmth of his breath.

"The one who isn't Bella," I said.

"I have no idea what you're talking about," Teague said, and pushed past.

❦

As we walked back together, he told me he wanted the Realm Between the Realms dismantled permanently and the generator disabled. There was no need, he said, for a VIP area: the whole park was in a way a VIP area. I nodded, told him I'll take care of it. We walked the rest of the way in silence, side by side, me occasionally glancing at him, wondering what, if anything, I should say.

"Are you all right, sir?" I finally asked as we approached the door to his office.

He smiled. "Never better," he said and went in and closed the door behind him.

❦

I do not know what has happened to the girl. Perhaps she returned to wherever she came from. Perhaps her body is hidden somewhere within the Realm Between the Realms. Nor do I know what, if anything, has happened to Teague. Unlike the others, there is no sign that a physical change has occurred, no digit or appendage that seems as if it has been grafted from another body. And his eye color, I would almost be willing to swear to it, is the same shade as before. Perhaps there is more gray in what remains of his hair, but perhaps the gray was already there and I simply failed to notice it. Was his stride more tentative than usual as we made our way back to his office, or am I only imagining this?

I am not saying that I am convinced this man is not Teague. But neither am I entirely convinced he is Teague. There is nothing I can put my finger on, nothing to make me certain, and yet…

This concludes my report. Teague, now that the Realm Between the Realms is closed, seems to have lost interest in receiving it. Indeed, he may have forgotten he commissioned me to write it—or perhaps it was another Teague, the real Teague wherever he now may be, God bless his soul, who did so, and this Teague isn't even aware of it.

When I am finished, I will put this report away in a safe place. If Teague asks for it, I will decide then whether to rewrite it to remove these final sections or not.

How long I will stay in Teague's employ I don't know. Until, I suppose, I begin to feel unsafe — assuming I am sufficiently aware to know when that is.

This is a good job, I tell myself, the pay is good, I would struggle to find its like elsewhere. *I can be happy here*, I tell myself, *I really can.*

Or at least someone who resembles me in nearly every particular could be. Someone like me, but not quite.

OMNIPA

How to Survive a Birthday Party at the Dragonfly Dining Terrace

Gwendolyn Kiste

1. *Don't attend the birthday party at all. Avoid the whole area if you can.*

It's a Monday morning when I first hear the strange flutter of wings.

I'm on my way to work, twisting along Highway 302, and for a moment, it feels like the sound of flight all around me, something weird and near and ready to take to the sky. With a shake of my head, I try to ignore it, try to tell myself I'm just tired. Which to be fair, is the truth. I haven't slept well in weeks, even though I'm not sure why.

"Night Fever" blares on the staticky radio, and my hands shift on the steering wheel, the engine bucking beneath me. My '69 Dodge Dart needs a tune-up, but it probably won't get it, not if my empty savings account has any say. I've been out of high school for more than two decades, but I don't have much more money now than I did my senior year.

I brace against the wheel, waiting for the buzz of wings to draw closer, but then I take the last turn on the road, and the noise is suddenly gone, dissipated into the early spring air. That's when I see it, the sign materializing before me.

OmniPark. This Universe Is Yours To Explore.

The sun in my eyes, I pull into the mostly empty parking lot. Every morning for the past eleven months, I've arrived nearly an hour before my shift, all because I don't like waiting in line for the monorail. OmniPark is in the middle of nowhere, but it might as well be its own city. Over one hundred acres set aside in the Texas plains, all of it dedicated to this strange park with its strange secrets.

But this morning, I'm not entirely alone. There's one other person waiting.

Sylvia, leaning on the hood of her orange Ford Pinto.

"Good morning," she says with a bright smile, as I stumble out of the driver's seat, my head still spinning from that noise. I want to tell her about it, but I'm not even sure how to describe it. I'm also not sure it was real.

We start across the lot, headed toward the front entrance when another engine revs behind us and a voice calls out.

"Hey, wait up." It's Anna, her short blonde hair falling into her eyes, her bag slung haphazardly over her shoulder.

Sylvia and I fall back until she catches up with us, her breath heaving.

"How was your weekend?" Sylvia asks.

"The same as always," Anna says, as we board the monorail, the three of us squeezing together to fit on the bench. This is the way guests arrive every day, thousands of them pouring into the park, but at least they won't be descending on us quite yet. We've got the place to ourselves for a little while.

The world zips by the Plexiglas windows. We take this ride every week, day after day, but if I'm being honest, so long as it isn't too crowded, this journey still gives me a bit of a jolt. Monorails. They feel like the future, like the promise of something space-age and new. But now, with most of the '70s in the rearview mirror, some people think the technology's starting to feel dated, like a promise that didn't come true. Too much of life ends up like that.

The monorail drops us at the front gates, and the three of us walk in together, nodding at the guard who doesn't know our names and we don't know his. There are too many people at OmniPark for us to know everyone. And besides, plenty of us don't last very long around here.

We're through the Entryway Pavilion with its marbled cathedral ceilings when a booming voice crackles over the loudspeaker, repeating the park's motto over and over again.

"This universe is yours to explore."

It's a good slogan. After all, OmniPark makes everything feel so *real*, each Realm carefully curated in its own pavilion. You can go to the bottom of the ocean or charge into the stars. You can venture back in time or venture into yourself, navigating the shadowy recesses of your own cells. There's a different section of the park for almost anything you can imagine, seven Realms in total, all of them equipped with rides and souvenir shops and cute little restaurants.

Anna glances around, her eyes narrowed, as though she's only seeing everything for the first time. "What do you think the point of this place is?"

I only shrug. "Why does there have to be a point? Isn't it just a theme park?"

"Like a more cerebral Disneyland," Sylvia offers.

"Don't kid yourself." Anna snaps her tongue. "They're up to something."

We don't argue with her when she gets like this. Besides, we know she's very likely right. There's always talk of disappearances and places in the park you shouldn't go. Spots behind closed doors that will whirl your mind until you don't know who you are anymore. Of course, those are just the rumors.

Sylvia and I take the first left turn toward the Realm of Life, waving goodbye to Anna. She works on the other side of the park at the Inventor's Mansion, arrayed in Victorian attire, while Sylvia and I spend all day here in our safari khakis, through this wide doorway, disappearing into another world.

The Realm of Life. It sometimes feels like everything happens here, and maybe that's true in a way, but it only happens to everyone else. Never to me. My own life is a static thing, an amoeba that never evolves. I've worked here since the day the park opened, and if my luck's any indication, I'll work here until the day it closes. Or the day I die. Whichever comes first. After all, I'm at the brink of middle age and employed at a theme park like some teenager on summer break. I should be further in life than this, but it feels like every direction I turn, I only end up in the same place.

But I'm getting ahead of myself. Truth be told, it's been less than a year since OmniPark unlocked its main gate and welcomed in all the wide-eyed, raucous guests. The park's birthday is coming up next month, and we'll all be on hand to celebrate.

We don't have to clock in for almost an hour, so Sylvia and I wander through the Realm together, following the first path, vines crawling over everything, their wicked embrace tighter than a noose. I run a hand over one of them and remind myself it's only ordinary greenery. Nothing more and nothing less.

"Where should we go next, Rachel?" she asks me, and I already know she doesn't mean in this Realm. She means for real.

With a grin, I reach into my back pocket and pull out a weathered paper map, the one I always carry like a talisman. Sylvia huddles with me, as I trace all the highways that lead away from this place.

"California," I say. "Or Canada. Maybe even Florida."

"Florida sounds nice," Sylvia whispers, a flash of hope in her eyes.

This is a game we play, the two of us make-believing where in the world we might travel. We're always looking at this map, at places near and far, cities we've never seen, forests and lakes and swamps where the animals might as well be as old as the ones in this Realm.

"Do you think we'll ever really leave?" Sylvia asks, but I don't say anything. This is the one thing I'm hoping for, but it seems too far away to matter. We have no money to go anywhere and no clear plan to get there. Sometimes, though, it's certainly fun to dream.

The two of us hesitate at the edge of a waterway. Here it is, the main attraction in our Realm: Palaeozoa. The guests take a river safari through a shrouded jungle, everyone bobbing along the cool blue water in a glass-bottom boat. I've only been on the ride one time when management gave the staff run of the place for the evening, and my flesh prickled the whole time, my body flinching at every bend. Anna insisted there was a very specific reason for that.

"Somebody spiked the employee punch, I'm sure of it," she told us later, but even if she was right, that wasn't the reason the ride gave me the creeps. I could be stone-cold sober and not enjoy sea scorpions and enormous millipedes attacking me from every direction, all of them animatronics that look too real for comfort. I don't know why anyone would spend a day of their leisure time with a bevy of prehistoric pests, but hey, I just work here.

Sylvia, on the other hand, thinks it's all a morbid delight. She plays one of the so-called Biologists, which is really just the fancy term for the Realm Ambassadors who pretend to take everyone back in time to meet a litany of oversized creatures. The gag is that on each river ride, she gets knocked out of the boat and into the water by a giant dragonfly. She has to run in the back between rides and change clothes in a hurry, her hair still damp the next time she gets dunked in the river.

"Terribly impractical," I tell her, but she just giggles.

"It's fun, though," she says and gives me that big grin of hers.

I, on the other hand, work as a waitress at the Dragonfly Dining Terrace. It's an open-air restaurant located at the end of one of the trails, just before the gift shop, everything decorated with giant winged insects that watch over us like they're our protectors. We serve mostly light fare like salads and nuts, but you can also order a few bizarre menu items like fried crickets and grasshoppers. Some people dine here just to challenge their family members to eat bugs. Good wholesome memories.

We keep wandering the Realm together, winding past animatronic insects the size of mopeds, until a voice comes on the loudspeaker to tell us it's almost opening time.

"See you later," Sylvia says and squeezes my hand.

I tuck the map back in my pocket, ready to turn down the Eastward Trail when that sound returns, buzzing deep into my marrow like it belongs there.

I look back at Sylvia, my chest tightening. "Do you hear something?"

She tilts her head, listening for a moment. "Like what?"

"Like wings," I whisper. "Like something ready to take flight."

"Of course I do," she says with a laugh, motioning all around us. "This place is filled with it."

I laugh too before starting toward the restaurant, dread still churning in the pit of my belly.

2. *When in nature, be sure to pay close attention to your intuition. That's the only way you'll get out of this party alive.*

My shift is almost halfway done when a shadow flashes at the end of the trail. I whirl toward it, convinced it's the same thing that's been following me all day.

But it's something much more banal. A couple of the Technosophers, the bioengineers who work behind-the-scenes at the park. They come by at least once a week, cataloging how the plant life is flourishing along the trails. But that's not the only thing they're watching. They're always taking notes about us, like the workers are specimens too.

I drift forward on the patio, the sun in my eyes again. "May I help you?" I ask, but they just shake their heads and move on to the souvenir shop.

A man wearing a *Disco Sucks* t-shirt leans back in his chair. "Can I get some service over here or what?" he hollers, and I do my best not to roll my eyes.

"What are you having?" I ask, strolling over to his table.

"The fish salad," he mumbles, and when I turn to walk away, he grabs my ass.

"Hey," I say, my jaw set, "I'm not on the menu."

He puts up both hands in mock surprise. "Sorry."

This time, I roll my eyes, and I don't care who sees it. It's 1978, and we should be long past men groping women, but apparently, some things never change. Out in the world, in cities like San Francisco and New York, there are people fighting and hoping and protesting for a better way, but that might as well be happening in another universe. It takes a long time before progress makes it all the way down to West Texas.

I'm ready to take my break when my boss Jake lines me up with the other servers, handing each of us a small pale tablet. It's one of the special vitamins the Technosophers have created for us.

"To keep you going," Jake tells us, and I should say no, but one after another, we all swallow our pills like they're a delicacy. He takes one too.

The rest of the day lazes by, and I gaze up at the sky, as unforgiving as eternity. Odessa, Texas. I've been here all my life, born and raised. Part of me still can't believe a place like OmniPark was born here too. There's such an uncanny magic on these grounds.

"It's dangerous," Anna always says, and she's not wrong. There are whispers all over town about the owner Dalton Teague and where he got his money and why he's used it to build this place. But with the park comes plenty of jobs, and with jobs comes hope, a commodity that's long been in short supply around here.

Still, that doesn't stop the gossip among the staff, their endless talk about the odd things that happen behind closed doors.

"Sometimes people come in the gates," Anna whispers, "but they never leave."

At least that's the story. I have a tendency of brushing it off when she tells us things like that. If I've learned anything in my time on this earth, it's that urban legends have a nasty way of pretending they're facts.

And I've heard plenty of urban legends in my day. I'm past forty years old now. No husband, no kids, and no regrets — not about that, anyhow. Ask the locals, and they'll tell you my way of life might just be the worst crime a woman can commit in West Texas. I think the worst crime is not leaving people alone, not letting them be who they are, what they are.

"There ought to be more than one way to live," I always say, but nobody ever hears me.

It's after closing time when the melody of fluttering wings returns. It vibrates through me, my skin feeling suddenly electric, everything in me ready to take flight.

I pretend not to notice. After all, like Sylvia said, it's probably just the animatronics buzzing out their final swan song of the evening. I'm letting this place get to me. So I grit my teeth and wipe down all the tables and balance the drawer before untying my smock and tossing it in the laundry bin in the back. By the time I come out, Sylvia is already waiting for me.

"You want to walk out together?" she asks, as if it's honestly a question, as if I would ever tell her no.

"Sure," I say, and we head past the ferns clotting on the path and the giant dragonflies suspended from a concealed pulley system, their gigantic eyes staring out blankly into the empty evening.

Anna meets us near the front gate. "So," she says with a conspiratorial grin, "the latest rumor is that this whole place is closing the day after our one-year anniversary."

"Closing?" Sylvia asks, a tremble in her voice. "For good?"

Anna gives us one of her patented told-you-so shrugs. "Of course, nobody knows for sure."

"Well, I think you're wrong," Sylvia says. "And anyhow, you have to be wrong, because I'm still planning to get transferred to the Realm of Dream someday."

"If they ever finish it," I say, and something tugs in my chest, a distant ache at the thought that Sylvia might leave the Realm of Life. She's the only thing that makes my shifts bearable most days.

In the parking lot, Anna climbs into her Ford pickup, but just as soon as the engine turns over, she rolls down her window. "Do you want to stop off downtown for a beer?"

Sylvia shakes her head. "My mother's expecting me home."

Her cheeks blossom red, because she knows how ridiculous it sounds. A grown woman not allowed to go out with her friends. Sylvia is the same age as Anna and me, but she might as well be a high schooler out past curfew. There are rules for women who break the rules, the ones who don't settle down like a proper lady should. Her mother never lets her forget that.

"Maybe some other time," I say to Anna, and she waves goodbye before pulling out onto the highway and disappearing into the night.

It's just me and Sylvia now, standing together in an empty lot. Once again, the urge rises up to tell her about the thing that's been following me all day, the thing I can't seem to shake.

"I'll see you tomorrow," I say instead, and she grins back at me.

"Have a good night, Rachel."

We turn away from each other, the night like a veil above us, and I do my best to ignore the call of something strange and faraway.

✗

3. *In the preparations leading up to the birthday party, do everything you can to raise the alarm. Or just try to get a running start.*

The next few weeks blur together, the soundtrack of wings never far behind.

It's the middle of May, the dry heat already hanging heavy in the air, as I board the monorail on a Friday morning with Sylvia and Anna, all of us laughing together. They're my only two friends at work. In a way, they're my only friends at all. My life practically doesn't exist beyond these gates. There's not a lot out there in Odessa, and there's certainly not a lot for someone like me.

There's not a lot for Anna either. She still lives in an old family home with both her parents, though they hardly notice when she's around. Sylvia lives at home too, taking care of her mother, a task that might as well be a full-time job of its own. I've been to her house once, and her mother just shrieked at us the whole time.

"You don't belong here," she'd say with a grimace, and I wasn't sure if she was talking to me or to her own daughter.

At the Realm's wooden gates, Sylvia and I bid farewell to Anna and slip into the Realm of Life. Today's no regular day. We're closing early, the guests shooed out by two in the afternoon, all for us. As a thank you, they've given us another "Ambassadors' Night" — a.k.a., free run of the park. It's only one week before the park's official birthday party, and I'd rather be at home taking a nap, but my boss Jake tells us everyone's expected to be in attendance.

"Dalton Teague himself might be stopping by," Jake says, as though we're supposed to be impressed. If you ask me, all rich guys are the same. The only thing that distinguishes this one is that he happens to be the rich guy who signs my checks.

Once the guests are gone for the day, and Dalton never shows up, jubilant chaos breaks out across the park, employees making crude announcements over the loudspeakers, the Realm of Man employees taking over the Realm of the Cell and vice versa, the rides going haywire. There's bottomless bowls of punch in every Realm, and glassy eyes to match.

Sylvia and I stand back for a while, watching the others.

"People come here every day on vacation," she whispers, "but sometimes it feels like we won't ever get to leave."

"I know," I say, and the paper map crinkles in my back pocket. For years, I've wanted to travel, to flee this oppressive heat, but I never had the money or the friends. Now at least I have friends, but they don't have their freedom. There's always some reason standing in our way.

Anna soon finds us, and we imbibe with the others, everyone gossiping about the boss from the Realm of the Deep and how he's taking his title of "Captain" just a bit too seriously.

A figure darts past us, half hidden behind outcroppings of primordial onyx and flint. With that receding hairline and his frame, gaunt as a ghost, it's easy to recognize him, even at a distance: Elijah Shattuck. The worst of the Technosophers — the one who never really sees you, only sees the scientific potential in you, always scribbling notes on that clipboard of his.

"How are we feeling today?" Shattuck asks us. A smile twitches at the edges of his lips.

"We'd feel a whole lot better if you stopped staring at us like that," Anna says with a sneer. At this, he grumbles to himself, makes a quick note, and scampers off.

The hours slip by, slowly at first and then in an instant. The park is strange after dark. Of course, it can be plenty strange in the daylight too, but even the corners and the crevices that seem safe at high noon become something else once the sun dissolves in the Texas sky and all we've got is moon and stars and faith to guide us. Not that you can see the stars clearly from here. The whole park is enclosed around us, with towering pavilions over every Realm, sealing us in like a tomb.

And I'm not the only one who feels uneasy here. We're still in the Realm of Life at closing time, the last ones left, when Sylvia can't help but shiver. "I don't like it here sometimes."

I let out a small laugh. "I'm not sure I like it here at all."

"I swear they spiked the punch again," Anna says, her words slurring together. "Or those damn vitamins."

My head spinning, I have to agree with her. "But why would they do that?"

"Because we're their little experiments. Their captive audience." Anna takes a deep breath, as if she's practiced what she's about to say next. "My cousin's got a place in California. She's really cool, an old hippie-type who lives in the woods. She said I could come stay with her. We could all stay with her."

Anna hesitates before adding, "We could be happy there."

Her head down, Sylvia clasps her hands in front of her. "What about our lives here?" she asks. "What about our families?"

"What about them?" Anna watches our faces, panic setting in, as she realizes we're not taking her up on her offer as fast as she'd hoped. "I'll meet you both at the Entryway Pavilion."

And with that, she vanishes out through the souvenir shop. With a sigh, Sylvia goes to the breakroom to get her purse, and I wait for her on the empty patio.

I gaze at all the décor arraying the trailhead. The dragonflies are my favorite, not just because the restaurant was named after them. They're such odd creatures, but beautiful too.

Sometimes, at the end of my shift, I'm sure I see them, flitting about, just for a moment, just long enough that I'm convinced they're real. Nobody knows where all this stuff came from, the fake creatures concealed along the paths. From the design labs in the back, I guess. Weird things happen there. Experiments that no one talks about, the kind with "Top Secret" labels on all the samples and manilla folders. But then again, weird things happen everywhere at OmniPark.

I close my eyes, the mechanical lullaby of the oversized dragonflies nearly lulling me to sleep. That's when I hear it, a voice somewhere beyond the greenery.

"You know the ones we want. The ones nobody will miss."

At this, my eyes snap open, searching the trees and the paths and anywhere the source of the voice might be hiding, but I'm still alone, only the animatronic insects buzzing pleasantly all around me.

"Hello?" I call out, but nobody answers.

4. *If you insist on attending the birthday party, then there's only one piece of advice left before it begins: hold your breath and try to wait it out. Maybe you'll make it through. Or maybe you won't.*

On the morning of the party, the whir of wings becomes too much to bear.

I'm in the parking lot when it starts. The rumbling beneath my flesh, the crack of bones in my spine. I double over, my knees nearly giving out next to my clunker car. I've finally clawed my way back to standing when I see Sylvia, her face wan.

"Something's wrong," she says, and Anna is with us now too, looking just as pallid.

We barely make it to the monorail, the three of us helping each other along. When we get through the Entryway Pavilion, the two Technosophers who have been skulking around the Realm of Life are waiting, checking in each employee, distributing pale vitamins to everyone.

When they spot us, they instantly perk up. "Those are the ones," they whisper to each other, and pull us out of line.

I huddle with Anna and Sylvia, tucked back near the entrance to the Realm Between the Realms.

"These are for you," the Technosophers say and hand us each a large green pill.

Anna scowls. "Why are our pills a different color?"

"Different vitamins for different people."

We should tell them no, but we're too tired to fight with them. Besides, from the sour, solemn expressions on their faces, it doesn't seem like we really have a choice at all.

One by one, we swallow the pills, and the Technosophers nod in approval. "Enjoy the birthday party," they say.

We're back in the courtyard, my skin still buzzing, all of us weak-kneed and wobbly.

"Let's just get through the day," Anna whispers, but as we go our separate ways, part of me is afraid we won't ever see her again. I take no more than three steps before I turn back, ready to call out to her, to tell her to stay with us, but she's already gone.

The gates have hardly opened when the eager families with their sticky fingers are already swarming everywhere.

"Happy birthday, OmniPark!" a voice on the loudspeaker announces every fifteen minutes, just in case you forgot.

"It'll be over soon," Sylvia says and tries to sound cheerful about it, but I see it there in her eyes, how we're drifting away from ourselves.

"It's this place," Anna told us, her whispers barely concealed on the monorail this morning. "They're going to keep us for their own if we're not careful."

I'm worried she's right, the way she's always right. But for now, we've got a job to do. Here in the Dragonfly Dining Terrace, I've got thousands of cupcakes to distribute, fried crickets nestled atop every dollop of buttercream icing.

"But I don't want to eat a bug, Mommy," a little boy whines.

"That's fine," his mother says and plucks the insect from the cupcake. She glances around for a moment before popping it in her mouth, her secret snack.

I could stop any of these guests. I could beg them to help me, to help Sylvia and Anna too. But what do you say to them? Do you tell them you willingly took pills, even though you didn't know what they were? Do you explain the buzzing all around you and beneath your own skin? How do you tell a truth so wild without making it sound like a delirious lie?

There are celebrations on every trail, in every Realm, balloons and streamers and cake-smeared faces, but once again, I stand back from it. The day is almost over, all the guests trickling out the exits when at last, I feel it. The thing that's been brimming in me for weeks now. Maybe even for a lifetime. It only takes a second, my body splitting open, a flutter at my back. My hands clench into fists, the pain searing through me until all at once, there's no pain at all.

"Rachel, where are you?" Sylvia's voice calling out from down the trail.

"I'm here," I heave, as she comes stumbling out. Anna manages to join us too, the three of us gathered together on the patio, stunned at what we are.

At the wings that have sprouted from our backs, as delicate as stained glass.

"They're beautiful," Sylvia whispers, running her hands along the edges of mine. "*You're* beautiful."

"So are you," I say and start to smile. We should be more afraid, but a strange sensation is stirring within our bones. It's as though this place has set free something that was always waiting and wild within us.

But we don't have much time to revel in this, because we're suddenly not alone. The two Technosophers are here now, and they're closing in.

"You," they say, marveling at the monsters they've made of us.

Today was a special kind of celebration, one that went way beyond the park's birthday. This was a celebration of us, of their experiment. Of what we could become.

And we were always what they were looking for. According to them, we're not worth missing, the three of us as disposable as park garbage. We can disappear, and even our families will mostly just shrug their shoulders and move on. The perfect specimens.

We try to back away, try to run, but the agony of transformation has left us weaker than before, our legs still uneven beneath us.

"Why?" Sylvia asks, her breath wheezing in her chest, her wings spreading out wider, brushing against the thick ropes of ivy in the trail.

"We want this ride to be as accurate and realistic as possible." The Technosophers advance toward us, casting long shadows over our faces. "You're all going to help us with that."

"But we still look like us," Anna insists, her gaze darting about, searching for the nearest exit. "We don't look like your specimens at all."

"That's because you're not quite finished yet," they say, "but we'll fix that."

I already know beyond reason where they'll take us. Back into the rooms behind the scenes, beyond the Realm Between the Realms, beyond everything, where they'll hide us, tinkering with our bodies, force-feeding us more pills, molding us until we're perfect. Until we fit right into whatever strange experiment they've been planning — something we aren't meant to understand.

It's just like Sylvia feared — we'll never leave here. We'll become part of this place.

But then I hear it again. That distant flutter of wings. The one that's been following my every step, beckoning to me.

"Please," I whisper, and whatever has been living in the gloom is more than happy to oblige.

All at once, the lights start flickering, and through the darkness, the whole Realm comes alive, the sea scorpions and dragonflies and millipedes no longer theoretical, no longer made of resin and acrylic paint. They're real.

And they're hungry.

I grab hold of both Anna and Sylvia, and together, we cower in the corner of the restaurant, crouched behind the wooden tables, our wings tucked into our backs.

We close our eyes the moment the Technosophers start to scream.

5. *Congratulations on surviving the birthday party at the Dragonfly Dining Terrace. For your own safety, we hope you've learned your lesson. We also hope you don't stick around for another year. Or even another day.*

When the lights stop flickering, and I look again, all I see are Sylvia and Anna. It takes a long moment for me to realize we're all alone. There's no one left who knows about us, about what we've become. Not yet, anyhow.

We wait until we're sure everyone has gone home, but we already know we can't stay here now. Maybe we can't stay anywhere, but if we linger much longer in this park, then someone is bound to figure out what happened. Then they might claim us as their own. As OmniPark property.

"Where will we go?" Sylvia whispers.

"Any place we want," I say, because it's finally true. Now that every other choice has been stripped away from us, there's nothing holding us back.

I take out the map that's still in my pocket, and Anna points to the spot where her cousin lives in California.

"She'll be happy to have us," she says, "no matter what condition we're in."

I almost laugh. After everything that's happened, Anna is still getting her way.

When we're recovered and ready, we make a small circle on the patio and gaze upward at the clouds hovering there. I smile to myself, because I can feel it. Our thin wings are stronger than they look. Everything about us is stronger than we ever realized, our bodies shining and buzzing and new.

We don't need a monorail now. With our arms outstretched, we take flight, all of us leaving the Realm of Life at the same time, the moonlight glinting off our translucent wings, and together, we wave goodbye to OmniPark, as we vanish into the endless Texas sky.

Advertising for Spicy Jellyfish Pops sold in the Map Room Gift Shop, in the Realm of the Deep, throughout the 1980s. Park guests reported that the candy produced a unique numbing/ tingling sensation on the tongue, which persisted for several hours.

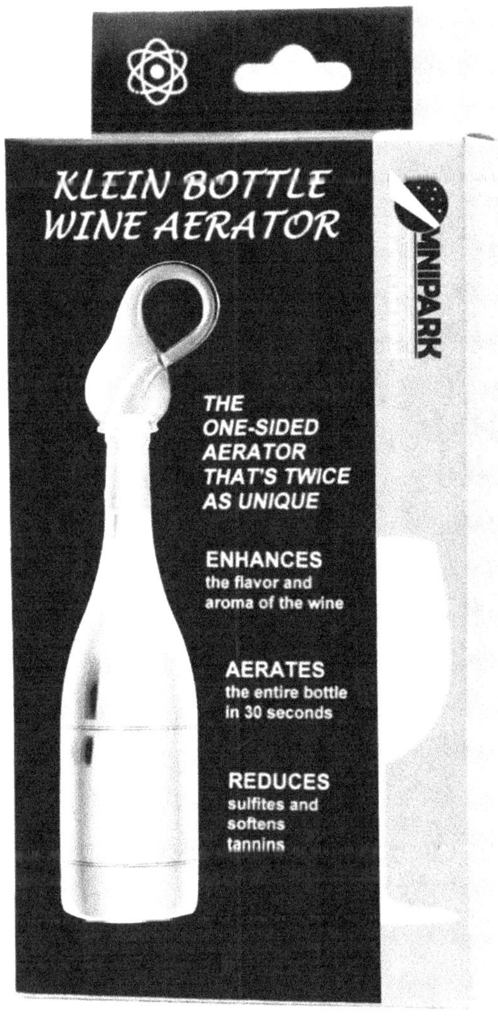

A Klein bottle wine aerator sold at the Everything in Particular General Store, in the Realm of the Particle. Often purchased as a gag gift, the Klein bottle's one-sided three-dimensional surface admitted no air, making aeration a physical impossibility. Even so, some park guests and renowned sommeliers insisted the device worked exceptionally well.

MILLS
POLICE

What You Can Do For the Park

Brad Kelly

John F. Kennedy, real as shoe leather, stood off in the corner smoking a cigarette, his brains blown out all over his dark blue suit. 1979, okay? The exit wound, it seemed, was sneaking glances at the door — Shattuck lurking in the hallway — but the eye that remained in his face stared right back at my dad. My dad, Deputy Sheriff (at the time) Tony Mills. And you have to imagine him here soaking wet, lean in that hard-labor way he used to be. Picture him with his fingers interlaced behind his head, stuck in a moment from which he could not dislodge himself while the hardest rain in a decade drummed hypnotically on the roof.

My dad, to John F. Kennedy: "You're going to have to explain all this to me, you know."

"Look," JFK said, the accent thin but familiar. "If you pay enough attention to the night sky — and the right kind of attention — you will see a craft from another world. A flying saucer, a UFO, whatever they're calling them. And if you stare into the darknesses of the woods with just the right desire to witness...well, you should not be surprised when a giant hairy ape steps out of the brush. Crevices in the ocean, you know, the depths of old cupboards, the empty desert. You think when you feel the presence of a monster in your dark cellar that the thing isn't, in one way or another, actually down there? And you consider yourself to be some kind of scientist?"

"I'm from the Sheriff's office," Deputy Mills said. He looked to the ceiling and then back. It was still JFK. At the right angle, you could see daylight through the wound. "Do you need medical attention?"

"I don't think there's anything modern medicine could do for me."

My dad had been a beat cop in Dallas, let's see, sixteen years before this. And even though he'd been posted to a barricade a half-mile from Dealey, he still spoke of Kennedy like a buddy of his who'd died on the job. He couldn't have done anything, of course, but I think that bothered him as much as if he'd been a second late knocking the gun from Oswald's hand. A few years later, my mother left him. She said that ever since Dallas, Dad spent most of his time in what she called his "little vacations." The next year he followed her to Odessa and took a job as a Deputy in this scrubland county. And it was common even in my every-other-weekend with him, back then, that I'd startle him out of a half trance and he'd apologize all over himself because he knew our time together was precious little.

He told me he'd spend a lot of his shift driving out on the forgotten roads. That old, old horizon unchanged for a million years before the Comanche. And the small he felt against that was peaceful, appeased him somehow, calmed the self-accusatory voice that'd been stirred up in him since Dallas. Ninety percent of the job was nothing but I do know that he made fine work of the other ten. He always got Christmas cards from folks I didn't know. Families from Midland and elsewhere that wanted him to see photos of their children. They said thanks again; they said they were eternally grateful.

Anyway, it must have been dizzying for my dad to find himself suddenly heading a murder investigation. Plenty of car wrecks and domestic disturbances and a handful of suicides — but a genuine whodunnit?

"Dr. Ralston," my father said. That's how this JFK had been introduced to him. "Did you kill Dr. Miguel Garza?"

"Absolutely not. He was my friend."

"And how did he meet his untimely end?"

The pummeling of rain on the roof and my father dripping on the tile floor. Back in a little meeting room that doesn't show up on the Park maps.

"It's quite possible Shattuck killed him," JFK said, as if translating a message coded into the cigarette smoke. "Maybe he did the actual violence that came at the end. What I do know is that Miguel expired after a brief struggle with an aggressive cancer of the dream."

The name Elijah Shattuck drew a lot of water in Odessa and Midland back then. Dollar-wise, OmniPark may have been nothing compared to the oil industry, but it made our little scratch a destination. We suddenly existed to the world outside of West Texas. A lot of old-timers didn't care for that, I guess. And yet occasionally an outsider comes along, like Teague or Shattuck, and they aren't trusted, they're lampooned if not scorned in the local watering holes, but their alien nature, their mystique, well, it burnishes their nameplate maybe more than it ought to.

My dad never met Elijah Shattuck before that night. It turns out not many people actually have. He had an accent Deputy Mills couldn't quite place: it seemed English but only because it wasn't Texan and it wasn't Yankee and he spoke every word cut sharp as a puzzle piece. He was shabby under a labcoat white as talc, scrawnily thin and yet a paunch slung across his stomach like something on a harness. A great balding dome and eyes you felt like you could never quite see — a layer of gauze, obfuscation, between you and what he was thinking.

"Tell me," Shattuck said, talking to my dad just outside the door to the meeting room. "What does he look like to you?"

"I assume it's a costume thing. Though why anyone would dress up like that is beyond me. Just keep it away from the kids and I couldn't care less."

"But what does he look like?"

"He looks like JFK about two seconds after Oswald shot him in the head."

"Very interesting. What did the assassination of the president mean to you?"

Deputy Mills, soaked to the bone, had managed to keep his cigarettes dry and he took one for himself, then offered one up to Shattuck, who waved it off, disgusted. My dad lit up, took Shattuck's measure once again. I like to imagine him pacing a little in that hallway, like a dark-haired Columbo.

"Now, when you came out to find Dr. Ralston standing over Dr. Garza's body, was he holding anything? A weapon of some kind?"

"As you see there, I've written up a complete statement. If there's nothing else, I have quite a bit of work to do, Deputy."

"You always work at midnight, Mr. Shattuck?"

"Anyone who does anything in this world worth doing, Deputy, knows that it is the small and quiet hours in which most of it actually gets done. Hmm?"

"Is that right?"

"Indeed. You see, for you the Park…Well, perhaps you've been to the Park. Hmm?"

"We're fixing to. Me and my daughter."

"Excellent. For those who pass through the park, it is, I hope, an experience both thrilling and edifying. Hmm? We venture, truly, to make some small difference. But to me, and to a few of the others, OmniPark is not simply a job for which we punch a little card and then eat in front of the television waiting for the next day to punch it again. Hmm? We are, in fact, explorers. And this is our outpost out on the very fringe."

"Fringe of what?"
"Well, Deputy Mills...the fringe of reality."

Let me back up. If you're old enough to remember 1979 in Odessa, that was the year that Hurricane Gilda pounded Galveston into mush. By the time the rest of her got out here to the Petroplex, she wasn't a hurricane anymore but she'd brought half the ocean with her and seemed to be setting up a franchise.

My dad got the call up there at the Sheriff's office in Adams. The night shift didn't even have a dispatcher in those days. A call came in about an incident at the park and other than that it was hard to tell, static and scatter in the lines. The rain had been falling for a day straight and I guess a telephone pole south of town had washed out. Anyway, my dad shot down there about fifteen miles to OmniPark and he was floating half the way so that when he got there he knew there was no going home until daylight.

Since those days, OmniPark has come and gone. I think of it like a bazaar from an Arabic fairytale, blown in on a dust-storm and out on the next without a forwarding address. My father, Deputy Mills, parked in the public lot right up by the entrance. "Raining cacti and claypots," as my grandmother liked to say. The Park was normally lit up like a casino, like a second sun out there on the flats, but in all this rain the light simply did not throw, everything beyond the fence just shapes. When he turned to look back he couldn't even see his patrol car. I have to think that when the thunder cracked overhead he must have flinched. He tried his radio over and over again, hoping to talk to Odessa PD or maybe a trooper on the state police band but you could hardly ever catch them anyway. The best he could manage was a crackling half-second with a long-haul trucker. It seems there was too much electricity in the air.

He prowled around the front gates, hollering out that it's the Sheriff's office and then it's the Sheriff's office and somebody better damn well let him in. Finally, here came Elijah Shattuck speedwalking toward him from deep inside the park, an enormous umbrella shielding him from the very rare rain.

"Thank goodness you've arrived," he said. Something like that. "There must be no misunderstanding."

Shattuck, talking all the while, led Deputy Mills — his shoes squelching with every step — through an inconspicuous door near customer service and on by maintenance bays where they were working on servo arms and television sets and down; past those great wide windows looking out over the workshop where they dreamt up attractions. Not dreamt, built.

At the very back of the building, a young man lay face-down in the final tee of a long hallway with a short crossbar. Where the two halls met had become an improvised break-room where they'd installed a two-seater booth like out of a cramped diner. Stale cigarettes and a light overhead that buzzed accusingly and a body right there like a hole in the Park itself. The legs straight as bowling pins and the face, though half-hidden still and masked with blood, misshapen, lumpy even, broken up like you might thumb out the knots in a muscle. Full analysis would show that Dr. Miguel Garza died from intensive injury to his face and the attendant trauma to his brain. But other than the damage to his orbital bones, nose, jaw, teeth, there was not a scratch on him. It was as though he'd *allowed* someone to beat him to death. Blood had run down his face and dripped onto his heather-gray t-shirt and very little of it was on the carpet underneath him. So, Dr. Garza had been moved after he slipped out of consciousness. A door there just a few feet from the body, in front of which someone had placed a shelving unit half-stocked with binders. Some of this my dad noticed right off and some of it only came later and hindsight is clearer than the mud of the moment, but he knew the real situation had been obscured on purpose, set just out of view.

"I did not see it happen, of course," Shattuck said. According to my dad, Shattuck looked at the body of Dr. Garza dispassionately, as though he were just an arrangement of matter only curious for the way it broke the pattern of the carpet. "But I'd heard a ruckus from my office and I came out to find this scene. Hmm? Dr. Garza *in extremis*, if not already deceased, and Dr. Ralston pacing the room like a man possessed. The rest is here in my typed statement, officer."

"Deputy. And where is Dr. Ralston now?"

"I was not sure what to do. Hmm? I cajoled him, in his confused state, into a meeting room down the hall here. And I barred the door to ensure he stayed, as it were, put."

"Show me."

"Of course. But I must warn you that Dr. Ralston has...changed. Hmm? You may find it rather disturbing to speak with him."

"I find this whole thing rather disturbing, Mr. Shattuck."

My dad tells the story — when he's up to it, in close company — so deadpan you might think he hardly reacted at all when he saw JFK in that room. But there's just no way. One might laugh as though it were a hoax or a prank. Of course, a normal person would be repulsed by the wound, at least a little, but curious too because the man is just looking right back at you. Anybody would be unsettled though, everybody. Whatever that first instant was in the head of Deputy Mills, it wasn't long before he sat down and offered a cigarette. Ralston wouldn't even shake his hand and asked my dad to toss him the smoke and the lighter across the table, which was four tables pushed together like for a big meeting or a six-foot submarine sandwich.

They say a conspiracy just means "to breathe together" and it only takes two. And so Deputy Mills and JFK each took a few drags of their cigarette and blew the smoke out in common and, with hardly any words, my father made a tenuous bond with this Dr. Ralston. Though, to all eyes, Dr. Ralston had left the building.

"Can you tell me who that body is out there?"

"It belonged to Dr. Miguel Garza. A man with whom I've worked side-by-side for well over a year now."

"Can you tell me what sort of work you did together?"

It sounded like mumbo-jumbo to my dad at first. More like a sales pitch for the park as some kind of pseudo-religion than any kind of job description. The hallowed territory of science and the beneficent call to entertain. Drawing up from the barrenTexas scrub a vision of the future that will be and the past that could have been in a present crackling with life. *Et cetera.*

After a while, Deputy Mills stopped taking notes and simply watched him. The smoke from JFK's cigarette, as it streamed from his fingers, coiled into a tight spiral. And, says my dad, the spiral became rectangular, as though it were a tilework snake rounding itself tight against the cold.

"And what happened to you, Dr. Ralston?"

"Same as Miguel. Though he was its vector and I was merely collateral."

"You playing make-believe?"

"Are you familiar with the concept of lucid dreaming?"

"Sure."

"Well, then. Perhaps it is obvious."

"This is a dream?"

"It depends how you define such things."

The rain drumming on the roof. Shattuck leering outside the door. And that hole in Ralston's head like an optical illusion — impossible to look away from even as it pains your eyes and the headache grows. The smoke spiraling tight and hard-edged and geometric. He told me that for even the deepest of meditators, when their mind is blank it is still like a dingy and stained sheet you call clean. There are splotches and discolorations and pills of lint. Nothing is ever quite empty. I don't know that he would have ever had such a thought if he'd never entered the Realm of Dream.

"Alright. Back up," Deputy Mills said. "Forget all that. I've got two questions right now and neither of them has to do with Dr. Garza out there so you can keep getting your story straight if you need to. The first is this: what's behind that door y'all tried to hide? Maybe not you, but somebody. And the second: why, do you think, being specific, is Shattuck wearing a labcoat with a nametag says Owens?"

He wanted to play the two off each other, so my dad stepped out at some point and asked Shattuck for the nearest phone and Shattuck was all too happy to oblige, though he seemed a bit relieved that you couldn't get a dial-tone. A dead world out there. You could hear the rain on the roof though there was a floor above them. You could feel the pressure slump in your old bones if you had them.

The nearest phone was in one of the repair bays and after a couple attempts at dialing, my dad stood there with Shattuck between a rack of brake assemblies for rides and a greasy bench of components he couldn't have named for a million dollars.

"You have to recall, officer—"

"Deputy."

"Apologies. Hmm? You have to recall that we specialize in the illusion here. Special effects you might call them. Hmm? And just as your, uh, Luke Skywalker appeared to wave about a standing laserbeam, that was not in fact the case."

"You can see right through his head to the wall behind him."

"Ta-da. Quite a thing. Hmm? What else did you notice?"

"I don't know. What did you notice about him?"

"Your pardon?"

"To your knowledge, what were Dr. Garza and Dr. Ralston doing in the hours and days up until you found Dr. Garza's body lying there?"

"I believe they were working on a new effect for one of the Realms. What, specifically, I could not tell you."

"Can't or won't?"

"I am unable to."

"You're the only three in the park right now."

"I'm not sure I would say that Dr. Garza is *in* the park at the moment. Hmm? Though of course this is a question that has plagued—"

"Why you three and nobody else?"

And here Shattuck pulled his shoulders back a little and looked off into the corner as though posing for a photographer. He nodded his head with a proud sort of grimace.

"Some of us. Hmm? Some of us are far more dedicated to the vision than others."

"He put on the white coat," Ralston said. "Because sociological studies say that it confers an aura of respect. Sixty-two percent of the time, anyway."

As to the second question, Ralston was surprised to hear the door was blocked and accused Shattuck. He made a firm point, poking the air with his cigarette, that it was dangerous now through that door. Behind it was the lab for the Realm of Dream. This was, as Ralston explained, another attraction envisioned by Dalton Teague back when the park still only existed in his mind. And for all the well-intentioned, scientific enthusiasm of the other Realms — where you might learn about the deep history of mankind or the dynamic ecology under the sea — there was a darkness to this realm from the beginning. Teague rarely spoke of his own dreams — he was what T.E. Lawrence would call a "dreamer of the day." And dreamers of the day, so Lawrence said, are dangerous because they may act out their dreams with open eyes to make them possible. One thing that Teague wanted to make possible, at least at first, was an immersive experience indistinguishable from that of the deepest sleep. A waking dream you could control with your thoughts. Or at least the sense that this was the experience you were having.

Teague, according to Ralston, shut down the Realm of Dream project after an intense meeting with Shattuck. No one is quite sure what it was about. Afterward, unbeknownst to Teague, Shattuck kept the dream alive, as it were, off the books. He hired Garza and Ralston fresh off their PhDs from opposite coasts, making sure they didn't know anyone else who worked at the park, and paid them through a company he'd founded to obscure his rogue expenses, diverting whatever would go unnoticed from the research budget in order to fund the Dream.

"Sounds like embezzlement," my dad said. "A little above my paygrade, to be frank."

"It's important background," Ralston said. "We were successful in our task. We brought the dream into the waking world. But it was a nightmare. So it was going to be very convenient that Garza was dead and gone. And, as for me, Shattuck could say I was the murderer — before you got here, he suggested that I ought to run off. Head out into the desert: New Mexico, maybe Arizona. Me gone and Garza buried and perhaps it'd be like it never happened."

"It was going to be very convenient. Until?"

"Until I called you."

"You called me?"

Ralston pointed at a phone mounted to the wall.

"I called you on that phone right there and as soon as Shattuck heard that, he barred the door so I couldn't leave."

"Did Shattuck kill Garza?"

"I can't say for sure. I wasn't there at the very end."

"Where were you?"

"I was lost in a maze of very attractive women, Deputy."

"I'm sorry?"

"It's a lonely life, being a secret Technosopher out here in the middle of nowhere."

While my dad considered all this, they smoked another cigarette and the tables at which they sat became his desk back at the station. He dug his eyes with his thumbs and yet it was still there, as though his desk — his paperwork, his typewriter, his little framed picture of me, the desk calendar that showed ranch scenes of West Texas — had stretched to accommodate this meeting table within it. And in the lacquered pine of the desk-top, in a dream, he'd been gouging whorls and abstract flowers, words in unknown languages, with his trusted pocketknife.

They aren't little vacations at all. What it is is that my dad takes a deep breath, holds it a moment, and when he lets it go, he dissolves into a state of objectivity, or something much closer to it. I think after the assassination, it was the only way to stop the what-ifs. And, then, see there's nothing to do when you're objective, there's just what can't be argued against.

So my dad took a deep breath and smoothed his wet hair against his head: "You're saying that I'm dreaming you right now?"

"You have to imagine me as if I'm. . .Deputy, are you familiar with Pink Floyd?"

"Sure."

"You have to imagine me like that prism on the cover. But when the light passes through me, I scatter it into the dream. The dream of the viewer. You see what *part* of your brain wants to show you."

"But Garza out there looks like an ordinary fella."

"Does he?"

"Except his face is all bashed in."

"I don't know how it all works, exactly. This is uncharted territory."

"The fringe of reality."

"It is now."

My dad moved toward the door. He kept as much of the room between them as he could. Looking at his shoes and his hands.

"Is it permanent?"

"I don't know. I should think not. What's happened to me is... second-hand. From Garza perceiving me. He got the full dose."

"Full dose?"

"Electromagnetic energy. At a very peculiar wavelength. What you see here. Me. That's just what Garza... what he did to me. Not on purpose, you understand. It could have easily been the other way around. Though, of course, Garza was always the smarter of us."

"I need to see the other side of that door."

"I wouldn't. Not until we know if the effect subsides or we've been able to strategize some countermeasures. Perhaps it's all contained now with Garza dead but I just don't know."

"Look, you might have a self-defense case here. If you just start playing it straight."

"I didn't kill Miguel."

"Then I'm going to have to go through that door. You have keys?'

"Elijah Shattuck has stolen my keys."

"Understood. One more thing for now."

"Yes?"

"I want you to give me a detailed description of Shattuck. Size and weight and face, if you can. His whole, what do you call it, affect."

Later, when I spent a lot of time at OmniPark, I often felt like dad was keeping a certain kind of eye on me. He, of course, was always concerned I hadn't been hurt or that I hadn't cut my hair with desk scissors again. But, and I noticed this long before I knew the story, he looked at me sometimes as though to make sure horns had not sprouted from my head.

When Deputy Mills stepped out of the meeting room, he glimpsed Shattuck hustling around the corner out of view, headed toward the front of the building where they'd come in. "Just hold your horses there," my dad hollered, echoing in those empty halls. A moment later, Shattuck came walking toward him, scarcely hiding his embarrassment, wringing his spidery fingers together.

"I caught you."

"I made no attempt to escape. Hmm? I thought perhaps you might enjoy a coffee."

"I'll survive," my dad said and jammed the chair up under the knob of the meeting room door. "Come with me."

While Shattuck paced about repeating himself, my dad did the best forensics he could. This amounted to feeling the back of Dr. Garza's head for contusions, staring at the carpet, and squatting there beside the body looking up and down the hallway and to the door like he was tracking wild game. A vague sheen to everything. A glassy distortion so slight he might have been making it up.

When my dad asked for the keys to the door that Shattuck (probably) had tried to hide, Shattuck protested. Said first there was nothing behind the door worth seeing and then that Deputy Mills needed a warrant. My dad kept staring as OmniPark's resident genius tried to bend reality around that door like some kind of trick of light: there were sensitive experiments behind that door that would be disrupted by changes in temperature. Dalton Teague was sure to kick off a lawsuit should an employee of the county yadda yadda. My father, when he told this all to me, said he wished Shattuck would have just tried to whack him in the back of the head with a board. At least that would have been a commitment to the actual happening of the world. But instead he kept circumambulating and building up arguments like this was all a thought experiment and he could think his way through the other end with himself on one riverbank and my father shaking his fist on the other.

Deputy Mills unsnapped the button holding his service revolver in its holster.

In one telling, Shattuck did try to flee. With short steps and his hands folded at his midsection, he ran like a butler who'd forgotten to polish the silverware. My father took big loping strides after him and kicked one of Shattuck's feet into the other and then pinned him to the thin-piled office carpet of the hallway. The key was produced forthwith.

"Look. You didn't kill Miguel Garza. I understand that. You haven't been close enough to the source of this thing or you wouldn't look like you're supposed to."

"Of course I didn't murder him, I—"

"Shut up. You didn't murder him but there's plenty of blame to go around. What I need to know, if it can be known, is right through this door you tried to hide like a child hiding his mess."

My dad moved the shelves and then he opened the door and just past this was another door, and around the frame of this one were scorchmarks like smoke had filtered out along the frame. But instead of a blackish haze, the wall was discolored by swatches of the wallpaper in my bedroom. The room at my mother's house where I stayed six nights out of seven. In, hold it, out. Trembling, though, he must have been.

What he says is that through the next door it was Dealey Plaza, but indoors, somehow. Confined like a laboratory reproduction, like a diorama under rafters at one-eighth scale. Do you think that when people make a scientific discovery it's always shouting eureka and jumping up and down? Or is it a little frightening, too? Knowing you've brought this novelty into the world but that its consequences might be out of your hands, that you might have no idea what happens next?

My dad didn't know what he was looking for and, if he were to find it, whether it would be real anyway. If he found a billy club lying on the floor and bagged it for evidence, in court would there be a whomping stick or a coke can or would they unseal that bag to find nothing at all. He said the room tried to turn into something else on him — what, exactly, he wouldn't say — but he just kept breathing, kept his eyes soft watching the space in front of him like a camera records everything without thinking on it.

He found a park bench there scattered with smashed-up pieces of gear: a vacuum tube like out of an old television. A telescope sort-of thing. Wiring harnesses separated from what they'd harnessed and so totally anonymous. The equipment was dream-proof, he says, but he could never confirm that with anyone who'd know. He trusted it was really there and who are we to question such a thing.

His theory, at this point, was that Ralston had killed Garza the way you might put out a fire with whatever was in reach. And then maybe Garza, grievously injured, dying, had stumbled toward the exit, maybe even out into the hallway. Maybe Shattuck thought to drag him all the way out into the scrub and bury him — hours with a shovel and those flimsy arms. And then maybe he'd tried to scare Ralston off, just like he'd said. Maybe no one would be the wiser. The Realm of Dream research a bust, worse than that, but Shattuck still Elijah Shattuck, the goddamn wizard of OmniPark.

That's not what happened.

Nearby the park bench where Garza had apparently taken that full dose, as Ralston called it, was a little half wall of cinderblock. Maybe it's in Dallas, too, I've never checked. At the foot of this was a pair of broken glasses and some other dream-proof tech my dad couldn't name and maybe nobody ever had. On the wall itself, and splattered below it, thick stains like blood. Except my dad said it wasn't blood at all, the way he saw it, but a black, black oil glassy with viscera, pulsing and bulging with an irregular heartbeat. And when he pressed a finger to it the coagulation screamed in pain.

I saw a lot more of my dad after that. My mom says it shook him awake, though that wasn't enough for her to see her way back to being with him. I only barely remember from before, so he's always been this man. A little taciturn unless he has to be, but for me there's wisdom in almost everything he says. "All those little sufferings keep you sane, you know?" he said, last time I saw him. "Otherwise you'd just float off into the air."

He became the head of security at OmniPark. That night back in 1979, Deputy Mills stepped out of the ersatz Realm of Dream to find Dalton Teague himself standing there. A bit alarmed, soaking wet in a pajama shirt. My dad had to explain to Teague what had happened: Shattuck running the secret lab. Their project derailing, refracting that room into something maybe the world hasn't seen before and maybe never will. We're probably better for it though what a ride it would have been. And then he had to explain to Teague that it wasn't Ralston who had killed this poor young technosopher, and it wasn't Shattuck either. Dr. Miguel Garza, it turned out, had seen the chaos he would make in the world — widespread cancer of the Dream — and, in his own kind of sordid heroism, he had smashed his face against the brick until his dream stopped.

Teague and Shattuck came to an agreement behind closed doors and at the end of it, Shattuck stayed at the Park. My dad found that hard to believe but he hadn't killed Garza and so it was a matter between them, as far as he was concerned. And the word was that Teague sent Ralston off to a cabin in the hills of Colorado. And then they bored under the laboratory until the building fell into the hole and then they sheathed the site with lead and concrete. Built a Coke stand over top of it. And I can't say for sure whether the effect was permanent, lots of loose ends lost when the OmniPark bazaar blew out of town. Maybe Ralston still lives out in the hills, looking like a different man to everyone he meets.

But I drive out in the scrublands with my dad on Sundays now. He's an old man now and I'm not so young. We wander out on those two-lanes with the horizon enormous and far. Oftentimes he'll point to something out there that he thinks is beautiful and ask me what it is. I tell him, that's a fencepost, Dad. That's a jackrabbit. That's a billboard some citified fool thought to build. And he laughs at this, laughs and laughs and says "ain't that the darndest thing?"

The Technosophers' Ball

A. C. Wise

It had been a joke when he'd first suggested it — the Technosophers' Ball: a chance to gather within the Realm of the Stars before it opened to the public, and celebrate a job well done. Hank had been picturing a few beers, some snacks, nothing fancy. Giving it such a lofty title struck him as funny, but somehow the rest of the team had taken the idea and run with it. From there, things had snowballed — they should at least have wine along with the beer and dress up a bit and why not make it a masquerade, even? After all, they'd designed an entire universe for OmniPark's guests to enjoy; when would they ever get a chance like this again?

Hank stood in the park's Entryway Pavilion, gazing at the colorful murals adorning the walls. But all he could think about was everything that might go wrong tonight. He'd been stupid enough to let himself get swept up in all this excitement, picturing how he and Julia would hold hands as they rode the "rocket ship" up to dock with the space station they'd helped design, how they'd stroll around Orbit One Central and how, against a majestic backdrop of spiraling galaxies and gas giants, he'd take a knee and propose.

That had been his plan. But it'd gone wrong straight from the start.

They'd been sitting at the small kitchen table in their apartment, finishing up their morning coffee when Julia had sprung up, dropped a kiss on his cheek, and gathered up her keys and bag.

"I have some errands to run. Meet you at the party?" Julia moved toward the apartment door even as she asked the question.

"Um. Sure." Hank couldn't think of an excuse for why they needed to arrive together that wouldn't tip Julia off and make her suspicious that he had something special planned.

The scene he'd pictured — Julia helping him with his tie, having a glass of wine while they dressed, and splurging on a cab so neither of them would have to drive — melted away as she stepped out the door.

Hank stood in the Pavilion's silent, cavernous interior as the last light slipped from the sky over OmniPark and the first stars emerged. Was he making a mistake? Was Julia's decision to arrive separately a bad omen, or was he over thinking things? Even though the day's dry heat had given way to a temperate night with a soft breeze, he still sweated inside the crisply-pressed suit he'd rented at the mall. On the display mannequin, the suit had looked simple and classic, but now he was afraid he looked like an usher at a funeral in plain dark gray with a tie in thin, alternating stripes of black and white.

He traced the contours of the ring box in his pocket, pacing a circle around the Pavilion's interior. What if Julia didn't like the ring? What if he got tongue-tied and flubbed the words? What if she didn't want to marry him?

"You worry too much, Hank. You can't control everything. Just relax, let life unfold, and see where it takes you." He heard the words in his head, such a common enough refrain that the words sounded as real as Julia's voice. As if she was right here next to him.

Hank stopped pacing and unclenched his fingers from around the ring box. Better to get it over with, like ripping off a band-aid. He turned away and strode toward the entrance to the Realm of the Stars. No more stalling. He opened the door, expecting the satisfaction of hinges squeaking, or even laughter and music from the party leaking out into the "rocket ship" area, but only silence and darkness greeted him. A new fear hit him: He'd gotten the date wrong. The whole idea of the Technosophers' Ball was a joke the rest of the team was playing on him. No wonder Julia had sent him on his own.

No. He was overreacting. The party would be inside, past the entry where guests would board the ship to carry them to the space station. Hank stepped inside, waiting for his eyes to adjust to the dimness. Emergency lights shone at the far end of the rocket ship chamber, but the fact that the main lights were off made him tense up and glance around nervously as if he was a trespasser here. The door clicked shut behind him, and Hank flinched, startled, his pulse skittering, more sweat dampening his armpits. He was being ridiculous. The door had merely slipped out of his hand, the sound of it closing echoing in the stillness. He listened to his breath rasp, and forced it back into a calm, even rhythm.

How often he'd teased Julia for her imagination, the way she could get utterly swept up in a project like the Realm of the Stars until she almost believed it was real. And now here he was, doing the same thing, jumping at an empty room just because he was already on edge.

A clear image leapt to his mind: Julia sitting at their small kitchen table, every inch of its surface covered in her sketches and watercolor paintings, concept art for the Realm. Light from the glass-shaded lamp fell over her. She had one leg crooked up, chewing on the end of her pencil, brow creased in concentration, pausing occasionally to scribble a notation on the pages spread before her. "Why don't you take a break?" He'd asked. "You've been at it for hours. The designs will still be here in the morning." Hank had slid into the space behind Julia's chair, resting his hands on her shoulders.

She shrugged free and leaned over the page in front of her, a map of stars Hank guessed would appear on one of the station's display screens.

"I just want to finish this one thing. Give me a few more minutes." Julia's shoulders hunched with tension, even though she'd refused to let him rub them.

"How much more could you possibly have to do?" Hank's voice rose with a tone of irritation he couldn't tamp down.

He reached for the drawing over her shoulder and Julia swatted him away.

"Hank, please. This is important to me, okay? Mr. Lexington put me in charge of the art team. I can't turn in work that's just good enough. It has to be perfect."

"Right." Hank stepped back. "I suppose I wouldn't understand, because I'm just an engineering peon and not a team leader." He drew the last word out, giving it a mocking edge.

It'd been petty, he'd known it even in the moment, but her words had stung, a physical sensation like a hand reaching into his chest and squeezing, reminding him how they'd been hired at the same time, but Julia's career had advanced and his hadn't, eating at him with the thought that she might leave him behind.

"That's not what I meant, I just—" Julia turned in her chair to face him, but Hank cut her off.

"You'd think you were really planning a mission to space, not designing a silly attraction at a theme park. Come on, Julia. I've seen the script for the Nebula Quest ride, and it's absurd. A ship searching for a lost nebula accidentally jumping beyond known space and time? The science makes no sense and you know it. How can you possibly care about this so much? All I'm asking for is one night where neither of us does, thinks about, or talks about work."

Julia leaped to her feet, sending her chair careening toward Hank, who dodged just in time. Her cheeks flushed.

"You don't understand at all!" Her voice rose in pitch. "You don't listen. This—" She waved her hand at the artwork and the star map sketch fluttered off the table at the breeze caused by her hand, spinning once before landing on the floor.

This time, Hank was quicker than her, snatching the sketch up and turning it to get a better look. He couldn't suppress the sound of disdain, halfway between a snort and laughter.

"You say your work matters to you, but these constellations are all wrong. Where are the Pleiades? And is that Orion upside-down? Did you even look at an astronomy book?"

Hank waved the page in the air between them, causing the paper to crackle with the motion.

"Just because you've never seen these stars—" Julia grabbed at the paper, but Hank didn't let go. She pulled and it tore between them.

Julia's face crumpled. Not tears, but worse: a pallor and trembling rage. He expected her to shout, but she spun on her heel, stalking to the bedroom and slamming the door behind her. Hank took a step after her, then stopped. Let her sulk. He'd sleep on the couch, and it'd all blow over by morning.

In the darkened rocket ship chamber in the Realm of the Stars, Hank released a breath. Julia was right — he didn't always listen. When she got that rapt expression on her face, talking about the wonders of the farthest reaches of the known universe, more often than not, he tuned her out. He'd told himself he was justified; it was ridiculous for a grown woman to talk about their work building a theme park attraction, as if the Realm of the Stars was anything more than pure fantasy. Sure, kids coming to the park with their parents might buy into it — but adults?

Well, he could put all that behind him now. They both could. Tonight would be a chance to start a new chapter in their relationship, a more serious one, and leave their past mistakes and petty squabbles behind. Just because she was prone to flights of fancy didn't mean Julia couldn't be serious too. She would be a wonderful wife, and a wonderful mother someday too.

Dark banks of screens caught his reflection as he moved toward the door to exit the rocket ship and enter orbit. Once the Realm opened to the public, they would be lit with mission control readouts, scrolling and bleeping above the guests as they traveled to the space station.

As he stepped through the door, Hank remembered the domino mask, his costume for the evening, in his breast pocket. He hastily pulled it out. The velvety material had crumpled, but he managed to smooth it over his face and tie the ribbons behind his head without catching his hair in the knots.

A wave of sound hit him. Bright laughter and the susurrus of conversation filled the room. The entire group of Technosophers who'd worked on the Realm wasn't that big, but scattered clusters of costumed bodies met Hank's eye everywhere he looked. A wave of dizziness swept through him. He'd seen the blueprints for this space station, but the area before him didn't map to those plans. The walls curved vertiginously, and the ceiling soared above him, levels rising like a series of stacked rings, as if he was actually on a space station. Hank felt simultaneously weightless and tugged downward by the spin creating artificial gravity, his body alternating between wanting to float, and a sensation like his shoes were magnetized to the floor, fighting him each time he wanted to lift them. Beyond the windows, just visible through the crush of bodies, he caught a glimpse of an agoraphobia-inducing sweep of stars — pinpricks of light against absolute black; and there at the edge of his vision, the blushing sunset colors of a nebula.

Hank braced himself against the wall, shaking his head. That was ridiculous. It was just a room. A cleverly designed room with meticulous attention to detail, but just a room nonetheless. If he looked closely, he would see the seams — the painted backdrops, the models, the clever tricks done with perspective and light.

A waiter carrying a tray of champagne glided past and Hank snatched a glass flute, sipping too quickly and coughing from the bubbles. It occurred to him that this too should be impossible. They'd all kicked in funds for the party, but surely they hadn't contributed enough for caterers and waitstaff. Could Dr. Teague have found out about their plans to host a secret celebration and generously offered to pay for the whole thing?

As he moved further into the room, he stumbled against one of the low benches scattered about the floor. The motion jostled the ring box in his pocket, reminding him to focus. He forced himself to breathe, fighting against the chest-tightening sensation of panic.

He caught sight of Julia and plunged into the crowd, dodging bodies as he tried to reach her. She was dressed in a ballgown and towering wig — a sculpted mass of white curls set with glittering pins in the shape of stars. Hank's rented suit itched, suddenly too tight across the shoulders, his shoes stiff and determined to trip him. Everyone else's costumes were so elaborate, and except for the domino mask, Hank might as well be on his way to church.

Julia waved. Before he could wave back, someone clapped him on the back hard enough to make him stumble.

"Quite the night, eh? Congratulations. We finally did it."

Hank couldn't place the voice coming from inside a cartoonish papier mâché moon with a rocket jammed into one of its eyes. The sphere balanced precariously on the wearer's shoulders, wobbling as though the person inside shook with silent laughter. He wondered briefly if it might be Mr. Lexington, who he sometimes suspected had less-than-pure motives for giving Julia her promotion. More pettiness, more unnecessary suspicion - Julia had received her promotion because she did good work, but that didn't stop Hank's mind from spinning out his insecurities and doubts. Like how he worried Mr. Lexington was mocking him during the presentation last week, when Julia assured him the man had just been asking an honest question. Like how he wondered now if everyone agreed on a theme for their costumes and not told him so they could make him the butt of a joke.

Hank's shoulders tightened, but before he could respond, the moon-man had moved on. Julia no longer stood where she'd been either, and Hank had the paranoid thought the man in the moon had specifically distracted him so she could slip away. Why hadn't she waited for him?

As Hank followed the curving ramp to the second level of the station, another wave of dizziness swept over him, fuzzing his vision at the edges and making his head spin, leaving him gripping the hand rail. The space station should only be a single ring with the shopping area in the center, and windows with video screens giving the illusion of additional rooms. It was the same thought he'd had when he first entered; the space around him didn't match the blueprints Hank shouldn't have been able to climb at all.

No. He must be mistaken. Obviously the space station had at least two levels. He was on the second level now, peering down at the floor below with its scattering of benches and people. Only now there were also rows of hydroponic plants, as if to aid in a real space station's oxygenation, and display terminals softly lit up, as if the people who lived and worked on the station might use them to call up information. The room held even more people than when he'd first entered, and they were all so elaborately dressed. One man rippled with ever-changing bands of light, while the woman standing beside him wore some sort of mirrored suit, giving the illusion he could see the wall behind her.

Hank pushed away from the railing, wheeling around to follow the curving hallway. He needed to catch up with Julia. If he kept going this way, he would reach the Nebula Quest area. Surely that's where she would be. Not only was it the crown jewel of the Realm, she'd been obsessed with the story ever since they'd been given their scripts in order to start design work.

As silly as it was, Hank admitted to himself that he could see the appeal. If Julia wanted to believe in bad science for the sheer joy of it, who was he to say it was wrong? As a kid, Hank used to stay up late at night, reading pulpy adventure novels with lush jungles and dinosaurs on the covers. Even after his mother made him turn out the light, he took the emergency flashlight out of his bedside table and read them under his blanket. The stories with daring scientists and impossible ancient beasts were always his favorites, despite knowing even as a kid that dinosaurs had been dead for millions of years and no one would ever discover one in some forgotten jungle. That didn't mean he hadn't enjoyed them. How could he begrudge Julia enjoying this?

He squeezed the ring box in his pocket. Sweat dampened the small of his back and stuck his shirt's cotton to his skin underneath his jacket. His legs ached from the climb. Even if he'd been mistaken about the building having two floors instead of one, he must be at least four or five floors up by now, which was impossible. Hank clenched his jaw, sending an ache from the muscles there all the way up the side of his skull. He refused to let himself look over the rail to see whether the sense of distance was merely in his head. He'd only had one sip of champagne. He couldn't be drunk. Was there something else wrong with him? Was he running a fever? Hallucinating?

It was one thing to resolve to be more understanding of Julia's flights of fancy; it was quite another to lose the distinction between reality and a fantasy altogether. He wasn't on a space station, the stars outside weren't actual stars. Believing otherwise was...

"We've discovered something incredible, Hank. I don't know how, but it's more than just an attraction building. There's a door..." Julia's words rose in his mind — a half-remembered conversation.

He'd hardly been paying attention, going over the design schematics for the Nebula Quest ride when she'd rushed in, eyes alight with excitement.

Julia's cheeks were flushed, and she bounced on her toes as she stood in front of the kitchen table where he worked.

"I'm in the middle of something, Julia. I need to get these designs turned in first thing tomorrow morning for Dr. Teague's approval."

"Hank, this is important." She spoke more quietly now, no longer bouncing in place.

"This deadline is what's important." He'd gestured at the work arrayed in front of him.

"Could you listen for just a moment, Hank. I'm trying to tell you—"

"Later. After I'm done." Hank turned his attention back to the blueprints.

Julia stood there a moment longer, and then he'd heard her cross their apartment back to the door, leaving again and closing it softly behind her.

He should have listened to what she'd been trying to tell him. Whatever it was she thought she'd found while working in the Realm of the Stars building might explain the impossible things he was seeing now.

He caught sight of Julia disappearing around the next curve in the corridor. The endless spiral upward had finally flattened out into a level hallway, and Hank broke into a jog, pushing past a costumed astronaut and someone dressed as the sun, surrounded by a ring of planets. The dark blue fabric of Julia's dress glittered with winking points of light as if a galaxy of miniature stars sparkled in the folds of her skirt. She looked even more ethereal than before, moonlight woven through the elaborate curls of her hair. The hem of her dress, her feet beneath it, scarcely touched the floor.

"Julia!" Hank pulled up short just before colliding with the moon-headed man who stepped in front of him as he reached for Julia to get her attention.

"Slow down. Enjoy the party." The voice, muffled by the head piece, was stretched flat, almost mechanical. It no longer even sounded human.

Hank tried to push away from the hands on his shoulders, trying to steady him or hold him back. Whichever direction Hank stepped, another partygoer pressed in to block his passage. Julia, absorbed in conversation with someone Hank didn't recognize, hadn't turned his way yet or noticed his effort to reach her.

The air grew syrupy between them; thick, as if the gravity had increased; pinning him down. Hank braced his hand on the wall to keep from falling, squinting as he tried to make out the costume of the man standing next to Julia. It wasn't... He wasn't...

Not a costume. Not a man.

The realization stole Hank's breath. The man, he — *it* — was a scribbled patch of sky, night-black and pinpricked with violent stars. His edges make Hank think of Julia's torn star map. Except they jittered, making Hank's eyes water, moving in ways no human should.

Nausea rose from Hank's stomach, clawing at the back of his throat. Everything spun around him as the thing, the rogue scrap of universe, turned his way. Turned without moving. Turned despite not having a head or a face and certainly nothing like eyes. But that didn't stop the fact that whatever it was looked at Hank, its gaze piercing him and seeing him all the way through, a weighty regard that flayed his skin from his bones.

The star creature bent its head closer to Julia, leaning in to be heard over the noise of conversation in the hall as it spoke. Hank couldn't hear what it said, but Julia inclined her head as if agreeing with something the star-made-man asked her. A shout of warning locked in Hank's throat, emerging as a wheeze. Hank blinked stinging tears from his eyes as the thing next to Julia folded back into the shape of a man, tall and dressed in a sharply-pressed suit the same dark blue as Julia's dress.

Gravity betrayed him, releasing its hold all at once, and Hank staggered forward, dropping to one knee against the hard concrete floor.

"There you are." Julia turned to him at last, smiling warmly and extending her hand. "I've been looking everywhere for you. We're just about to leave."

She gestured back toward Nebula Quest's door. It blurred in Hank's vision, like the shard-of-sky man. It was a door, and yet it was also an airlock, or a gateway, or...

He clenched his eyes shut against the overlapping layers of reality, heaving in a deep breath. When he opened his eyes after another breath to calm himself, Julia was still smiling at him, hand still outstretched. His jumbled brain insisted she was waiting for him to slip a ring on her finger; he was on one knee not because he'd tripped, but because he was about to propose.

"You can't go." Hank reached into his pocket for the ring box, but his hands shook and it snagged on the fabric. "You have to stay here with me."

"I tried to explain, Hank. I tried to explain so many times. All I can do now is show you, if you come with me."

Julia moved the hand held out to Hank closer to him, but he didn't take it, still fighting with the ring box caught in his pocket, afraid to tear the fabric if he pulled too hard.

"You can't," he said again.

Julia's expression faltered: disappointment, as if she pitied him.

"I wish you'd come with us." Her tone matched her expression — melancholy, as if what she was actually saying was goodbye. "It's going to be so beautiful."

Julia turned. Her skirt flared out as she did, brushing against his hand as he finally freed it from his pocket. He reached to catch the hem and hold her back, but missed.

The distance between them warped impossibly. Julia was already light years away, an object at the edge of a black hole. He stretched toward her and she fell farther and farther away without ever seeming to move. He wanted to shout after her, insist she change her mind, or even that he could change his mind if she'd let him. But she'd given him that chance before, throughout their relationship, and he'd repaid her with dismissal, petty jealousy disguised as teasing. She'd given him his last chance, and somehow he knew there'd never be another.

Hank saw her in a series of frozen slices of time, like panes of glass, marching away from him. He watched the repeating sequence as she turned and looped her arm through the arm of the shard-of-sky man and stepped through the door to Nebula Quest; through a gateway to eternity.

Hank rose, his legs wobbly as he made his way past the people still crowding the hallway to the Nebula Quest door. Through the doorway, multi-colored neon tubes arched over the entry to the ride, suggesting a futuristic launching area. Hank shouldered past the people waiting in line, twisting his body sideways to slide through the polite gaps they left between them, ignoring them when they called after him for cutting the line. He stumbled into the boarding area just in time to see Julia and the scrap-of-sky man in a two-seat car moving along the track.

Hank grabbed the shoulder of the man in front of him, pulling him out of the line and climbing past him into the car he'd been about to board. He pulled the lap-bar down and locked it into place.

"Sorry!" He waved an apology he didn't mean as the car clacked forward. "You can take the next one."

It was a tracked ride; it couldn't deviate in direction or speed, but that didn't stop Hank from leaning forward, willing his car to go faster, to catch up to Julia and the star-man. A woman's voice emerged from hidden speakers, introducing herself as the Navigator and explaining their mission to search for a lost nebula. His car swung around and Hank's stomach lurched. He fought the urge to be sick, though it had nothing to do with the dizzying view that now filled the screen in front of him: Earth from above against a vault of familiar stars. Hank strained forward as far as the safety bar would allow, trying to see into the other cars, but the vehicle's curved shape blocked his view.

The floor of his car vibrated, the sensation shivering up through his soles to his calves, as if vast engines drove their mission ship through the stars. He'd designed the system himself to combine with the way the cars circled around and around the same section of track, making it seem as if they traveled vast distances through hyperspace, jumping first from Earth to Pluto and then beyond their solar system. A whole new view stretched across the screen now, the blues and golds of the Crab Nebula like a ring of fire expanding outward. Hank tugged at the lap bar, but there was no give.

Another swooping turn around the track, adding to his sense of disorientation. Now the screen showed a chain of stars like spilled milk, shaded pale blue, green, and mauve. They shimmered across the screen, giving the sense of a universe that lived and breathed, stretching outward into an unknown vastness. He couldn't match what he saw on screen to anything he'd ever seen in astronomy books. A shape appeared on the screen, blocking out the stars. Hank jerked backward, breath hissing as panic contracted his lungs. All jagged edges, the shape poured itself from the screen to one of the other ride cars in a fluid arc like spilled ink, water spurting from a fountain, electricity jumping between two coiled wires.

It was the shard-of sky-man and as Hank watched, locked in his own ride vehicle, he darted from car to car, unrestricted by lap bars or distance, as the screen whirled through increasingly rapid changes. Planets Hank didn't recognize, nebulae crawling with shimmering light in colors he couldn't name, flashed across the screen as the ship jumped farther and farther beyond the possible, beyond the reality Hank knew. Panic clawed at him. In each car the star-man visited, Hank imagined an offer being made. The same offer Julia had made to him earlier in the hallway.

"I wish you'd come with us. It's going to be beautiful."

Julia had tried to tell him. She'd found a door to somewhere else. She hadn't just been caught up in the wonder of the ride's story; it was real. In the cars around him, Hank pictured the living scrap of night sky twisting around the other riders, swallowing them whole.

Part of Hank wanted to call out to the star man, to beg him to visit his car. But he already knew it was too late. He'd already refused. No matter how many times the creature arced from car to car, it would always pass over him. He'd turned down the offer once, and it wouldn't be repeated.

Pressure built behind his eyes and his throat rasped as he hauled in a breath, dangerously close to tears. The unhinged voice of the ride's narrator grated against Hank's ears. How could she keep talking about their last-ditch effort to punch through time and space and leap back home? But of course, the narration had been recorded months ago; there was no pilot, only a mindless tape. Hank squeezed his eyes shut, fought to get his breathing under control.

Brakes hissed, bringing his car to a gentle halt. Hank opened his eyes, disoriented, unable to make sense of the disembarkation area. He'd been in the depths of space, beyond the known galaxy, and now bright lights illuminated the painted gray concrete platform where guests exited their cars and the metallic gates that funneled them out the door and back into the main attraction building.

Hank blinked, stumbling from Nebula Quest's doorway and back out into Orbit One Central. He'd been gone a thousand, thousand years. His throat felt parched, sandpaper-rough, as if he'd been sobbing. He'd traveled beyond the edges of the known universe and a small handful of his colleagues — two of his fellow engineers and a man from the sound department stood chatting, holding paper plates of food and sipping from plastic cups, as though nothing unusual had happened.

Hank scanned the room. The layout matched the blueprints he remembered, a ring with shops where OmiPark's guests could buy souvenirs, and the Cosmonaut Cafe, currently closed, where they could buy freeze-dried ice cream and other snacks. The overhead lights washed everything mercilessly, leaving the Realm of the Stars looking like a mundane imitation of the place Hank had just returned from. A plastic mask in the shape of a cat's face lay abandoned on a nearby chair. Hank glanced at his watch; it wasn't even 9 p.m. yet, but exhaustion weighed heavily on his shoulders. If Julia had exited the ride ahead of him, surely she would be here with the others. Scanning the room, Hank didn't see her anywhere. Nor did he see the man with the moon on his head, the astronaut, the woman in the mirrored suit, or the man rippling with light. He certainly didn't see a man who looked like a living shard of the night sky, moving in ways that nothing from this world should.

None of the fantastic costumes he'd witnessed earlier were present, only a few domino masks like his own, and the cat mask abandoned on the chair. Julia's name ached in his throat. He couldn't bear to ask anyone if they'd seen her exit Nebula Quest. He was too afraid of the answer.

Hank slunk through the room without talking to anyone, making his way to the Realm's exit. Back outside at the silent Entryway Pavilion, Hank tipped his head back to look at the sky. Scrubby, dishwater clouds obscured the moon. Hank's hand went instinctively to his pocket, stomach dropping when he found it empty. The box must have fallen out. His hand clenched against emptiness. He could go back and look for it, but he supposed it didn't matter now.

A rough chuckle scratched at his throat, dangerously close to turning into more tears. He scanned the sky one last time, trying to imagine Julia up there, the ring winking on her finger like a star.

But all Hank could see were the clouds.

ECTOR POLICE DEPARTMENT
WANTED PERSON REPORT

Ident. No._______

Date **8-31-81**   Reason Wanted **MISSING**   Offense No. **U-91**

Name **Unknown**   Address **unknown**   Phone_______

Color_______ Sex **female** Age **~19** Birthdate_______ Alias **Nickname - Denise/Denny**

Ht. Ft. **5** In. **1** Wt. **90** Hair **brown** Eyes **brown** Teeth **prominent** Comp. **splotchy**

Speech or Voice **Non-verbal**   Scars, etc. **horizontal scar across forehead**

FILL OUT FOR WANTED PERSON

Warrant Issued Yes_______ No_______   Warrant No._______

Wanted By_______   Department_______

Reported By_______   Date_______ Time_______

ADDITIONAL INFORMATION

I was working as the sole OmniPark Investigator on Aug 31, 1981 at approximately 10:40 am, when I was notified by a park employee of a missing person and possible crime scene at the newly constructed Realm of Man. Upon arrival it became clear the crime was more likely grand theft and not a missing person, [sorry Rose, I'll retype this report using the proper form tomorrow] involving one of the animatronic characters in the "Great Ten" positioned near the entrance of the The Story of Man attraction. The initial notification was reported by a craft service staff member who had worked in the bldg for several weeks and thought the character another living employee. On entering the area, I was unable to find any electrical switches and had to use my flashlight to view the darker recesses. The scene was in a well trafficked part of the pavilion. The figure had been on a platform that was approximately four feet above ground level behind a row of stretched animal hides. All electrical connections appeared to have been severed and the character was missing. There was considerable red-tinted fluid in the area which I assume was hydraulic fluid for the character. It appeared the lines were still pressurized when they were severed. The area was unsecured and open to anyone. The employee who initially reported the incident insisted that the character was not animatronic, but a living person wearing effects makeup who spoke in pantomime. They asserted that they had developed a relationship over the past few days and were highly concerned about the character's whereabouts. When park officials arrived they said the character had malfunctioned and been designated to storage in the Park Archives. It was at this point that the reporting employee became emotional and attacked the officials. I restrained the employee and detained them in my patrol car. I have left a message with OmniPark administration to see if they wish to press charges. They have not returned my call.

Typed By **Lester Rhodes**   Date **8-31-81** Time **1:30 PM** Broadcaster_______

Located By_______ Location_______ Date_______ Time_______

30900-013

Wanted Person Report from the archives of the Ector County Police Department, 1981. The report describes an officer's investigation of a disturbance in the Realm of Man, leading to the arrest of an (unnamed) OmniPark employee who appears to have been mentally ill. No further records of this arrest are known to exist.

18 %
LIVE
Harper Sharp @OmniParkIsReal
KleptoSkeptic: haha holy shit ok!
KleptoSkeptic: damn Sharp you really went all out
Biggest_Ounce: no
SonOfTeague: Harper I dont like this
Comment...
SEND

Angel of the Prairie

Brent Winter & Jesse Bullington

ADAwesome®
Real-Time Descriptive Video and Audio, Closed Captioning, and Chat Transcripts

Biggest_Ounce: Anyone else think it's ironic the subtitle company doesn't voiceover it's own waiting screen/

Biggest_Ounce: ?

KleptoSkeptic: *its* own waiting screen

Biggest_Ounce: THANK YOU

KleptoSkeptic: NO THANK YOU

SonOfTeague: where is everyone? Pls tell me its not just you two

Biggest_Ounce: *it's* not just you two

KleptoSkeptic: *it's* not lol

SonOfTeague: -_-

KleptoSkeptic: For realsies, that paywall was bananas, I'm surprised you technopeasants had the apes to get in.

SonOfTeague: why's the channel's biggest troll dropping so much crypto if your you're sure its fake???

Foreground — Low-resolution close-up of Harper Sharp's face. The light is bright on Harper's face and dim elsewhere. Harper appears excited; they are sweaty and shaking. Their forehead is smudged with a dark substance.

Background — Interior of a small, dark room.

Harper says: This is it, Omnifam! Your enby is in! Welcome... to OmniPark!

Foreground — Out-of-focus 360-degree pan of small, dark room.

Harper says: I can't hecking believe this. The Realm of Time. We're in the hecking Realm of Time!

Son0fTeague: OMFG they actually did it!!!!

KleptoSkeptic: are you FUCKING kidding me???

KleptoSkeptic: That could be any walk-in closet in the world

Biggest_Ounce: Sharpie, we can't see shit

KleptoSkeptic: Harper said they wouldn't check the chat midstream. Now you know why lol

KleptoSkeptic: Sonny? Thoughts????

Son0fTeague: Give them a sec jesus

Son0fTeague: if it was fake theyd put a lot more work into make it convincing

Biggest_Ounce: Don't wanna take klepto's side EVER but I dumped my savings for this.

Biggest_Ounce: If it's really OP why didn't they start the stream outside

KleptoSkeptic: BECAUSE IT'S A HOAX.

KleptoSkeptic: Even if Omnipark WAS real it'd have been demoed forevs ago.

KleptoSkeptic: Thought that was canon even for you kool-aid drinkers.

Biggest_Ounce: jfc we're never gonna see Sharpie or our $ again are we

AI VOICEOVER:

Foreground — Blurry and dark as Harper crosses room.

Harper says: So I'm guessing right about now Klepto is talking maximum excrement and Ozzie is losing his. Y'all probably thinking this is just some janitor's closet since I didn't stream my entry. Tried, but some private security goons rumbled me soon as I cleared the last fence. Y'all didn't miss much — outside is mostly trashed. Abandoned amusement park that could be anywhere, nothing to prove we're really at OP... But in here, well, see for yourself.

Foreground — Quick-acting waterproof door set into rear wall comes into focus. Above wheel is OMNIPARK LOGO and large block text reading: IN CASE OF EMERGENCY KEEP TEMPORAL CLEANROOM SEALED

Harper says: Don't know if yinz can read that, so let's shine some light on this shiz.

Foreground — Glare obscures screen

Harper says: True facts, I'm not big into urban exploration videos. Other than my own, obvs. Y'all know from my previous vidjas I never considered myself an explorer until I started looking for OP... but once I started digging into the history, I knew I had to find it IRLs, 'cause there's something *real* special about this place. At least I hope there is. So let's find out.

Foreground — Brightly lit room comes into focus

SonOfTeague: Sharpie wouldn't con us no way

KleptoSkeptic: hey maybe they *are* reading the chat!

KleptoSkeptic: What's up grifter

Biggest_Ounce: WTH is that?

SonOfTeague: Submarine hatch?

KleptoSkeptic: This bish about to go down periscope with our apes

SonOfTeague: sTFU KLEPTO

Biggest_Ounce: yeah chill. maybe this isn't bukk

AI VOICEOVER:

[Audio — Switches being flipped; electrical humming]

Foreground — Tracking shot of bank of computer terminals built into wall on either side of watertight door. Monitors flicker as they turn on.

Dark porthole set into wall above computer monitors. Portable automobile jump starter sitting on floor next to computer terminals, wired to power outlet.

Harper says: Heck, we don't have much time. Wow. SuchWhat irony!. MuchWhat cringe.!

Foreground — Camera hovers over jump starter power display. Percentage of available power reads 94%... 93%... 92%... decreasing approximately one percent each second.

Harper says: Now I told you OmniPark doesn't look like much anymore. See for yourself.

Foreground — Camera blurs, refocuses on porthole. Through aperture, a narrow view of moonlit landscape with piles of debris, exposed rebar, rusted raised train trestle.

Harper says: But if my research is correct...

Foreground — Camera blurs, refocuses on computer screen as numbers appear: 08.31.2003.

Harper says: Then we can visit OmniPark the day *after* the park permanently closed without warning. All my research points to this being an extremely important date, but why?

[Audio: Keystrokes. Humming intensifies, then slows to a halt.]

Foreground — Harper's pupils dilate. Their mouth falls open. Camera blurs and then refocuses on porthole in wall, now brightly lit.

[Audio: Distant laughter, shouting, mechanical grinding, loud pops]

Foreground — Camera moves closer to the porthole. Through it, a thronged amusement park at night comes into focus, lit with sodium bulbs and punctuated with fireworks overhead. Camera zooms in on glowing waters of fountain.

KleptoSkeptic: Not bad. Glad to see you spent a little of our money on SFX

Biggest_Ounce: STFU

SonOfTeague: STFU

[Live Stream Continues on Next Page]

AI VOICEOVER:

Foreground — Camera focuses on a man standing on a raised dais in front of the fountain. Crowd of thousands of adults and children encircle him, holding hands.

Harper says: Is that him? Has to be... but if this is the day after the park closed, he should already be dead, and why are there so many—

Foreground — VISUAL TRANSCRIPT ERROR

[Audio: Screaming starts, drowning out all other exterior sound]

[Audio: Harper gasps]

Foreground — View blurs as Harper drops camera.

Son0fTeague: omff

Biggest_Ounce: no

KleptoSkeptic: haha holy shit ok!

KleptoSkeptic: damn Sharp you really went all out

Biggest_Ounce: no

Son0fTeague: Harper I dont like this

Son0fTeague: im gonn b sicj

Biggest_Ounce: no

KleptoSkeptic: can't believe you sprung for practical effects *and CGI, must've cost most of our crypto!

AI VOICEOVER:

[Audio: Screaming stops]

Foreground — Computer monitors flicker as camera is retrieved and directed at jump starter, which displays 18%.

Harper whispers: What did he do. What did he *do*?

[Audio: Weak groaning and cries from beyond porthole]

Foreground — Jump starter displays 17%.

Harper whispers: No. Wait. This didn't happen. It couldn't have. I wouldn't be here. I wouldn't be *anywhere*.

[Audio: Groaning and cries grow louder]

Foreground — Jump starter displays 16%.

Harper whispers: I shouldn't have come here. This was a mistake.

Foreground — Jump starter displays 15%.

Harper whispers: Maybe... did I change things?

Foreground — Jump starter displays 14%.

[AUDIO TRANSCRIPT ERROR]

Harper shrieks: Oh fuck it's coming!

[AUDIO TRANSCRIPT ERROR]

KleptoSkeptic: If I didn't have it on pretty good authority the world didn't end in 2003 I'd be convinced, bravo Sharpie!

Biggest_Ounce: no

KleptoSkeptic: some of my subtitles are shitting the bed, you guys make it out?

[SonOfTeague has left the chat]

Foreground — Jump starter displays 13%

[AUDIO: Harper takes deep breath, holds it]

Foreground — Camera view shakes. Jump starter trembles on the floor. Display reads 12%.

[AUDIO TRANSCRIPT ERROR]

Foreground — Jump starter and computer terminal vibrate wildly. Display reads 11%.

Harper shouts: Obvs! Fuck!

Foreground — Jump starter bounces on floor. Display reads 10%.

[Audio: Rapid keystrokes]

Harper shouts to be heard over [AUDIO TRANSCRIPT ERROR]: I was saving this as a surprise for my elite tier backers—

[AUDIO TRANSCRIPT ERROR]

Foreground — Jump starter bounces so hard it almost flies out of frame but is tethered by wires to the outlet; it lands face down.

Harper shouts to be heard over intensifying [AUDIO TRANSCRIPT ERROR]: — end of the stream, but not the end of everything!

Foreground — Jump starter stops bouncing and slowly rises into the air, hovering at the ends of its connecting wires.

Harper shouts: — Google drive! All my sources, the documents, everything! Again, *impossible* to forget URL, it's [AUDIO TRANSCRIPT ERROR]

KleptoSkeptic: oh come on really?

KleptoSkeptic: Tell me you got the drive address, BO

Biggest_Ounce: no

Foreground and background — Blurry motion as Harper picks up phone and runs to door.

[Audio: Humming stops]

Harper pants: Have to stop him! Have to try! Must've!

Foreground — View blurs as Harper holds phone in teeth for a close shot of sweaty hands turning wheel at center of watertight door.

[Audio: Harper grunts; metal groans]

Foreground — VISUAL TRANSCRIPT ERROR

[AUDIO TRANSCRIPT ERROR]

KleptoSkeptic: WHAT'S THE URL HARPER

KleptoSkeptic: Your gag only works if you give us whatever phony docs you uploaded

KleptoSkeptic: Harper

KleptoSkeptic: ...

KleptoSkeptic: You believe this shit, Ounce?

Biggest_Ounce: no

[Biggest_Ounce has left the chat]

KleptoSkeptic: I'm going to sue your fake ass all the way back to the Dark Ages, Harper Sharp.

[Live Stream Has Ended]

How I Spent My Summer Vacation
By Dennis Payne
Grade 5
Mrs. Hamrick

OmniPark is a theme park that opend in 1977. A man named Dalton M. Teague bilt it with his own mony. Thats what my dad keeps saying. "He bilt it with his own mony. Why spend that kind of mony bilding a theme park in the middle of no where?" Every summer since 1977 Ive asked my dad if we can go to OmniPark. In 1977 he said, "You bring your grades up next year and well talk about it." In 1978 he said, "We cant go when your Mothers sick, but as soon as she gets better well go to OmniPark to celebrate. I promise." Now its 1979 and Mom didnt get better. We had her funeral a couple weeks after school got out. So now theres nothing to celebrate. But dad took me to OmniPark anyway.

I like OmniPark because I like the idea of exploring. Thats their offical motto. "The univers is yours to explore." My favorite units in history are when we talk about the explorers, like Columbus and Majellan and Desoto. Those guys were so brave that they were willing to saile their ships off the edge of the map where everybody thoght there were sea monsters. I want to be brave like they were. But now everythings mappd out. Ever since Columbus discoverd that the Earth is round, none of the maps have monsters at the edges anymore.

At Omnipark at least you can go on a ride thats like a explorer journey. I mean youre not exploring the Luisianna territory like Desoto did, but youre exploring the Relm of the Cell. Or the Stars. Or Time. That was the Relm I wanted to go to the worst. I wanted to go back in Time to when mom was ok and stay there forever.

On the way to Omnipark I said, "Dad do you think Dalton M. Teague can send me back in Time?"

"Sure bud." He didnt even look at me when he said it. Thats what he does wen hes not lisening. "Sure bud." He does that to me all the time. Then after dinner he comes to my room and nocks on the door and says, "You now you can all ways talk to me if you want to." Wen he does that I say "Sure dad."

We got to Omnipark and it was great. Except it also wasnt. I mean it was great because I was finally there. I got to ride a real monoraile and it was like riding into the future. I got to walk threw the garden in front of the Inventors manson and look at all the statues looking at clocks and watches and hour glasses. I got to walk into the manson and look at all the mashines and books and everything.

And it also wasnt great because it was like none of it tasted good. Ever since Mom died that was how everything in life was. No flavor. Like the time she let me make a bowl of instant grits for breakfast. I didnt burn the house down or anything but it didnt taste good because I forgot the salt. That was how I lernd the word flavor less. And that was how everything in life was now. Including Omnipark.

In the manson Dad said "Hey bud. You want to go ride the Time Mashine?"

I said "I want to look around the librery first." He said okay and he went to the parlor to get a ice cream. I didnt really want to look around the librery. I just wanted a moment to myself. Thats what Mom used to say: "Would you like a moment to yourself Denny?" Like wen she could tell I was sad or mad or just wanted to be alone. I would say yeah and go to my room and shut the door so dad wouldnt bother me. I could stay there as long as I wanted and wen I came out again Mom would smile and kiss me on the head like everything was okay. And it was.

I walked up the stairs to the librery. There was like a million books in there. Adults were walking around looking at the books and the exibits in big glass jars. Little kids were running around like it was a playground.

Then a big deep gong went off all threw the mansion and a voice came over a speaker and said "The time has come to enter the Time Mashine." That was how you new the next ride was leaving soon. The librery cleared out and it was just me in there. I went over to a big globe standing in a corner by a closet door. I spinnd it around and wached the continents and oceans roll by and thoght about the explorers saileing all around the world and finding every piece of land their is. They walked all over every continent and discoverd all the natives and stuck their flags in the ground and clamed the land. And now its all done. And theres nothing left to do but go to school and watch TV. And wen you grow up you go to work every day. And have a flavor less life till you die too.

Then the closet door busted open and a person jumpd out real fast looking kind of crazy and scary like they migt have a "screw loose," like dad says about the bums at the bus station downtown. I couldnt tell if it was a he or a she but he/she was like my dads age. They scared the bejeepers out of me and I nocked the globe over onto the floor. I lookd around to see if anyone saw me do it but the library was still emty.

The crazy looking person said "Hey wait wait wait. Dont run away. Just tell me what year it is." They kept looking around like they were lost.

I said "Its 1979."

They said "1979. Christ. I wasnt even born yet." They reachd in their pants pocket and pulld out a flat rectangle thing and tappd on it with one finger a few times, and then held it up in front of their face and lookd at it. "I thoght so," they said. "Im at least forty five years old now. Jesus Christ."

I said "Are you the Inventor?"

They said "The Inventor. Your talking about the Relm of Time. Is that where we are?"

I said "Yeah. This is the library. Where did you come from?"

They looked around at the library and then at me and now they looked even scareder. They said "Hold on. Whats your name? Is your name Danny?"

I said "No it's Denny."

They said "Oh eff it's you." Exept they didnt say "eff." They said the other word that dad told me never to say. Mom used to say it sometimes when dad wasnt around, like if she droppd a plate or something. Then she would wink at me and say "Our secret." I would wink back at her to show I understood. That was how I lernd to wink.

"Oh eff, it's me!" they said this time. Then they laughd a sound like I never herd before. Not a funny laugh. It was like they had a screw loose and there mouth got confusd and made the wrong sound.

Then they got all serios and said "Look. Denny. Whatever you do dont go in that door." They pointed at the door they came out of.

I said "Why not?"

They said "Look kid. Do you like your life? Do you like living here? Your parents? Your home? Your school?"

I said "Not anymore. Not since Mom died. Everythings flavor less."

This time they said the s-word and rubbed there head with there hands and looked dad-tired.

"Right" they said "Of course. I'm sorry, Denny, I forgot."

"It's OK" I said because you have to be nice to crazy people.

"You now I tried looking you up before I found this place. To ask about the park but also just to say sorry. Like about your mom. And that coming hear wasnt good like you hopd it woud be. But I coudnt find you."

Dad came in and said "Hey bud. How about we go get in line for the next Time Tunnel ride?"

The person who came through the door winkd at me. I winkd back. Then they went back throgh the door and shut it behind them.

Dad said "Who was that? And what happend to that globe?"

The globe had crackd open where it hit the wooden floor. I said "That person did that when they came threw the door. I think they work here."

Me and dad walkd toward the Time Tunnel but I lookd over my shoulder one last time at the closet door and the globe where it crackd open and I decided I woud come back someday and go threw that door and see what was on the other side. Maybe Mom or maybe the weird person or maybe something else. Maybe something bad. I didnt care what I found as long as it wasnt flavor less.

Dear Mr. T,

The Traveler has just departed. Although I braced myself for the encounter by reading this letter top to bottom half-a-dozen times, the tremor you detect in my calligraphy proves that intellectual armor of foreknowledge may yet be pierced by human nerves.

It went like this: I entered the newly completed cleanroom — making sure to leave the door open behind me — to greet our very first guest. They were trembling on the floor, overcome, I expect, either by the reflection of their wizened face in the chrome door or the strain of operating the wheel to open it. In either event, time had not been kind to them.

Anticipating this delay, I had brought a stool with me. I settled in with my notebook and pen.

Them: It's really you.

Us: It's really me.

At this they twisted with some difficulty into a seated position on the floor, running a hand through their thinning hair.

Them: Mr. Teague. I come with a warning. A serious (coarse word) warning. About the park, about what happens if you keep it open.

Us: Do tell.

So they did, in great detail, though it took some time, for there were tears. You alone know what profound effect their words had on me, for their account is not spelled out in this letter, and each new revelation brought with it fresh rapture, culminating in the final revelation, the final validation of all our plans: I now know exactly what steps we must take at the end of it all, if we are to succeed.

Them: So that's why you have to close the park.

Us: *Before* August 31, 2003, you mean.

Them: Yes. And... I don't know if this is, like, bad form or whatever, but you... well, you die. Sir. Your heart. In 2001, two years before the park closes. But that's what I don't understand. When I set the cleanroom for the day after it closes, on August 31, 2003, you're there. You're in the middle of the crowd when the... but how?

They trailed off, lost not in time but that far vaster realm of possibility that you and I know by the name of interdimensionality.

Us: Well, maybe this visit is accomplishing what Evelyn cannot by inducing me to finally take better care of my old ticker. Maybe I eschew the steak tartare and resume my calisthenics routine and live to 104. Maybe—

Them: Excuse me, but if the park stays open, you don't live to 104. *Nobody* lives past August 31.

Us: So you say. But that's the problem with prophecies: you can't prove them until it's too late to prevent them.

Them: But you said you believed me.

Us: And I do.

Them: So you'll close the park? If you live past 2001, you'll still make sure the last day is the 30th?

Us: I will make no such pledge. You don't even know what you're asking. A lifetime of time travel and you don't understand a thing.

Them: I understand what a paradox is. And we're in one, Teague.

Us: Poppycock. You seem to think time is some great branching tree, and when you find yourself on a rotten limb, you attempt to climb down to where it meets the trunk, to prune it away before it can infect the whole.

Them: Are you saying that's not how time works?

Us: I'm saying time does not "work" at all. It simply exists, as part of the great unbroken and unbreakable whole of spacetime. That's why everything that has happened and will happen *must* happen.

Them: What makes you so sure?

Us: I have physical evidence. I use this lock box (I tapped my shoe against the chrome housing at the base of the console) to receive letters from my future self. In thirty-odd years, when I am an old man, I may remember that you and I had this conversation; but will I remember it accurately? Will I be able to transcribe it verbatim and place the letter in the cleanroom to warn the me-of-today? Of course not — better to preserve it in the moment. Hence these trusty writing tools, which I shall employ as soon as you depart.

Them: Well… but how do your letters get into the future?

Us: The old-fashioned way. I have a very sophisticated filing system.

Them: Why not use your fancy time machine?

Us: There are no machines; only ports of call. Some, like our little sanctuary here, are artificial, but most are as natural as black holes or quarks or anything else that existed long before we had a name for them… or a name for anything. When we still dwelled in caves, even then we knew there were thin places in the world that we'd best avoid. Steer clear of the deep dark wood on the winter solstice or be lost in the Seelie Court, where you spend but a night and return to find a hundred years have passed.

Them: So you're telling me what? OmniPark is built on top of a fairy ring?

Us: In a sense. You see, my father made a number of unwise investments many years ago and brought our family to the edge of ruin. Yet no matter how poor we became, he held onto this plot of land. One of his hired men tried to swindle him out of it early on, apparently, and in the ways of we obstinate Teagues, that convinced him this little spot on the globe was important, that he was meant to have it. And lo, time has proven him right, even if he didn't live to see it — or all the vast acres I've added to the family plot.

Them: Proven him right how?

Us: The unique properties of this building site amplify the cleanroom's function, which is to stand apart from the flow of time, not to move through it.

Them: So the cleanroom didn't bring me here.

Us: No, you brought yourself here. You chose to open the door because you weren't satisfied to merely gaze upon the past. You had to take that extra step, to physically feel new shores beneath your feet, no matter the risk. Am I warm?

That earned a wry smile of acknowledgment.

Them: So what's the (coarse word) *point* of it all? In my day we all thought Dalton M. Teague was the greatest explorer of the 20th century. But now you're telling me that even though you've figured out a way to travel through time, the only thing you use it for is to trade (coarse word) *love letters* with yourself.

Us: Oh, I've been tempted to do more than that; but it's far safer this way. I'm afraid your plight provides ample illustration of the dangers involved. Although I must say I admire your courage. It makes the denouement of our encounter all the more regrettable.

They tried to speak, but after a word or two it started coming out backwards.

Us: I do wish you hadn't forced our hand. When I left the door ajar behind me, I contaminated the cleanroom. Therefore, my train is now pulling forward, while you've already purchased a ticket headed in the other direction. Our time has come to an end. Disappointing, from a scientific perspective. But quite a relief from a practical one, as you would have certainly made an attempt upon my life once you realized you couldn't convince me to abandon my plan.

The wracked expression on their face seemed to indicate they still could hear me as they vanished completely. That, or falling backwards through time hurts terribly. Fortunately, we shall never find out.

Ours,

Dalton M. Teague

IX XI MCMLXXVI

Post scriptum — I almost forgot: The code for the cleanroom door is 08312003. In this case, PS stands for paradox side-stepped!

Henri Schlumberger
Prospecting Team Lead
Société de prospection électrique
Paris, France

November 19, 1927

Wilton Teague
President and Chairman of the Board
Teague Holding Company
803 Amundsen Street
Midland, Texas

Dear Mr. Teague,

We have completed the geophysical survey of the borehole you specified, located approximately 9.45 miles SW of Odessa, Texas, at 31° 48′ 21″ N latitude and 102° 26′ 43″ W longitude (see borehole survey in Appendix A). We conducted the survey by using our proprietary electrical resistivity technology--the first of its kind in the world. This involved lowering an electrical probe down the borehole and using it to send current through the surrounding rock formations. The electrical resisitivity encountered by the probe allowed us to determine the mineral composition of the formations below the surface with a much higher degree of certainty than is possible from examining core samples. We then used this information to determine whether extractable oil reserves are likely to be present at the site.

As you no doubt recall, I questioned your decision to perform an electrical coring test at this precise location. The physical core samples you took from nearby boreholes returned disappointing results, and I saw no reason to believe this location would prove any more rewarding. In reply, you stated that the impact of a meteor on the adjacent plot of land, where an impact crater is located, may have influenced the mineral substrate under the borehole parcel so as to make fossil fuels more accessible.

To test this theory, our geologist contacted local university faculty to learn more about the meteor. Professor S. H. Dillard of the Department of Geology at the University of Texas, Ector County, told him the crater was formed by meteor impact some 60,000 years ago. Since it was made it has filled in with so much dirt and vegetation that today it barely registers as a shallow bowl about 200 meters in diameter. Professor Dillard confirmed our geologist's surmise that any fossil fuels would be buried far too deep for the meteor's impact to have affected them.

Thus, I decided that before we lowered the probe into the borehole, the survey team and I would further evaluate the site to see if we had missed anything about the local geography, geology, hydrology--anything that might explain the survey site's appeal to you.

After we arrived at the borehole and began taking rock samples and scouting for water sources, a most unusual occurrence took place that I have already mentioned to you; this letter will now provide additional details. I hiked down into a small declivity, looking for signs of oil residue in the soil, when I heard a faint croaking that sounded like an animal. I listened more closely and followed the sound to a thick clump of creosote bushes. Behind the bushes I beheld the most singular vision I have ever seen: an emaciated corpse lying on the ground--a corpse that moved and spoke to me. "*Go away*," it said.

I immediately went to the person's side to render aid. So ancient it was, so gaunt and drawn by age and deprivation, clad in rags so tattered and rotten, I could not tell whether this pitiable creature was white or black, male or female. All I knew was that it was not yet a corpse, although such a fate was no doubt imminent.

I knelt down and assured the person I would help them. "What is your name?" I inquired. The sunken, lidless eyes searched my face for a full ten seconds before the croaking response came: *"I don't remember."*

I told the creature not to worry; we would help it. I sat back for a moment and began to think about how best to transport this individual to an infirmary in Odessa, but then it beckoned me closer with one knobbed claw-hand. I bent over it, and it drew a deep, trembling breath, as if preparing to speak. Then its hands flashed out with surprising speed and wrapped around my neck.

I tried to prise its talons from my throat, but the creature was possessed of an unnatural strength that resisted my efforts and cut off my breath. I was quite unable to call out for help. For a few moments I wondered if my end was nigh. During that small eternity, the corpse put its face close to mine and wheezed, *"Don't let Teague build it here! Anywhere but here!"*

These baffling statements might have been the last words I ever heard, but fortunately two members of my team heard the sounds of my struggle and came to my aid. Once I had been freed from its clutches, the creature let its arms fall to the ground and its head loll to one side, and it neither moved nor spoke again.

By the time one of our number returned from town with a police officer in tow (see police report in Appendix B), the corpse had become one in fact as well as in name (see coroner's report in Appendix C). For my own part, I wondered how this person knew you were the one having the site surveyed. As you've said, you understandably kept that information a secret, and I can assure you my team and I respect our clients' confidentiality to the utmost.

Despite this unusual turn of events, we had a job to do, and we proceeded to perform the electrical coring survey. In my professional opinion, the results of this survey indicate that fossil fuels are highly unlikely to be present in the borehole's vicinity (see electrical resistivity well log in Appendix D). Nor did our additional site survey discover any other attributes that would recommend it for oil exploration.

I recommend no further development at this site. To be frank, I would recommend you divest yourself of this property at the soonest opportunity. I am not a superstitious man and have all but convinced myself the "corpse" I encountered was a withered old prospector or sharecropper who felt a claim to this land, a claim your interest impugned upon... but even if that is all there is, desperate men are known to have desperate friends, and given the geological bankruptcy of the site, I see no utility in holding onto it.

From our previous discussions on the practicality of exploring this site in the first place, I understand you are not a man who appreciates being told what to do, even by the men you hire to do just that. But pray think a moment what vast expense you should have spared yourself if you had heeded my original counsel that this plot is barren of fuel? I know my business, sir, as you know yours, and it is my professional opinion that no good shall come of retaining a barren property where lurking revenants curse your name.

Sincerely,

[signature]
Henri Schlumberger

Hannah Miller

[1839-1925]

The flood of German immigrants into west Texas in the 1830s carried with it the origins of our next unfairly forgotten folk poet. Hannah Miller (born Müller) was the only known surviving child of Werner and Kathe, homesteaders who staked their claim outside what is now the city of Odessa. What little we know of Miller's hardscrabble life and her fantastic imagination is contained in a single untitled chapbook of revolutionary (for the time) free verse, discovered by the executors of her estate upon her passing. The editors are proud to print it here for the first time.

Went back out again
Every birthday since
Lifetime of doubt
But tonight
There you are
Lashed by saltgrass
Proving me sane
Breaking my heart
Crying like an animal
My angel of the prairie

You are radiant
You are unchanged
Untouched by years
Hairless, timeless, sexless
But oh how you wail
Banshee of Odessa

Am I dead

A younger girl would be afraid

Is this death

As I was once

Anything but this

A figure made of moonlight

No no please anything but this forever

But now I have grown too old to fear death
Even when I behold its very face

I call out to you

You see me

I see you

You see me

You smile the words
The birth of what became that old calm
That old beauty

I see you
More
I know you
We are old friends

Are you G_d?

To be asked such a question by an angel
But if I remember right
I asked you the same thing
A lifetime ago

I am Hannah
The scared girl you called by name
And told your mysteries to
A lifetime ago

A lifetime

You roll the word out
Chew it up
The fear within it not drained
But boiled clean
Simmering into excitement
Your draught of choice

When first we met
You said you would not remember
So you bid me write a letter
To bring back here when you returned
To daub the tears you knew you'd shed
On an old woman's birthday

Sixty years since I've made you smile
Worth the wait
Wise ghost of my youth
Scared spook of my croning
Now wise again
To see I have no letter
In my trembling hands

Lost
I admit
Somewhere along the life
And you laugh
As you said you might
And we sit
And I share what scraps
Have caught in the blackthorn

And you pretend to remember me
Just as I pretended to forget you
And in your frailty
The fear I soothe with assurances we have met before
I understand you are not the angel of death
I always took you to be

And then I start to lose you again
And your fear comes back
And so does mine
For I know what's coming

Long ago you warned me
If one day there is an Odessa here
Then someday there will be nothing anywhere
And the lights shining through your fading form
Are those of the town that bears that name

All my father took from your warning
Through a daughter's lips
Was a pretty name
To christen the fold
For his growing flock

But you and I know what becomes of sheep

And this time it is my turn
To comfort you as you go
Telling you how brave you were the first time I lost you
When you told me the explorer's heart is not guided by a map
But pulled by what may lie beyond its borders

So look for me again
Daubed on cave walls
Chiseled in mammoth's bone
And dragon's tooth
Until my warning is heard

Or I come back around
To try again

We turn away from Odessa
And I see new stars through your smile
Then you're gone

For now

Autographed copy of the "P is for Pterry" children's book sold in the Realm of Time circa 1991, when the long-running Time Tunnel attraction was replaced with a new ride narrated by a cartoon pterodactyl named Pterry, geared toward a younger demographic, and accompanied by a major merchandising push in the Realm's gift shop. It is rumored Teague begrudgingly endured the character.

And What I Saw There Saw Me

Jonathan Maberry

-1-

August 3, 2024

The professor knelt in a patch of shade, deep in the forests of Oregon's Blue Mountains.

The rain had faded to nothing overnight and now the sky was a faultless blue. Professor Collier disliked intense sunlight. The shade was cool and damp and soft. Birds sang in the trees, but there was a sleepy quality to it. It was the same with the deer she'd seen earlier. They moved slowly as if half in a dream.

She could understand that. This whole forest was like that and had been for a very long time. The air smelled different than in other forests. It was earthier, fecund, vital, but also with a slowness to it, as if time here realized that the manic energy of the cities was the aberration. Here things were not still, but the speed at which life unfolded was unhurried. The sea was like that, too. Glaciers as well.

"Same planet, different worlds," she murmured. The accuracy and poignancy of the old phrase made her smile.

She bent and placed a liver-spotted hand on the ground, and, for a very long time that's all she did. Her palm flat, eyes half closed — listening with senses other than her ears. Beneath that cool, musky ground *it* waited. Patient beyond anything people could relate to. Growing at its precise and measured pace as it had been for more than eight thousand years ago. When it was born — calving off of another of its species — it was the middle of the Holocene Age. Early tribal groups were making tools out of copper, having yet to discover the process of crafting bronze. Before Sumer, before the Akkadian Empire. Long before Egypt, Greece, Persia, and Rome. The thing that slept beneath the forest floor had lived, thrived, grown.

The professor smiled and whispered a single word. "Soon."

Around her the forest became suddenly very quiet.

Liz Collier smiled at that, too.

-2-

July 3, 1975

"Take a breath, Ms. Collier, and I will try to explain this again. No need to laugh or scream. And, please, don't throw anything else from my desk across the room."

Liz sat there, staring at the man. Dalton Teague. He was fit, middle-aged and looked like a kindly grandfather who had some interesting history. A broad smile below very clear, sharp eyes.

She cast a nervous glance around the Park Management office. The other three people there sat silently -- either shocked at her reaction or embarrassed on her behalf. Likely both. The glass ashtray she'd hurled lay in glittering pieces below the file cabinet, and the second from top drawer bore an astray-shaped dent.

One of the silent watchers was Evelyn Teague, Dalton's wife. She was gentle, affable, and agreeable.

On the other end of the couch was Luke Cho, a pilot. Of sorts. The nature of his job was tied to Liz's reaction. And Liz still didn't think she had overreacted. Not even a little.

The other person in the room was Professor Mitch Albertus, Liz's thesis advisor. His smile looked reptilian, as always. Every time Liz had made the trek to his office for a conference, she'd felt the urge to count her fingers afterward. Or take a bath. He was exactly as good-looking as he thought he was, and her academic and future professional career dangled on his whim. He was acutely aware of that, too.

Liz swallowed dryly, licked her lips, and said, "I'm sorry, Dr. Teague—"

"Dalton, please."

"I'm sorry, but you're talking about time travel."

Teague beamed. "Yes, we are. And that's why we asked you to sign those papers. Now you can understand why we *need* a nondisclosure agreement."

"Oh, I can certainly understand that," said Liz. "It's the only thing keeping me from calling an ambulance to take you in for a psych eval."

"Behave," said Evelyn. Still smiling, but not meaning it.

Liz turned to her. "Excuse me, Mrs. Teague, but nothing in that NDA requires that I believe any of this bullshit. And nothing requires me to be polite."

"Common courtesy?" Evelyn suggested, arching an eyebrow.

"Common courtesy when I'm the subject of either some kind of freaky practical joke or locked in a room with crazy people? I'm not sure that's in the good manners playbook."

"Okay, Liz," said Mitch, "let's dial it down. They're paying you to be here."

"And I haven't cashed the check," Liz snapped back. "They can have it. It's in my purse. I'm happy to give it back and then leave this place, because whatever is going on here is unfair, improper, and absurd."

"Unless," said Teague, "it's all true."

Liz gave him four seconds of her best ninja death stare. "True? Time travel? Sure. And what else is true? Magic? Teleportation?"

"Magic? No, my dear," he said. "Teleportation? Please don't throw anything else, but... we are literally working on that."

Liz got to her feet. "That's it. I'm out of here."

Mitch moved to stand between her and the door. "Sit down," he said. When she didn't, he took a breath. "Liz, *please* sit down. Hear them out."

"Mitch, are you actually *buying* any of this?"

"In point of fact," he said, "yes I am."

"How?" she barked.

His smile wavered only a little. "Because I've *been* there."

"Where?"

"The past," he said.

"Bullshit."

"Actually, no. And I can prove it."

"How? Some fake artifact? A phony dinosaur bone?"

"No, because you wouldn't believe that kind of thing," said Mitch. "And, though it might surprise you to hear it, I have too much respect for you to try any kind of hustle."

"Then how?"

"I have samples in my lab here that can't be faked," Mitch said, "But you'd need time, a dedicated lab space, and equipment to verify their authenticity. You'd need to do radiocarbon dating, DNA comparisons, and a bunch of other tests. That would take too long, and I doubt you'd believe it even then. So, the best and easiest way is to take you there. Cho and I."

Liz stared at him. "Take me where? To the past?"

"Yes."

"The *actual* past."

"Yes. And way, way back. A billion years, to the first appearance of fungi."

"And that just tells me you're messing with me, Mitch," she fired back. "The oldest known fungi have only been dated to five hundred million years."

Mitch's smile changed, becoming both more excited and a bit warmer, more human. "That's exactly the kind of thing that will convince you, Liz. We've found, with no chance of uncertainty, that fungi — let's call them ur-fungi — developed at least a billion years ago. I collected samples of *ourasphaira giraldae*, a process-bearing multicellular eukaryotic microorganism. I harvested it by my own hand a billion years ago in the era where the Mesoproterozoic transitioned into the Neoproterozoic. Liz, listen to me... this fungus may have existed before plants! That's earthshaking. It's Nobel Prize and it's the two of us made for life. It's everything we got into science to discover."

"And you want me to believe that," said Liz. "You want me to accept that as truth and not out you for participating in a hoax?"

"Miss Collier," said Evelyn Teague, "that check in your purse is for fifty thousand dollars. Why don't you go cash it? And once you have the cash in hand, come back and tell me why we would give you so much money just to play a trick on you."

Everyone looked at her.

Liz said, "Jesus Christ."

-3-

July 22, 1975

Liz Collier stood with Mitch Albertus and Luke Cho in a machine shop. Set on rails in front of them was a vehicle approximately the size and shape of a Volkswagen minibus. On the front right fender was its name.

The Chariot

Mitch had explained that Cho picked the name because he'd been a huge fan of the TV show *Lost in Space*. There were six seats inside, though only three of them were going on this trip. Liz licked her dry lips as they approached. Over the last two weeks Liz had gone through more than three dozen simulations, ranging from what Cho called 'rock'n'roll' trials, where a version of the chariot was on steel beams that literally rocked it in all directions, to milder trials that allowed Mitch and Liz to learn how to operate it.

The Teagues had explained everything about OmniPark, and gradually Liz had come to accept that their wild claims were not only real, but greatly understated. Parts of her mind felt numb, and more than once Liz wondered if she had been hit by a car or had some kind of neurological accident and this was all a dream.

The test run for her — which was Cho's thirty-first trip and Mitch's fifth — was scheduled for the next day.

Liz looked at the Chariot and shook her head.

"Now what's wrong?" asked Mitch.

She flapped an arm at the machine. "Even if this thing works, why has anyone risked using it? You of all people should see the inherent dangers, Mitch. I need to understand why you're good with all this."

"Because I believe in what the Teagues are doing. What they *want* to do."

Liz snorted. "What? Sell tickets so people can time travel?"

"That, sure," he said. "But I'm talking about observing the literal process of evolution from its beginnings. And, of course, collecting samples."

"Right," she snapped, stabbing a finger in his direction. "*That's* my point. How can you risk it?"

Mitch sighed. "There's nothing to worry about."

"How can you even say that?" gasped Liz. "If we were to take a plant, or fungus, or — god help us — a more complex life form, then how can we be sure that there wouldn't be a cascading crisis of cause and effect?"

"Because the Teagues have already thought that through."

"Oh sure, you mean the Ray Bradbury speech."

"Well... yes."

She rolled her eyes. "Jesus, Mitch, you have your issues, but I never before thought of you as naïve."

In one of their first staff meetings, Teague had told them a key part of the OmniPark protocols for time travel was inspired by a short story by Bradbury. That story, "*A Sound of Thunder,*" dealt with a similar model, where tourists were taken back in time and were forbidden to take any kind of sample of something alive — insect, tree, dinosaur — unless it fell within a volcano's known path of destruction. The argument being that those creatures could not play any meaningful part in evolutionary history because they would die within minutes of the time team's visit.

He also said that in other Realms at OmniPark, where robots were given a degree of self-guidance with a new form of artificial intelligence, some of the behavioral software in place was directly inspired by Isaac Asimov's *Three Laws of Robotics.*

"You're risking all of human history on a couple of short stories?" growled Liz.

"No, I'm saying that those stories — written by visionary writers — were based on a reasonable insight into cause and effect. Teague and the Technosophers working on the Time Tunneler technology spent as much time working out the do's and don'ts as they did designing the tech. The last thing the Teagues need is to build an educational theme park that destroys humanity. Bad for business. It's why they use animatronic invertebrates here rather than bring back live specimens. Last thing anybody would want is a *real* giant dragonfly chomping on the guests."

"I know that last part was a joke, Mitch," said Liz, "but it's not funny."

Mitch bridled. "Well, maybe consider the benefits, because timidity isn't going to get you that Ph.D. You know as well as I do that research on human fungal pathogens has historically taken a backseat to that on other infectious diseases. And that's due to the persistent misperception that fungi mainly cause superficial infections. You, of course, know better."

"But—"

"No, listen for a change," he snapped. "We live and die on grants. Lately, with the economy the way it is, we're seeing smaller grants and shorter timetables. The country has barely recovered from the oil crisis and we're still *in* a recession. Instead of encouraging pure research, the grant committees have strongly hinted that results — workable results — are what they're really looking for. Why? Because more and more of our grant money comes from corporations who are using the grant process to shortcut their research. That's a fact of life, Liz, and it's not going to change. Expanding into new areas of research and development is the wave of the future. This is 1975 and the Teagues plan to open the park gates in two years. By then they need to prove the model's efficacy, and we are part of that process."

"What are you saying? That we forget the purity of academic research in favor of corporate needs?"

"God, talk about being naïve," he said. "Yes. That's exactly what I'm saying. We do that so that *we* are fully funded. So that *we* can use that funding to go farther, dig deeper, learn more, and bring results to market sooner than we could ever hope to do in the university setting."

"Are you really that greedy?"

For a moment Mitch Albertus looked genuinely surprised and visibly hurt. "You think this is greed? Good god, Liz, this is us being given what amounts to a blank check to do the kind of research we've always dreamed of. And, in doing it at this accelerated rate, and with the access that time tunnel technology allows, we can go to the very source of the development of disease forms. The original bacteria, viruses, and fungi that evolved into the diseases that plague humanity or attack crops. We can harvest the purest disease forms and from that build entirely new classes of treatments. Instead of treating symptoms, Liz, we can start seriously thinking about eliminating diseases entirely."

Liz looked down into her coffee cup for a moment. "That sounds great, Mitch. Not joking. But at what cost? What if there's a mistake? I *read* Bradbury's story — and in case you didn't, it did not end well. You can have the best protocols and the best intentions, but then there's human error — and that's its own kind of force of nature."

Cho seemed to find something suddenly fascinating on the fender of the Chariot and used a sleeve-cuff to polish it away.

Mitch looked hard at Liz. "You can stand here in your disapproval and timidity," he said quietly. "Or you can look at the bigger picture and embrace the truth that the benefits outweigh the risks by several orders of magnitude." He shook his head. "I'm going to the crew room to begin prepping for the trip. Maybe I'll see a brilliant, fearless, visionary scientist there. Or maybe there isn't one around who has the nerve to join me. I wonder which it will be."

With that he turned and walked away.

Liz watched him go. His erect posture, stiff back, fists balled with frustration at his sides.

"You officious prick," she muttered.

Five minutes later she exhaled slowly and deeply and followed.

-4-

July 24, 1975

Liz had heard everything about the trip through the Time Tunnel. She knew the details, understood the physical stresses, grasped the disorientation. What she did not expect was... nothing.

Cho removed the special platinum starter key from where it was looped around his neck on a chain, slid it into the slot, fired up the Chariot, told Liz and Mitch to hang on, dialed up the power and...

...and they were there.

The whole process took almost no time.

Which, only in retrospect, made sense.

-5-
1,006,918,487 Years B.C.E.

It took a very long time for her to want to leave the Chariot.

Some of that time was spent staring at the vehicle's chronometer.

Some of it was spent hyperventilating.

Some of it passed as she looked out of each of the Chariot's big windows at the world. At this version of the world.

Her mouth formed words, but her lungs forgot how to give them voice.

Finally, Mitch touched her shoulder with surprising gentleness. "Yeah," he said. "I know."

Cho looped the starter key around his neck and handed Liz her helmet.

"Make sure it's snug and sealed," he cautioned. "Atmospheric science is more my field than yours. Stop me if I'm telling you something you already know. Short version is that life evolved along with Earth's atmosphere. It took a lot of time for tiny photosynthetic organisms to produce enough oxygen to react with the methane in the atmosphere to transform it into a more permanent state. So, about a billion years further back than we are now, that methane haze cleared and the sky turned blue."

Liz, dazed, looked up and saw that the sky was, indeed, blue. A rather odd shade of it, though. Nearly indigo.

"Since then," continued Cho, "photosynthetic bacteria—"

"We get it," said Mitch, cutting him off.

They got out of the Chariot and stood in an area defined by a pool of light created by a continuous row of bulbs around the roof of the machine. All through the training, Cho had insisted that they did not step even an inch beyond that clearly-defined circle of illumination. It was their safe zone, and Cho nicknamed it the Sundial. A small meteor would hit that spot in less than fifteen hours.

Liz, feeling a bit like she was in a trance, murmured, "Look at all the life..."

Cho and Mitch exchanged knowing smiles. Each of them had experienced a moment like this. Each of them had been dumbstruck. Each had been terrified. Each had wept. Each had come to an understanding of what awe truly meant. Liz knew this about them, and had thought, until now, that they had been exaggerating — telling tall tales to ignite her enthusiasm.

Now, though, she knew they had each understated things. She felt herself trembling and forced herself to remain calm. She took several steadying calming breaths. She kept raising one hand to touch the visor of her helmet, and each time seemed surprised to encounter plastic, metal, and glass.

"I don't…," she said. "I can't…"

"Yeah," said Mitch. "I know."

There was a bright light off to the east and they turned to watch several shooting stars scrape fire across the dome of the sky. Five of them. Four disintegrated entirely. One, the largest of them, punched down through the resistance of atmosphere and slammed into the side of a volcano like the fist of God. Part of the upper cone blew apart, sending chunks of half-melted rock whipping across the troubled sky. Glowing lava spewed from the fractured rim, raining down on the landscape and setting countless fires. Within seconds the majesty of the volcano was redrawn into an image of hell itself. Massive pillars of burning ash spiraled upward like the hands of Lucifer reaching in vain for forgiveness from an angry God.

Liz's heart pounded on the inner walls of her chest and she cried out softly. "Jesus…"

"Don't worry," said Cho, then he nodded to where the meteor had struck. "That one was Big Red. The damage it does to that volcano will be catastrophic, but we'll be long gone by then. Actually, Wile E. Coyote — the one that will impact where we're parked — is about five times bigger. Later there'll be another medium-sized one, Roadrunner, which will hit way over there to the southeast. When we see that one strikes, then it's our cue to head back home."

Liz turned and gazed at him, blinking slowly. "You really *have* been here before."

"Yes, ma'am. And the first time I saw all this I was feeling what you are right now. Stunned. The word 'awed' really doesn't cover it. Not sure any words from our vocabulary could, because this wasn't really meant for us to see. We're in the forge that nature used to smelt and forge our world."

"It's humbling," said Mitch quietly. Liz cut a look at him. His usual haughty sneer was gone, replaced by an almost innocent wonder. But also a kind of sadness that she could not quite define. Maybe it was that coming here had shifted his own life and attitudes into a different perspective. She wondered how many trips of this kind it would take before the humility he felt here infused every part of his life back in their present. Liz knew for sure that she would never be the same after this.

Never. How could she? How could anyone, really?

"I know just about every rock and pool in this whole area. Or, at least, everything that I can see from the Sundial."

Liz seemed to snap out of her trance. "You never strayed beyond the Sundial?"

"Me? Oh, hell no," laughed Cho. "Two reasons. One, we sent sensors back first and that's how we found this spot where the meteor hits. Second... this place is awesome but it's also scary as hell."

"Scary?"

"Yeah. Stop for a second, turn your helmet speaker up, close your eyes, and just listen for a minute or two."

"Why?"

"Just try it," said Cho.

She did, and gradually her relaxing senses were able to edit out the sound of her own breathing so she could hear what the world sounded like.

She expected it to be incredibly quiet. And it was. For a few seconds.

Then she heard the sounds.

Strange noises.

Not the hiss of gas from volcanic vents. Not the whistle of wind as it moved across a landscape made of shattered rock. She tuned that out, too.

What she heard was a deep, low, wavering noise. It was not stationary, which made no sense since everything here was so still. But that howl — for that's what it sounded like to her — had a plaintive quality to it. Melancholy, lost, and in unended despair. Liz thought that it was more like the kind of cry the very last creature would make at the other end of time. It was the loneliest sound she had ever heard. It called to mind a fragment of a song lyric. A Simon and Garfunkel song from a few years back — *El Candor Pasa*. She could not pull the exact line from her memory, but it was about a man tied to the ground giving to the world, in his despair, the saddest sound.

This was that. The saddest sound she would ever hear.

That thought turned her heart cold and it seemed to crumble beneath the weight of aloneness so deep, so complete and profound, that it was inexpressible in any language that would ever be. It was not even the kind of sound a lonesome animal might hurl at the empty air.

But at the same time...

There was something vital about it — alive in a way that did not ignite empathy. The sound was needful, angry, covetous, as if it knew in full measure what it needed but was driven close to madness because satisfaction was beyond its reach.

That insight changed the nature of what she heard, twisting it away from sadness to a kind of mournful rage. Almost anticipatory rage, which was a concept she had never before even considered.

She opened her eyes and walked a few paces to the edge of a slimy pool whose nearest bank was inside the Sundial's circumference. Liz knelt, with her gloved hands palm down on the moist dirt.

"I think it's coming from here," she said.

"What?" asked Cho sharply.

"Are you sure?" whispered Mitch.

Liz beckoned. "Come over here and listen."

They did, kneeling on either side of her. Cho sat back on his heels, clearly not wanting to get too close to the pool. Mitch leaned closer, eyes narrowing in concentration.

"I can hear it," he said. "It's..."

He left it unfinished.

"Where's it coming from?" asked Liz.

"I... I think it's coming from the pool," said Cho.

Mitch leaned even closer. Liz noticed a yellow-gray scum on the surface, covering most of the pool. Slow bubbles rose around its edges and popped softly.

"Liz," Mitch said with a tremor in his voice, "are you seeing this? Do you know what it is?"

She had to wrest her attention away from the howl. She studied the surface scum for a minute and then grunted. "It looks like... fungus."

"It does," said Mitch, peering at it. "And it shouldn't. This is the main reason I wanted to bring you here, Liz. This is your field. I want you to identify exactly what it is, because this could change so much about what we know — or thought we knew — about this branch of evolution."

Liz took a half step forward. That pool and that strange patch did more than intrigue her — it seemed to call to her as if it needed her — specifically her — to see it, to understand it. To *know* it.

On any other day, in any other place, those thoughts and feelings would have been silly, laughable, absurd. But not here. Nothing here could be ignored. No, she thought, correcting herself, nothing here could be *allowed* to be ignored. Science demanded it. Truth demanded it. And, on some level she could not yet begin to understand, that patch of... of whatever it was... demanded it.

"But we're too early for fungus," said Cho, breaking into her thoughts. "Right?"

Liz turned and looked at him. "If it is, then we will need to go farther back. This is already going to change so much, but we can't allow assumptions to guide us. We have to *know*. Which means we have to go back more and find out."

"We can't," said Mitch, and he looked like saying those words caused him actual physical pain.

"You don't understand," said Cho. "I brought you this far back because the Chariot doesn't seem to like going farther back."

Liz stared at him. "The Chariot doesn't *like* it? What does that even mean?"

Cho shook his head. "I don't understand it, and the team back home can't figure it out. No matter how we fiddle with the chronomatic drive, the Time Tunnel takes us here. It's like this damn spot is pulling us. And, no, don't look at me like that. I haven't lost my mind. I'm just telling you how it feels. Every trip to the deep past brings us right here."

"He's right, Liz," agreed Mitch. "Always here." He looked at that patch on the pond and repeated it in a soft, distant voice, "Always here."

Cho looked deeply uncomfortable and he gave Liz a weak, conciliatory smile. "Even so... I figured you could take some samples, and then we'd move up to 635 million years, which is where the first fungi were *supposed* to present. And then to 260 million years, where they were, according to Mitch, the dominant life form. So... I'm pretty sure you're wrong. Can't be fungi."

He produced a sample vial from a pocket.

"C'mon, let's take some samples and get out of here. This time zone really gives me the creeps."

He bent forward to dip the very edge of the vial in the pool a few inches away from the scum.

"We need to take samples of that, too," said Liz. "I think Mitch is right. That's some kind of fungus."

Mitch turned to her. "Look, guys, there's not a chance that it's—"

"Watch out!" cried Liz.

And the fungal scum suddenly leapt from the surface of the water and wrapped itself around his hand.

Cho panicked and flung himself backward. His scrabbling feet slid on the muddy bank and before Liz and Mitch could grab him, he fell into the water.

"Grab his arm," yelled Mitch. "For Christ's sake, Liz, grab his arm."

She hesitated for a terrible moment because the only part of him she could reach was the arm with the fungus wrapped around the glove. Cho uttered a high-pitched whistling shriek of terror. He thrashed in the murky water, beating and kicking, showering Mitch and Liz. Mitch jerked backward, slapping the water from his suit. Liz kept trying to reach Cho, but the greasy water covered her visor, turning the whole scene into a hazy nightmare. She pawed at it, but that only made it worse, reducing everything around her to shadow shapes that capered like goblins.

"For fuck's sake, man, we're trying to help you," growled Mitch, but there was a sharp note of panic in his voice.

Liz pulled on Cho's arm, but he was bigger and heavier than her and the bank was as slippery as oil. The speakers in her helmet were still turned up and so everything was too loud, too intense, too much. And yet with all of that, the howl continued. However, the pitch was sharper, higher.

Hungrier.

That word flashed into Liz's mind and it nearly made her let go.

"No, no, no," she said, speaking the denial to everything — the noise, the panic, Cho's terror, Mitch's flailing as he sought to brace himself to pull, and the bizarre aggression of the fungus.

Cho was half-submerged now and the patch of scum seemed to ripple of its own accord as it covered more and more of the man. It was all over his back, both arms, his chest.

"It's fighting us," cried Liz.

"That's impossible…," growled Mitch, but there was no force behind his words. The scum *was* fighting them. Or, at least, it was fighting to pull Cho down. That made no sense to Liz. How could anything have this level of aggression when there were no predators or prey in any conventional sense in an environment like this. It was impossible.

And yet the fungus pulled at Cho.

Suddenly a tendril of it, thick as Liz's wrist, whipped out of the water and slapped wetly across the visor of Cho's helmet. He saw it and his eyes bulged with new terror. Cracks appeared in the reinforced glass. They whipsawed across the face of it and they saw droplets of that greasy water splash on Cho's face. On his cheeks, his brow, his nose. And across his eyes.

"Pull him out," shrieked Liz. "Christ, Mitch, *he has the key.*"

And there it was. From her own lips, there it was. In the fragment of a moment from when Cho's visor began to crack, she knew. He was lost. Even if he survived this, even if they got him out, he was contaminated. They could never risk bringing him to the Chariot, let alone back to OmniPark. But the key…

The key.

That was what mattered now.

The comet would crash down and sanitize the area in hours. It would kill this strange fungus. It would incinerate Cho.

And if they did not get the key, it would kill them both.

It took Mitch about three full seconds to understand what she was saying, and what it meant. He looked at her. For another fragment of a second they just looked into one another's eyes. Sharing horror. Sharing grief. Sharing awareness of what they had to do.

On some level, even as he fought and screamed and wept, Cho understood, too.

He used his other hand to fumble at the chain. His pleading eyes were locked on Liz's as she reached to take the chain from him.

"I'm sorry," she said, her voice breaking as she reached for it, closed her gloved fingers around the chain. His body jerked sideways as she pulled it and for a moment her sleeve was caught on a jagged edge of his visor, but Mitch grabbed her arm and pulled her free.

And then the fungus tore Cho from their grip and dragged him down into the depths of the pond.

Liz fell back onto the bank and began kicking at the mud until her heel hit something firm. A rock. She used that to shove herself away from the pool. Mitch rolled over onto hands and knees and crawled like a sick dog.

They staggered to their feet and stumbled toward the Chariot as, behind them, the pool thrashed and boiled.

At the back of the Chariot they paused. Mitch fumbled with a lever and a high-pressure hose drooped out of its slot. He yanked several yards of it out, turned on the nozzle, and blasted Liz with it. Then himself. Repeatedly.

He let the hose drop and unceremoniously snatched the key from her hand, nearly tearing off her glove. They hurried to open the Chariot and scramble in. Mitch crawled into the pilot's chair and jammed the key into the ignition. He cranked it hard and the motors roared to life, drowning out even the howl that still filled the air.

"In five," he said. "Hold on."

As the temporal engines engaged, Liz looked out of the side window at the pool. The surface seemed to bulge oddly and then something broke through the scummy film. It looked like Cho.

But the visor was shattered and inside the helmet there was nothing but a roiling darkness. She glimpsed it for an instant and then the Chariot was gone.

She half turned to Mitch, to ask him if he'd seen it, too. But that question died on her tongue. Instead, she folded into the silence of shock.

-6-

July 24, 1975

They returned to the present.

Dalton and Evelyn Teague were there, waiting for them. Dalton's eyes were as bright and alert as a falcon's, his face filled with anticipation of new discoveries. Evelyn beamed with happiness at their return.

When the Chariot fully materialized, their smiles began to crack and fall away. They looked past Mitch and Liz. Looking for Cho.

Looking.

Not finding.

-7-

August 3, 2024

It was all a very long time ago.

The Teagues were as past-tense as OmniPark. It had opened, thrived, stalled, and died. Liz had gone back to the university with Mitch and gotten her Ph.D. She married Mitch, surprising everyone.

He had never recovered from that trip. He lived for only two years after they returned, then a rare form of cancer began eating him alive. Liz was at his bedside when the wasted thing that had been her mentor, her advisor, her adversary, and then her husband, faded. He was barely ninety pounds.

The doctors never could properly diagnose the cause. Cancer, they told her, seemed to be more of a symptom than the cause. And that was its own mystery. There was also some kind of fungal infection that none of them could identify.

Liz never told them about the pool. Once OmniPark shut down, she never mentioned that, either. As for the Realm of Life... its nature was changed to modern dioramas and animatronics. None of the tourists rode the Chariot back. In other Realms, yes. Not in that one.

When things went bad for the Teagues and the park was shut down, Liz was fine with moving on. She had other things to draw her focus, to fill her heart and mind.

Liz wrote extensively about fungi. She taught about them. Then she retired to a small cabin on the edge of the Malheur National Forest in Oregon and did her research in private, in solitude.

In 1992, a biologist she knew, James Anderson — along with two colleagues — made a discovery of a species of the fungus *armillaria bulbosa*, in a hardwood forest in northern Michigan. It was massive, covering 37 acres. The "humongous fungus" it was called in the press. That triggered a global search for other examples of that newly discovered species. The search inevitably led to the largest one of all, in the Reynolds Creek and Clear Creek, east of Prairie City. It was much, much bigger, covering nearly four miles.

Liz had come out of retirement to lobby on behalf of the fungus, and finally winning court cases to leave it untouched. After all, it was the oldest known species alive on Earth. After the influx of tourists came, saw, became bored with it, and left,

Liz resumed her retirement. She returned to the research she had been doing ever since returning from the distant past.

Now, she knelt deep within the thing. The day was fine and there was almost no wind, nothing to rustle the leaves. Even the birds had fallen still, as they often did when she came out there.

Liz removed her gloves and pressed her palms against the soft, springy ground. With the air so still, she could hear the sound that had come to soothe her. To speak to her.

It was nearly an hour before the mossy dirt between her splayed thumb and index finger trembled and then parted. A tendril, thick as her wrist, rose from the ground. It probed her fingers and then her wrist, pausing where an old scar was still visible, even after nearly fifty years.

"It's okay," she said.

A tendril changed its shape very subtly and a smaller length of it extended out and brushed that scar. Licking it. Licking her.

"Soon," she said, as she looked up into the sky. A plane was moving slowly across the blue. "Very soon."

In the stillness of the forest, Liz Collier raised her head and began to sing.

If anyone had been there, the song would have sounded very strange. Like a cry. Plaintive and hungry.

Like a howl.

She smiled.

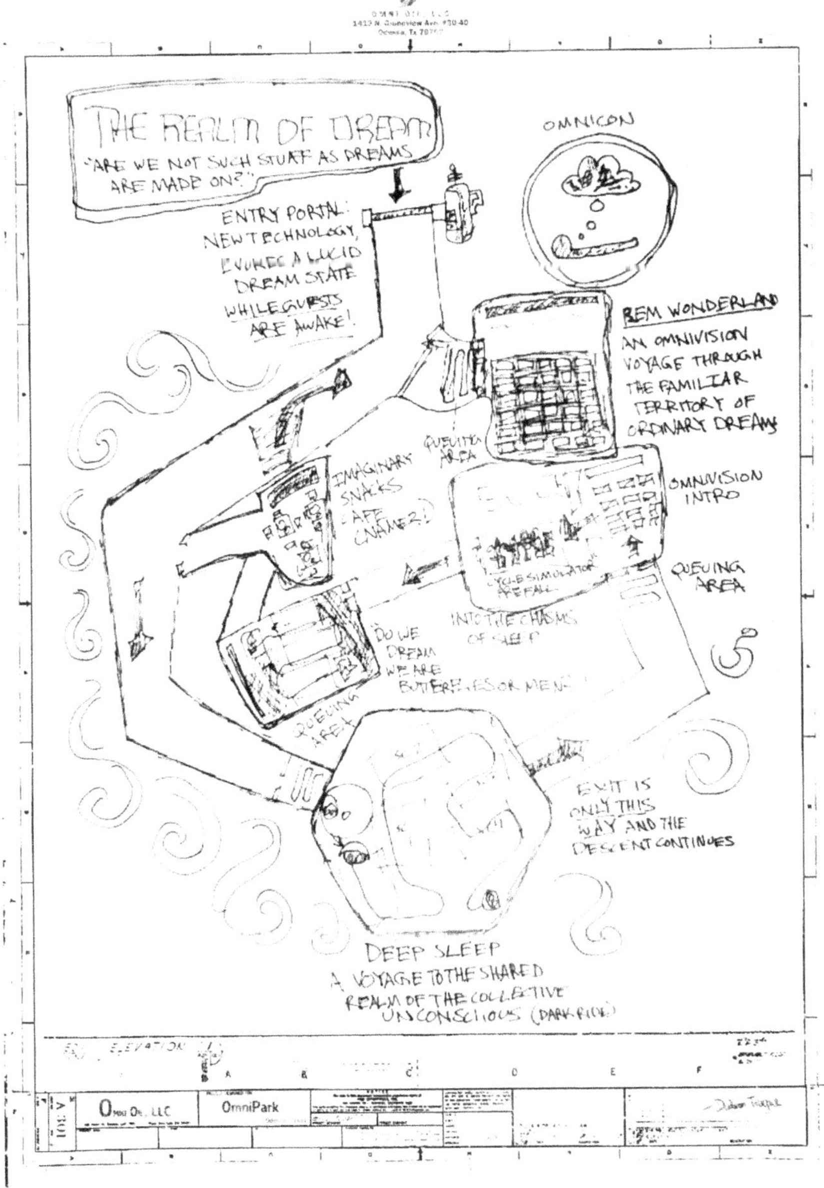

Elijah Shattuck's initial design sketch for a proposed Realm of Dream (pre-1974). The date of this sketch remains in dispute, due to the fact that it was drawn on the stationery of Omni Oil, Dalton Teague's petroleum firm, from which Teague retired in 1967 — seven years before the founding of OmniPark. This may indicate that Teague and Shattuck shared an unknown prior relationship, and began planning OmniPark much earlier than is generally accepted. Another possibility is that this document is simply a hoax.

Letters from Evelyn

Ben Thomas

In my dream, Dalton, I meet you in a garden scented with green sage and evening primrose, an improbable palm tree at its center. Small tangled oaks dance in the background. I sing you the words you already know by heart, lending perhaps a strangeness to their intonation from my locus of being. I sing to you of the ways we'd broken faith with the call we carried back to Odessa that October, so long ago. What do these accusations mean to you, I wonder? Will they remain once waking consciousness floods in after this dream ends? If I howl and bay against the chasm dividing us, my being's spent rage will fade to a wisp of a memory when our work here is done. And so I am reconciled to the fact that our time together will never mean more to you than the fading dream-memory it is.

November 6, 2001

I tear the red tape with trembling hands, ripping the envelope asunder, shaking rain from my umbrella and plastic poncho sleeves. Like you always said, it rains in Odessa for one week a year, and that week is keen to make up for lost time.

I had to tire-spin through pale muck to reach your old office at the Entryway Pavilion, my dear. You'd be proud of my facility with the gear-shift, even with these arthritic hands.

My chances of getting clear of this place before tomorrow are slim, so I poured myself two fingers of bourbon from the liquor caddy you kept for guests but rarely touched yourself. Why did you keep that thing? I wonder. Good memories, I guess, of those late-lunch meetings when we closed the contracts that paid for this park, thrilled as newlyweds buying a home. Which in a way is just what we were.

On your desk I find the banker's box right where Morrie said it'd be. I reach in and extract the first sheaf of pages my fingers brush: a collection of poems to your park. Our park. The first is a sonnet; a eulogy for the one Realm we never built. It reminds me there are sanctums to which even I, your own Evelyn, was never admitted.

Tears rise as I scan your tight-packed lines:

> Oh! and where will moonbeams gleam?
> Where in all the Realms of wake
> May we hang pennants
> 'bout the Realm of Dream?
> Where Science finds no anchorage;
> Psychology, neurology, satori—
> None has yet managed to cage
> Our cryptic and most all-elusive quarry:
> The upside-down awareness of each night
> When light's shut out and selves in dark take flight...
> Where among the Seven are you sought—
> Dream, whose very substance prismates thought?

The Realm of Dream: that puzzle piece that just wouldn't fit.

How many times did we sit on these gray art-deco couches in this skylit office, listening with practiced patience as our Technosophers deployed well-intentioned arguments for "The Realm of the Robots" or "The Realm of Woman?" One after another, you dismissed them with imperturbable courtesy: "Well, I'll give it some thought." And that would be the end of it.

You gave no reason because none dared ask it of you. Because this place was yours; ours — we who'd pumped a sultan's ransom from beneath that West-Texas caliche, trekked beyond the map's edge for seven years, and returned even richer than we'd left: a fairytale real enough to make the society pages.

Most people would've stopped there; cashed out and thanked the Lord for His abundance. Not you. Never you. With muscles still sore from Tibet and Tenochtitlan you hunched behind that drafting desk, ink-stained hands leaping across hand-drawn maps of the place that was to be. Till sunrise we'd sit curled on the balcony couch, talking of seven Realms in which the universe would lay bare her evanescent symmetry: Life. Cells. The sea. The stars. Humankind. The particle. Spacetime. Completeness in a perfect seven, that most holy of numbers.

How I loved your design, little as I understood it then.

How did we know it was time to assemble the Technosophers? Or did they come to you because they knew it was time to begin our great Work? Even wildcards like Shattuck and Egger fit as crucially into the equation as any widely divergent variables. Our thing could never have balanced without them.

That was the whole problem with the idea of adding onto the park, of course: the design was too structurally complete. The Seven Realms had come together as easily as falling asleep. Did you know rumor still holds that you made some pompous speech at that stakeholders' meeting in '74? On websites they say you spoke of gematria, invoking the cryptic significance of the number seven.

Bullshit. I sat right next to you, and remember your words by heart:

"Each of our Realms is necessary in its own way: each a frontier where we've peeled back the curtain just a little; used the tiniest bit of showmanship to remind our guests that it's all real. Every particle, every cell and fossil and star lays claim to its station in spacetime as surely as you or I do. It's all *really here*, do you see?"

I wonder now if, even as we nodded in agreement, any of us fully grasped your meaning. We'd devoted each of the Seven Realms to an aspect of the physical world that was — in your words—"*really there*." And what did that leave us to do with dreams, whose reality is undeniable, yet which are not *there* in the same sense neutrons and trilobites and planets are?

November 7, 2001

I woke on the couch in your office this morning, from a dream I remember only in fragments: standing beside you at the groundbreaking — then on opening day as a meager trickle of guests wandered in confusion.

"They don't understand, Evie." I remember your jaw was trembling. "They don't see what we've built for them."

Do you remember my hand pressed firm against your back? "Then we'll make them understand," I told you then. And we tried.

A year later we were hosting sheikhs and princesses in the Realm Between the Realms. All things seemed possible to me then, in the firework glow amid champagne foam and flying corks and smiles gleaming as the sequins on our evening gowns. We stayed late and rose early, meeting with Bachmeier and Olivetti and the rest to plot journeys to time's end, or beyond the edge of space.

Yet where we saw *infinity*, you looked *further* and saw a horizon we could not cross. The Realm of Dream remained, resilient in your mind's wanderings, in the soft humming moments at the ends of our days.

"There are places we cannot go, Evie," I remember you saying to me that October midnight, back when just a touch of dye still made my hair shimmer black, and only the merest hints of wrinkles creased your cheeks. "Places we'll never visit, not even if we build rockets faster than light."

I dropped my mink coat into the hands of the attentive young man in the foyer, then kicked off my Chanels, celebrating my barefootedness with a little dance on the granite tile. Odessa sparkled far beneath us, our park its radiant heart.

"You're thinking about time again." I strolled over to the bar, picking up where we'd left off with the Dukes Simoneta Gómez-Acebo y Borbón an hour or so earlier. "But that's why we built this place, isn't it?"

But you shook your head, loosening your black bowtie as you sank into the mountainous expanse of that leather couch facing the fireplace. "Not time," you told me. "Mind."

I dropped two ice cubes into the martini shaker and shook myself a dry one. "We already have a Realm for that. Which reminds me — those Kesey people scare off the families when they show up." I grabbed a stem glass and poured my drink. "And last time Channel 5 brought cameras. They're nice enough folks, but… us offering family entertainment, or claiming to…"

But you heard none of this. I turned to see you'd shrugged out of your dinner jacket, and you'd declined my offer of a drink with a silent hand-wave. Hickory fire danced in your eyes. You'd gone somewhere else.

I settled onto the couch next to you and waited, like always. Must've been about ten minutes before you spoke.

"Where do we go," you asked me, "when we fall asleep?"

A few seconds passed before you turned to me, clarifying that the question hadn't been rhetorical.

"Into ourselves, I suppose." I sipped my drink. "Back to old memories. To places that could be, and people who might be there." I smiled; reached out and stroked the stubble on your cheek. "You're not the first man to wonder what dreams are. Won't be the last, either. Is that what we need — a dream ride?"

"Not a ride." You shook your head. "A Realm."

My eyes widened. "Replace the Realm of Mind?"

You cracked your knuckles and turned back to the fire. "I'm not sure yet. But how can we call ourselves 'Omni' if we leave one-third of life unaddressed?" Your eyes rose to meet mine, dark in the warm glow. "I'll go there tonight, to Dream; and so will you. We all will, even if we don't remember it tomorrow morning."

I nodded slowly, taking time to find the right words. "We built all the other Realms on evidence. Tangible evidence, I mean. Fossils, satellite photos, particle traces. Who's ever brought back an artifact from a dream?"

A smile creased the corners of your lips. "Maybe I did," you said. "Maybe that's what this park is."

I had no answer for you that night, any more than I do now. That night I slid up closer to you and kissed you, and after I finished my drink we made love in the bed overlooking the flower garden, and if I dreamed anything that night I have no memory of it.

Later that year the Realm of Mind became that of Man. We gutted The Mystery of Consciousness; replaced it with a ride through human evolution; painted over the psychedelic murals with bison and elk in cave-wall ochre. Kesey and his Pranksters departed in unmerry disappointment, to the rejoicing of Channel 5 News and many God-fearing families across Texas, who brought their children and grandchildren in such numbers we had to schedule their ingresses to the Entryway Pavilion, like a church whose Sunday services multiplied with its worshippers.

That was around the time they started calling you "Papa." And though it escaped my notice then, I see now how those swift hours turned into years: we two adventurers gone gray at the temples, retiring at reasonable hours while the galas between the Realms roared on through the night. I didn't even notice you'd ordered the inner sanctum demolished until a week later. That in itself serves as a measure of our change.

I'm more tired now than I was then, yet here in your office sit all these notes and folios. Tomorrow I'll open another, and see what I find of you there.

November 8, 2001

Woke early again this morning, on the same couch in your office, with a sore back. It's getting harder to sleep through a whole night. I dream of waking beneath blankets I can't shake off; of brushing my teeth but seeing no reflection of myself in the mirror. Then I wake and repeat it all, asking myself if it's real this time, or if this, too, is a dream from which I'll open my eyes, taste sourness in my mouth, and begin again.

Cracking my aching back, I tear open another red-taped packet from the banker's box; spread a sheaf of blue-lined pages across your desk. "The Eighth Realm," says one of the headings, in your block-printed letters. Every millimeter dense with notes and plans and diagrams in the sharp 2H graphite we found at that stationery shop in Montmartre, for which you would brook no substitute.

We were older, I think, when you began to speak of Dream in this way, as a breaking of the park's symmetry, our balanced seven expanded to eight. A higher geometry. A paradox straight out of Gödel: our park, perfect in its completeness, yet incomplete for its blindness to the worlds beyond waking life. Nothing could be added; nothing destroyed. And still Dream remained.

"They still aren't seeing it, Evie." Out here at the ranch you'd found a bigger fireplace to gaze into. Your countenance was dark that night — I remember that exact phrase came to mind, your expression evoking visions of robed monarchs beneath heavy crowns. "The place is changing faster than I can keep up with. The more it changes, the less they understand."

I'd long-since swapped martinis for chamomile tea, which I sipped curled up next to you on the sofa, like on so many other nights. "We've ridden out a lot of changes," I said. "Made even more, if you can remember back that far."

You didn't return my smile. "Our time here has a limit," you said, and that sent ice crackling up my spine because you'd always spoken of death as a great adventure, an old friend — never an unwelcome guest, as on that night.

"I haven't done what I set out to," you said. "It's not finished."

This was the Dalton Teague we made damn sure the world didn't remember: not the rough-and-ready oilman of your war-hero years, nor the enigmatic globe-trotter always returned from a Do Not Travel Advisory Zone; me at your side, smiling, most of the time. No, not even the gray-haired captain of industry: that good old Papa Teague the world would recognize from that black-and-white CBS interview. Puff piece, but hence springs archetype all the same.

By then I knew what was on your mind when this mood took you. "It's not too late to build Dream," I said. "Have Elijah or Beth draw up some concepts. We've got plenty of land."

You shook your head. "It's too late. We've been around long enough, they've all got the idea this place is about the world outside — the distant past, the deep sea." You drew a deep breath and sighed like a tired old dog. "How much clearer could we have made it? 'This universe is yours to explore.' Dream would've made it clear what this place was really about."

"Folks like to look outward," I said. "That's why they come here. If they keep looking, some will realize if you look out hard enough, you find yourself looking in."

You turned to me, smiling like you were lifting a heavy stone. "We found it," you said, so quiet I almost didn't hear you. "Dream might've helped some of them find it, too."

I ran fingers through the white streaks of your hair; lifted your glasses off and placed them gently on the coffee table. "The ones who are supposed to find it, will," I told you then, and I still believe it now. "We built it the best we could. The rest is up to them."

Firelight danced on the tears in your eyes. "We could've done it better." Your jaw was trembling, and even as I pulled you close I knew you might as well have been back in the Himalayas, at that monastery whose name we never learned. What did you see, or hear, or touch, in that back room you entered all alone — the one place I could not go with you?

Maybe nothing at all. Maybe that was just the moment when it all clicked into place for you. When you understood what you had to do. What we had to do.

What I still have to do, now, after the park closes. The work I may never commit to paper, which you've left me to finish alone.

A part of me hates you for that, Dalton. But most of me just misses you.

The rain's coming down hard now. I feel sleep coming on.

Hope I'll find you there.

Yours eternally,

—Evelyn

Special Thanks to Our Premium Kickstarter Backers

Jesse Bullington
Matthew Carpenter
Howard Chang
Joseph Daniels
William DeGeest
Kristen T. Dennis
Landon Fitzgerald
Nikki Guerlain
Bettina de Guzman
Alicia Hilton
Ted Johnson
Martin Kearns
Steve Kostoff

Algie Lane
Chloe LeGendre
Frank Lewis
Ethan Lightle
Rex Long
Jeremy Mallory
Kaleb Maskill
Carver Rapp
Cindy Thomas
Griff Thomas
Whitney Trepel
Paul Trinies

HouseBlackwood.net

9 798218 333218

9 798218 333218